Teaching and Learning Algebra

Also available from Continuum:

Julia Anghileri: Teaching Number Sense
Marilyn Nickson: Teaching and Learning Mathematics
Adrian Oldknow and Ron Taylor: Teaching Mathematics with ICT
Mike Ollerton and Anne Watson: Inclusive Mathematics 11–18

Teaching and Learning Algebra

Doug French

continuum

Continuum

The Tower Building	80 Maiden Lane
11 York Road	Suite 704
London SE1 7NX	New York, NY 10038

www.continuumbooks.com

First published 2002
Reprinted 2008

British Library Cataloguing-in-Publication Data
A catalogue record for this book is available from the British Library.

ISBN: 978-08264-5221-3 (hardback)
      978-0-8264-7749-1 (paperback)

Typeset by YHT Ltd., London
Printed and bound in great Britain by Biddles Ltd., King's Lynn, Norfolk

Contents

Preface   vi

1. Learning and Teaching Algebra   1

2. Sense and Nonsense in Algebra   8

3. Beginnings   26

4. Developing Algebraic Skills   46

5. Patterns with Squares: Explaining and Proving   65

6. Functions and Graphs   81

7. Puzzles and Problems: Creating and Solving Equations   99

8. Proportionality, Growth and Decay   116

9. Links to Geometry   128

10. Trigonometry and Circular Functions   145

11. Sequences and Series   161

12. The Calculus: Differentiation and Integration   174

Bibliography   191

Index   195

Preface

Algebra is a vital part of mathematics and is increasingly accepted as an important element of the school mathematics curriculum for most, if not all, students. Algebra is a powerful tool for solving problems in the 'real' world, but besides its utility it also has an intrinsic interest through its application to puzzles and problems and to explanations and proofs within mathematics itself. However, as all mathematics teachers know only too well, many students fail to make much sense of algebra and fail to appreciate either its usefulness or its fascination. The purpose of this book is to explore the problems and the possibilities of teaching and learning algebra. It looks at the nature of some of the difficulties that students commonly experience, reviews many of the topics of the school algebra curriculum and suggests a variety of approaches to teaching and learning the key ideas.

Although there is much research and curriculum development related to teaching and learning algebra, these cannot provide simple recipes for success because teaching and learning are such incredibly complex tasks and algebra is a challenging subject. They do, however, provide a framework of evidence and ideas for the teacher to build upon in making the essentially pragmatic decisions of day to day classroom work. Ultimately, the way a teacher behaves is determined by their beliefs about teaching and learning and by the view that they have of the subject that they are seeking to communicate. Inevitably, therefore, this book is a distillation of my own thinking and beliefs which have developed over a long period as a school mathematics teacher and as a teacher educator. It is founded on a strong belief that mathematics is an intrinsically interesting subject which can only be learnt successfully when understanding is developed alongside fluency, and when students can see meaning and purpose in what they are being asked to learn.

I am deeply indebted to all my students over many years, both in school and university, because my ideas could not have been developed without a rich experience of working in a classroom. Equally, I am indebted to colleagues who I have worked with in school, university and the Mathematical Association, together with a multitude of other contacts and sources of inspiration. Finally, I should like to thank Anthony Haynes of Continuum who has been a constant source of advice and encouragement while I have been preparing this book for publication.

Doug French
University of Hull
d.w.french@hull.ac.uk
October 2001

Chapter 1

Learning and Teaching Algebra

No one can doubt the value of Geometry as an exercise in severe reasoning; and Algebra, though inferior to geometry in this respect, yet is needed to give perfect completeness to the knowledge of Arithmetic, and affords admirable examples of ingenuity.
(Ministry of Education, 1958, p. 4; quoting from the 1868 Schools Inquiry Commission)

WHY LEARN ALGEBRA?

To most lay people the defining characteristic of algebra is its use of symbols, but beyond that they would find it difficult to describe either what algebra is or what purpose it has. Indeed, many mathematics teachers find it difficult to answer those recurrent questions that students ask: 'Why are we learning algebra?' and 'What use is it?' Unfortunately, many people's experience of school algebra fails to give them a clear view of what algebra is. The questions arise because they acquire a very narrow and restricted image of the subject.

Algebra has its roots in both arithmetic and geometry, and has developed as a succinct system of symbols to describe relationships. At an elementary level, these relationships usually involve numbers, and their essential feature is that they express generality. When we look at the numbers 3, 6, 9, 12 and 15, our immediate response is 'the three times table' or 'multiples of three'. We know that the sequence continues as 18, 21, 24, and that if we went on far enough we would get to 99 or 300, or even 3 million. Our sense of the regularity or pattern is very strong and it is this generality that algebra seeks to describe and work with. We see that the three times table 'goes up in threes', but much more powerfully each number in the table is 'three times something', and that enables us with ease to say that the 300 is the 100th term in the sequence because it is 3×100. Although there is no need to express such a simple problem in algebraic terms the thinking involved is entirely algebraic. The 'something' is a variable standing for any positive whole number and is often denoted by n. 'Three times something' can then be written as $3n$ and the observation that 300 is the 100th number in the table arises from unconsciously solving the equation $3n = 300$.

The ability to express general numerical relationships in symbolic terms is very powerful. Once we know that all numbers in the three times table are 'three times something', or $3n$, we can determine *any* number in the sequence and we can use that knowledge to solve problems and explain surprising relationships between numbers.

Figure 1.1 shows the result of adding several different sets of three consecutive numbers. The striking thing about the results is that each is a multiple of three, and we might suspect therefore that adding three consecutive numbers *always* gives a multiple of three, but how can we be sure? In algebraic terms, using the variable n to denote any positive whole number, three consecutive numbers can be expressed as n, $n + 1$ and $n + 2$. Adding these together gives:

$$n + n + 1 + n + 2 = 3n + 3.$$

$1 + 2 + 3 = 6$	$7 + 8 + 9 = 24$
$3 + 4 + 5 = 12$	$9 + 10 + 11 = 30$
$49 + 50 + 51 = 150$	$22 + 23 + 24 = 69$

Figure 1.1 *Sums of Three Consecutive Numbers*

The general result $3n + 3$ tells us that whenever three consecutive numbers are added we obtain a multiple of three, but it tells us more than that. Since $3n + 3$ can be written in the alternative form $3(n + 1)$, we can see which multiple of three is involved: it is three times $n + 1$ which denotes the middle number.

Clearly, this property of consecutive numbers is very simple and could be explained without recourse to algebra, but it does illustrate some key aspects of an algebraic argument. A symbolic expression is set up to represent the sum of three consecutive numbers and then transformed into two different equivalent forms that provide further information to explain and extend the property suggested by the numerical examples. In general, any algebraic argument has this three part structure: *representing* the elements of the situation in an algebraic form; *transforming* the symbolic expressions in some way; and *interpreting* the new forms that have been produced. Expressing the elements of a situation in a symbolic form makes it easier to carry out the transformations of the second stage. Before the development of our modern symbol system, which is broadly in the form used by Descartes in the seventeenth century, arguments were either presented in a verbal form or in terms of the properties of geometrical diagrams. Many examples of this can be found in Boyer and Merzbach (1991), Fauvel and Gray (1987) and other books on the history of mathematics. The invention of symbolic algebra was a considerable breakthrough that made it much easier to understand and work on complex situations. The effort involved in learning to work with a symbolic system is considerable, but once the elements are mastered it provides a very powerful tool. As Tall and Thomas (1991) say: 'there is a stage in the curriculum when the introduction of algebra may make simple things hard, but not teaching algebra will soon render it impossible to make hard things simple'.

The essence of algebra is that it uses an economical and consistent symbol system to represent expressions and relationships which are then used in formulating arguments concerned with prediction, problem solving, explanation and proof. Prediction often involves finding a suitable function which can then be evaluated; problem solving involves setting up and solving equations; whilst explanation and proof commonly involve establishing and interpreting an algebraic identity. The problem of representing the relationships between sets of numbers, which can arise in many different ways, has led to the development of a variety of mathematical functions and their expression in symbolic form. The list includes linear, quadratic and other polynomial functions, rational functions, exponential and logarithmic functions and the circular functions, sine and cosine, together with other functions related to them. Indeed, one could say that algebra is the study of functions and their application to a wide range of phenomena both within mathematics and from the 'real' world.

There are two broad reasons that can be advocated for learning algebra: the first is that it is *useful* and the second is that it is *interesting*. Algebra is clearly *useful* in a direct sense to those whose work is in fields like science, engineering, computing and, of course, in teaching mathematics. Only a minority of students will find employment of this kind, although as it may not be clear who will be in this minority until they reach the later stages of schooling, it is important that opportunities are kept open. However, the majority will find very little direct use for algebra either in their work or in their play and it is misleading to argue otherwise. Algebra is also useful in two less direct senses: firstly it provides a valuable training in thinking skills and a respect for rigorous argument and, secondly, it gives insight into the explanations of a wide range of phenomena in the world. The first is not a sufficient reason because the same can be said of other aspects of mathematics and, indeed, of most, if not all, other school subjects. The second is true in that citizens who are well informed and interested in the world have more to contribute to society and perhaps have more satisfying lives, a point that is well made by Usiskin in pointing to the value of learning the language of a country you are visiting:

> If you visit Mexico but do not know Spanish, you can get along, but you will never appreciate the richness of the culture, and you will not be able to learn as much as you could if you knew Spanish, ... And perhaps most importantly, you will not even know what you have missed. (Usiskin, 1999)

This does, however, reflect even more the second broad reason for learning algebra which is that it is *interesting* in itself, as well as on account of its utility. We do not ask children to learn about music, art and literature because they are in any way directly useful, but because they are potentially interesting and enjoyable. They give insight into different aspects of human endeavour. The same is surely true of mathematics and its vital component, algebra, which, to quote from the passage at the head of this chapter, 'affords admirable examples of ingenuity'.

Sadly though, we know that any suggestion that algebra is either useful or interesting is at variance with the experience of so many students, even when they are reasonably successful in mastering the requirements of the school curriculum. We are not very successful at imparting to students the real nature and power of algebra to predict and solve and prove. This failure deprives them of the opportunity to make an informed choice about whether algebra is something whose study they should pursue. Cockcroft (1982, p. 67) said that 'mathematics is a difficult subject to teach and to learn' and that could be said of algebra with even greater force. In the next two sections of this chapter I examine what algebra students should learn and the crucial question for this book of how students might learn algebra with greater success and enjoyment.

WHAT ALGEBRA SHOULD STUDENTS LEARN?

There appears to be a remarkably wide consensus across the world concerning the content of the school algebra curriculum, as will be seen by examining the mathematics curricula of the wide selection of countries compared in Howson (1991). There is no reason to think that this has changed dramatically since Howson's book was published. The English National Curriculum, DfEE/QCA (1999), has introductory sections which refer to problem solving, communicating and reasoning and the detailed content section for algebra in key stage 4 (fourteen- to sixteen-year-olds), which is not encountered in full by all students, has the following headings:

> use of symbols, index notation, equations, linear equations, formulae, direct and inverse proportion, simultaneous linear equations, quadratic equations, simultaneous linear and quadratic equations [one of each!], numerical methods, sequences, graphs of linear functions, interpreting graphical information, quadratic functions, other functions [which includes cubics, the reciprocal function, simple exponential functions and circular functions], transformation of functions, loci.

The post-16 curriculum for advanced level mathematics, which is only studied by about 10 per cent of students, extends this further to include the calculus with material on polynomial, rational, circular, exponential and logarithmic functions.

In the United States the Principles and Standards for School Mathematics, NCTM (2000a, pp. 222 and 296) in the sections on algebra for grades 6 to 8 (eleven- to fourteen-year-olds) and grades 9 to 12 (fourteen- to eighteen-year-olds) states that programmes should enable students to:

- understand patterns, relations, and functions;
- represent and analyse mathematical situations and structures using algebraic symbols;
- use mathematical models to represent and understand quantitative relationships;
- analyse change in various contexts.

These statements are expanded with lists of expectations that, although not as detailed as the English national curriculum, cover a similar range of topics, including items that appear in the English advanced level curriculum but, as in England, only a minority encounter the whole curriculum. Data in NCTM (2000b, p. 103) suggest, for instance, that only about 13 per cent of students do courses described as pre-calculus and calculus.

Lists of content are, however, very deceptive because they do not indicate the relative importance assigned to different topics, how effectively they are learnt and the emphasis given to broader aims related to prediction, problem solving and proof referred to in the first section of this chapter, which appear in various forms in DfEE/QCA (1999) and NCTM (2000a). Text books and assessment items offer some information about the way in which curricular requirements are interpreted, but they can only give a partial view, although they are likely to indicate the general form in which the vast majority of students are presented with the curriculum. There is clearly a vast difference between what is intended, what is taught and what is learnt, and there can be no doubt, as stated in RS/JMC (1997), that 'more research is needed to understand the relationship between what algebra is taught and what algebra is learnt'.

In a semi-facetious way, it is perhaps instructive to think about the two sets T, representing what is taught, and L, representing what is learnt, shown on a Venn diagram in Figure 1.2. The naive assumption of the writers of curriculum lists is that we might achieve a situation where

$L = T$. Some people might imagine that in practice $L \subset T$, or even, for some students, that $L \cap T$ is empty. It would certainly seem sensible to try to minimize the content of $L' \cap T$, those things that are taught but not learnt. However, whatever might be true about $L \cap T$, the reality is that the set $L \cap T'$ will never be empty. Students will always learn things that they have not been taught, whether they be misconceptions or, much more positively, aspects of a topic that they have found out for themselves. We should surely aim to expand the desirable elements in $L \cap T'$ and reduce $L \cap T$ by fostering our students' ability to learn independently.

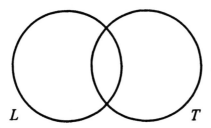

Figure 1.2 *Learning and teaching on a Venn diagram*

Whilst there is widespread assent to the topics that should be included in an algebra curriculum, there is much less clarity about more diffuse issues related to aims and to the contexts in which algebraic ideas should be presented. Problem solving is considered to be very important, but there are clearly substantial differences in what people mean when they speak of problems, and there is little consensus on how best to help students learn to solve problems for themselves. The essence of a problem is that you do not know how to solve it when you first encounter it, because if you did it would not be a problem! It has nothing to do with whether it is presented in words or whether it relates to the real world, issues which are usefully discussed in Pimm (1995, p. 158). Many so called problems in text books are not really problems at all: they are direct applications of a routine procedure that has just been rehearsed or else they are presented in a structured format that sets out the steps required to find the solution. Nonetheless, even when detailed instructions are given for solving a problem, some students inevitably still encounter difficulties.

Obviously, these issues are not clear and simple: one person's routine task may be a serious problem for somebody else. If a young student does not remember what 7×8 is and they have no immediate strategy for working it out, then it is a problem, but, if they realize that they can start at 8 and add on more 8s, it ceases to be a problem. Another student, faced with the same problem, may decide to work backwards from 10×8 or to add 8 to 49 because they remember that is 7×7. We would recognize that the second student displayed more sophisticated problem-solving skills, whilst no doubt regretting that this important fact had not been remembered in the first place. Problem solving is not just a matter of finding solutions, but a constant striving for more economical and elegant routes to solutions. That applies from the early stages of learning arithmetic right through to the more challenging problems encountered in an algebra course.

Helping students to become better problem solvers is an important aim in learning algebra. It is much more difficult to achieve than proficiency in using routine algebraic skills, although that appears to be difficult enough. Problem solving cannot be taught as a separate skill: it has to be learnt alongside other things as a gradual building up of experience through the acquisition of a variety of strategies. Thus, the appearance of the phrase 'problem solving' in a list of curricular requirements has to be interpreted as a long-term aim that should pervade all algebraic learning.

HOW SHOULD STUDENTS LEARN ALGEBRA?

There is a strong prevailing tradition in algebra teaching whereby the teacher introduces students to a new topic by demonstrating 'worked examples' and then seeks to reinforce the procedures involved through extensive practice exercises. These exercises are usually isolated from activities that could give meaning and purpose to the algebraic ideas and operations. Although there has been an increasing emphasis on looking at numerical patterns and on using graphical calculators or graph plotting software to investigate the properties of functions and graphs, these do not necessarily have a significant effect on approaches to learning skills or to using algebra in solving problems and explaining numerical properties. Innovations often become additions to the curriculum which either displace some existing practices or else sit uneasily alongside them. Text books and forms of assessment have a considerable influence on classroom practice, but they are often an uneasy compromise between conflicting approaches and where they differ significantly from existing norms they are largely ignored or rejected.

The way that algebra is taught is influenced profoundly by teachers' beliefs about the nature of the subject and how students should learn it and, also, by a whole host of external constraints. There cannot be a definitive answer to the question as to how students should learn algebra, but one can point to the nature of the difficulties by looking critically at current research and examining practices in the light of the evidence it provides. There is an underlying tension for teachers between a view of mathematics as a body of knowledge and as a way of thinking. The former leads to lists of topics to be imparted to students in some way and the latter leads to somewhat vaguer demands for problem solving and proof. There is no question of having to choose between these two elements because both are important, but it is far from easy to achieve the right balance between the two.

Traditional approaches to teaching algebra are characterized by a lot of time being spent on learning skills before attempting to apply them to problems. This tends to give predominance to the body of knowledge and sees the way of thinking as something that follows after acquiring that knowledge. An alternative is to start with problems, which will often be linked to specific topics, and learn necessary ideas and skills through working on the problems, so that mathematics comes to be seen as something to think about and make sense of rather than as a set of rules to be remembered. These two broad approaches are not exclusive and it is likely that good teachers will use a blend of each, but the relative emphasis given to the two aspects and the extent to which they are inter-related has a strong influence on students' perceptions and performance.

Swan (2000) describes some ideas for algebra lessons designed to encourage students to 'construct and reflect on the meanings for expressions and equations' particularly through discussion rather than by generating a lot of written output. A typical task consisted of a set of cards, some giving algebraic expressions and others giving equivalent written statements. The intention was that students should work in small groups selecting pairs of matching cards and justifying their choices. In assessing the impact of these materials, he points to the importance of creating an appropriate classroom culture by contrasting two teachers who used the same materials. The first gave little introduction to the tasks and the students 'simply worked individually . . . as if it were a practice exercise and learned very little'. The second teacher made the purpose of the tasks clear and emphasized the need to take time and think about what things mean rather than just work through the tasks. This teacher 'discussed the difference between working for *fluency* at skills (which requires practice) and for *understanding* meanings (which needs discussion – to see another's point of view)' He explained to his students that fluency is concerned with doing a task 'without conscious effort' and that understanding is something you have to keep working at and never 'finish'. Swan comments that over time many of the students had developed an awareness of different 'ways of knowing' and the means of developing these for themselves.

The purpose of this book is to offer approaches to the teaching and learning of algebra which seek to balance these two important elements of fluency and understanding in order to make algebra both more accessible and more congenial. It is based on the firm belief that students will only learn to understand and use algebraic ideas effectively if they are constantly challenged to think for themselves. This implies that problems and the explanatory role of proof should feature strongly at every stage of learning algebra and that discussion and reflection have an important role alongside more conventional written tasks. These are recurrent themes in the chapters which follow. The crucial role of understanding is discussed in Chapter 2, which looks at conceptual difficulties and other underlying issues as a background to identifying effective teaching strategies. In succeeding chapters I have tried to relate these ideas to various aspects of school algebra. Chapter 3 focuses on activities that are appropriate in the introductory stages and Chapter 4 is devoted to the essential task of ensuring fluency with skills, alongside an appreciation of algebra as a powerful tool for explaining and problem solving. The remaining chapters from Chapter 5 onwards consider standard topics drawn from the algebra curriculum. They look at the particular challenges they present to the learner together with approaches that incorporate and extend those considered in the first part of the book.

There is a very real difficulty about any systematic attempt to discuss learning because it is a frighteningly complex and messy business that resists being organized into neat curriculum packages. Wheeler (1996, p. 149) has this to say about it:

> Almost all educational research and development seems to be built on the assumption that learning is an evolutionary business, an evolution, moreover, which should be gentle, regular, and sustained. When I reflect on my own learning, I find few instances of such a gradual and continuous increase. On the contrary, learning appears to me to be very largely a discontinuous, non-linear, business. ... Learning seems to me certainly never additive and almost never convergent. It coalesces and disintegrates, it continually backtracks and recasts itself, as if it were some hugely complex, on-going experiment that never concludes.

It may be entirely appropriate to organize the curriculum and teaching in an essentially linear way, but we must never delude ourselves into thinking that learning will follow the same path. The uncertainty and unexpectedness about the paths that learning can take is what makes teaching such a frustrating and demanding task, but it is also one reason why it can be so stimulating and endlessly fascinating.

Chapter 2

Sense and Nonsense in Algebra

知其然，知其所以然

Know how, and also know why. (Ma, 1999)

UNDERSTANDING

Many students fail to make much sense of algebra and see it as lacking in both meaning and purpose. Motivation is clearly influenced for the worse when students find ideas difficult to understand and the only apparent purpose for the subject is to do the questions in the next test. Vague suggestions that algebra is useful later when they have learnt more of it do little to generate enthusiasm if current tasks lack intrinsic interest. This is not restricted to those who fail to make progress with algebra. Arcavi (1994, p. 24)) notes that it may also apply to those who appear to be successful: 'Even those students who manage to handle the algebraic techniques successfully, often fail to see algebra as a tool for understanding, expressing and communicating generalisations, for revealing structure, and for establishing connections and formulating mathematical arguments'.

At an early stage, students commonly acquire wrong ideas about the meaning to be attributed to letters, expressions and equations. Although much good work has been done in recent years to encourage interesting approaches to algebra, particularly through exploring number patterns, this is not always followed up in algebraically fruitful ways. Finding a formula to represent a pattern should not be the end point of a task, but the start of further work to extend the power of algebraic ideas and motivate the development of appropriate skills that students can use in solving interesting problems. The approach in many textbooks is to provide endless exercises in manipulation unrelated to any meaningful context. This places the emphasis on remembering procedures, rather than reinforcing the link between letters and numbers and developing an understanding of the ideas and how they can be used.

The need for understanding in learning mathematics is crucial, something which is recognized in a powerful statement in *Principles and Standards* (NCTM, 2000a), which is the major resource and guide for those concerned with mathematics education in the USA and the successor to earlier documents (NCTM, 1989 and NCTM, 1991):

The vision of school mathematics in *Principles and Standards* is based on students' learning mathematics with understanding. Unfortunately, learning mathematics *without* understanding has long been a common outcome of school mathematics instruction. (NCTM, 2000a, p. 20)

The mathematics component of the *National Curriculum for England*, DfEE/QCA (1999) is not so bold in asserting the importance of understanding. None the less, the programme of study for each key stage is headed 'knowledge, skills and understanding', something which is paralleled by references to 'factual knowledge, procedural proficiency and conceptual understanding' in NCTM (2000a, p. 20). It is thus widely accepted that understanding is an important element in teaching and learning mathematics and this applies with equal force to algebra as a vital element of mathematics.

The idea of understanding is not as straightforward as its everyday usage would suggest because it may mean different things to different people. Skemp (1976), in discussing the idea of understanding in relation to learning mathematics, suggests that a distinction should be made between two types of understanding. He refers to these as *instrumental understanding* and *relational understanding*. In the simplest terms instrumental understanding is concerned with knowing how – something which is referred to as 'rules without reasons' – whereas relational understanding involves knowing why as well as how.

Ma (1999), in her interesting and important study contrasting the subject knowledge of elementary school teachers in China and the USA, notes that many of her Chinese subjects referred to an old Chinese saying: 'know how, and also know why', in describing their approaches to teaching mathematics, whereas her American subjects concentrated almost exclusively on 'how'. The parallel with Skemp's instrumental and relational understanding is strong. Ma suggests that this marked difference in approach may offer some explanation of the wide disparity in mathematical performance between students in China and the USA. Mathematical performance in the UK is often compared unfavourably with a number of countries in the Far East and Eastern Europe (see, for example, Kaiser, *et al.*, (1999) and there may be uncomfortable parallels here with the contrast that Ma makes between the understanding that Chinese and American teachers seek to develop in their teaching.

The distinction between the two types of understanding is not as clear cut as simple definitions might imply, but it is none the less a useful working idea for discussing teaching and learning. Instrumental understanding is a relatively superficial quality which is observed when a routine task can be fulfilled satisfactorily, whereas relational understanding is more subtle and is never complete. It develops and deepens as an idea is experienced in a variety of forms and linked to other ideas. It is also less obviously demonstrable or measurable, because different individuals inevitably have differing and partial pictures of the complex web of ideas that constitutes mathematics. It would seem to be self-evident that to learn mathematics effectively it is essential to aspire to relational understanding, but, even if that aspiration is accepted, the route to achieving it is far from obvious or simple.

Another useful idea that Skemp discusses is that of *mismatches* between teachers and students in terms of the sort of understanding that is appropriate in learning mathematics. A teacher may discuss mathematical ideas and set tasks with the intention of encouraging the student to understand relationally, whereas a student may only want to understand instrumentally by seeking to remember procedures that give the right answers to exercises and examinations. It is commonplace to find students who have come to see school mathematics as formulae and procedures to be remembered rather than understood in any relational sense. This may be because they have been taught by teachers whose teaching aims only at instrumental understanding, but it may also arise in spite of a teacher's best efforts to encourage a deeper response, because learning involves such a complex of factors.

A mismatch of the other kind may arise where the teacher teaches for instrumental understanding, causing great frustration to the student whose wish is to understand why things are so – to understand relationally. Holt (1958) speaks of students being either *producers*, whose aim is to get through the tasks set by the teacher and get right answers, or *thinkers*, who want to question and develop what is, in Skemp's terms, relational understanding. It would be nice to think that there is no longer any truth in Holt's observation 40 years ago that schools in general are not particularly congenial places for thinkers, but I suspect that his comment is still valid when applied to many mathematics classrooms and, perhaps, particularly when algebra is the topic.

Another connection, noted by Gray and Tall (1993), is to the work of the psychologist Ausubel (1968), who drew a distinction between *rote learning* and *meaningful learning*. This again has obvious parallels with Skemp's instrumental and relational understanding. Rote learning is characterized by a strong reliance on memory to remember apparently arbitrary facts, whereas meaningful learning is concerned with placing facts and ideas in a coherent overall structure, an essential feature of relational understanding. A major attraction of relational understanding is that it reduces the demand on memory by creating a framework in which facts that have been forgotten can be retrieved. It would not be an exaggeration to say that much school algebra teaching at all levels encourages rote learning and, at best, instrumental understanding, and that this is singularly ineffective as a way of developing students' powers to use and apply algebraic thinking and encouraging a positive attitude towards the subject.

Ausubel also stresses the importance of teachers ascertaining what students already know and building on that knowledge. Algebraic understanding is inextricably linked to students' prior understanding of number and numerical operations, because algebra at an elementary level is concerned with generalizing arithmetical relationships. The links need between symbolic results and the numerical results that underpin them need to be reinforced constantly. The flexible thinking and relational understanding that can be developed by encouraging mental calculation is particularly valuable in this respect, because calculation strategies have an underlying algebraic basis. An understanding of negative numbers and fractions and an ability to perform operations fluently with them are essential precursors to learning many aspects of algebra. Difficulties with them are often a substantial barrier to progress.

Some of the difficulties in developing relational understanding, encouraging thinkers and promoting meaningful learning as students attempt to learn algebra undoubtedly lie outside the classroom and are beyond the control of individual teachers, but the policies a system adopts about learning can be influenced and what happens in the classroom is to some degree within the control of the individual teacher. It is therefore important to identify some of the difficulties and explore ways in which they might be resolved.

MISCONCEPTIONS AND ERRORS

Misconceptions and errors are valuable indicators of the state of a student's understanding and provide important information on which teachers can build in discussing ideas and designing classroom tasks. Some misconceptions arise frequently and are widely recognized, but students can be very inventive in their failure to understand and the reasons for errors can sometimes be difficult to discern. The major difficulty with algebra, particularly in the early stages, lies in acquiring appropriate meanings for symbolic statements and most of the misconceptions that follow arise from this.

Kent (1978) gives the example of a student, Margaret, who was perplexed by the equation $3x - 7 = 5$ and unable to solve it, but then went on to assert confidently that $\frac{3x}{4} - 6 = 2$ has the solution $x = 2$ and that it was 'daft' to try to solve $x + 3 = 15$. In the second case Margaret had taken $3x$ to mean 'thirty something' so that $x = 2$ made 32, which was the correct solution in her terms. With x interpreted as a digit in this way her difficulties with the other two examples are immediately clear, because subtracting 7 from 'thirty something' cannot give you 5 and a two digit number is need to solve $x + 3 = 15$. Margaret has a perfectly consistent way of giving meaning to the expressions used here, but it conflicts with the conventional interpretation.

Booth (1984, p. 31) quotes an interview with fifteen-year-old Wayne who is asked to explain the meaning of y when he is attempting to add 3 to $5y$. Wayne says: 'y could be any number; it could be a 4 making that $(5y)$ 54.' He then gives further evidence of multiple confusion by going on to say: 'Or it could be a 5 to the power of 4 (written correctly as 5^4), making it 20'.

The difficulties here are to do with *juxtaposition*: how do we interpret the two symbols 2 and x when they stand next to each other as in $2x$? Teachers may tell students frequently that $2x$ means $2 \times x$, but juxtaposition is given a variety of different interpretations in different contexts, both within mathematics and elsewhere, and it is necessary to learn the appropriate conventions. The possibilities for confusion are all too clear if the reader considers the meanings that might be conveyed by each of the following:

$$27 \quad 2p \quad 2^3 \quad 2g \quad 2\tfrac{1}{2} \quad 2A$$

For instance, $2g$, depending on the context, may mean 2 grams, twice the number displayed on a green dice or the weight of a mass of 2 kilograms, where g represents the acceleration due to gravity, whereas $2\tfrac{1}{2}$ means $\tfrac{1}{2}$ *added* to 2, and $2A$ may be the number of an apartment or a way of referring to an exercise in a text book.

The research conducted by CSMS, reported in Hart (1981), produced evidence of the poor level of performance of students on algebraic items involving *simplification*. With a very large sample of students it was found, for instance, that 77 per cent of thirteen-year-olds and 87 per cent of fifteen- year-olds could simplify $2a + 5a$, whereas only 22 per cent and 41 per cent, respectively, could give a correct response when asked to add 4 to $3n$.

Students often acquire the erroneous idea that letters stand for objects, and this leads them to interpret $2a + 5a$ as a request to add 2 apples to 5 apples – which not unreasonably gives them a correct answer of $7a$. However, that kind of interpretation is not at all helpful when it comes to adding 4 to $3n$, and an expression like bc is totally meaningless if b and c are thought of as bananas and carrots. Letters are used to stand for numbers, so we could legitimately have b as a number of bananas and c as a number of carrots, but bc would still lack meaning. It may be that linking letters to the names of objects like this is not a good strategy in the early stages of learning algebra.

I observed a lesson where a twelve-year-old student had written $7k$ as the answer to $2k + k + 4$ in a text book simplification exercise. The teacher had some difficulty explaining what was wrong. If pupils interpret k as kangaroos, then their instinctive thought is likely to be '4 what?', and the obvious answer is 4 kangaroos, giving $7k$ altogether. When this is coupled with the fact that $3k + 4$ does not look like an 'answer' in the students' terms, it is perhaps not surprising that such errors occur. However, if k is understood to be a number, then substituting some values in the expressions $2k + k + 4$, $3k + 4$ and $7k$, as Figure 2.1 makes clear, shows that the first two expressions are not equivalent to the last.

k	$2k+k+4$	$3k+4$	$7k$
1	7	7	7
2	10	10	14
3	13	13	21
4	16	16	28
5	19	19	35

Figure 2.1 *Substituting to reveal an error*

It is not sufficient simply to tell a student that their response is wrong and then to show them the correct way of proceeding by referring, for instance, to a phrase such as 'gathering like terms'. They need to appreciate why a response does not make sense and to develop a variety of means of checking for themselves to decide whether an answer is correct or, at the very least, plausible. H.G.Wells (1910) in his novel *The History of Mr. Polly*, describing Mr.Polly's experiences at school, states that 'he was always doubtful whether it was eight sevens or nine eights that was sixty-three (he knew no method for settling the difficulty)'. Most students have even greater problems 'settling the difficulty' with an algebraic problem!

In the context of science teaching, Adey and Shayer (1994, p. 62) suggest that *cognitive conflict* is an important component in promoting students' cognitive development. They describe such conflict as 'an event which the student finds puzzling and discordant with previous experience or understanding'. Misconceptions and errors are important growth points for students' learning if they are shown to be in conflict with results obtained by approaching the problem differently. At the simplest level this involves encouraging students to ask whether an answer is sensible or to check it in some way and then to think again where there is a conflict. However, the skilful teacher may choose deliberately to engineer a conflict in order to challenge students' thinking.

Confusion caused by interpreting letters as objects can arise in many ways. A frequently quoted example comes from Clement (1982): he asked university students to produce an equation relating s, the number of students, to p, the number of professors, when they were given the statement: 'There are six times as many students as professors at this university'. The common error was to give $6s = p$, rather than the correct form $s = 6p$. In a similar way, it is all too easy for students to translate the statement that a week is seven days into the plausible looking $d = 7w$. However, if w is supposed to stand for the number of weeks and d the number of days, taking a value of 7 for w creates obvious cognitive conflict by suggesting that 7 days are the same as 49 weeks! The formula should be $d = 7w$, which is counter-intuitive unless it is seen as a relationship between two sets of numbers rather than between the two objects, weeks and days. Arcavi (1994, p. 27), in a comment on Clement's work, states that the problem is less one of falling into the 'linguistic trap', but of failing to realize that anything is wrong, through a failure to develop a 'symbol sense' which includes 'developing the healthy habit of re-reading and checking (e.g., by simple substitution) for the reasonableness of the symbolic expression one constructs'.

Early in their course, I asked a group of student teachers to each write down a formula linking m, the number of miles, to k, the number of kilometres, using the usual approximation that 5 miles is equivalent to 8 kilometres. The two most common answers, obviously based on the erroneous notion that $5m = 8k$, were $m = \frac{8}{5}k$ and $k = \frac{5}{8}m$ (or their decimal equivalents). I asked them what that would give for 8 miles and was, at least, pleased that the answer of 5 kilometres worried them! As with the weeks and days problem, it is necessary to think about the relationship between sets of numbers rather than between words. Realizing that 1 kilometre is equivalent to $\frac{5}{8}$ of a mile is the key to arriving at a correct relationship in the form $m = \frac{5}{8}k$ and similarly for the alternative form $k = \frac{8}{5}m$.

Another misconception is illustrated by a student teacher I observed who was trying to get a class of thirteen-year-olds to express the mapping in Figure 2.2 algebraically. Having helped the class to recognize that the numbers on the right were each one less than the corresponding numbers on the left, the teacher asked how the relationship could be written if x was used to represent the numbers on the left. Rather than $x \rightarrow x - 1$ the first response was $x \rightarrow w$, presumably using the fact that the letter w precedes x in the alphabet.

$$x \rightarrow ?$$
$$2 \rightarrow 1$$
$$3 \rightarrow 2$$
$$4 \rightarrow 3$$
$$5 \rightarrow 4$$
$$6 \rightarrow 5$$

Figure 2.2 *Find the mapping*

The difficulty here is that a student has come to think that the numerical values attached to each letter follow the order of the alphabet. This is perhaps a little better than believing that each letter stands for one particular number, a view that can be encouraged by exercises involving coded messages that use the simple substitution $a = 1, b = 2, c = 3$ and so on. A striking example is given in Johnson (1989, p. 136). Frank is being asked by an interviewer about the meaning of the formula, $V = l \times b \times h$, for the volume of a cuboid. He begins by counting up on his fingers to determine that l is the 12th letter of the alphabet. After some confusion, in which he inadvertently replaces the 12 with 10, he decides that V is equal to $10 \times 2 \times 7 = 140$, which does use the correct positional value for b, although he miscounts for h. He is then totally mystified by his answer as he realizes that there are far fewer than 140 letters in the alphabet – a good example of cognitive conflict!

The use of the equals sign is another source of difficulty. Both Kieran (1999, p. 349) and Nickson (2000, p. 112) discuss research that shows that, initially at least, students interpret equals as an instruction to do something to determine a result rather than as a symbol that indicates the equivalence of two expressions. This arises in a natural way through the use of equals in numerical calculations. It is also encouraged by the presence of a key labelled with an equals sign on many calculators. More sophisticated calculators use the much more appropriate labels 'enter' or 'execute'. In an arithmetical context, it is common for students to write a statement such as $5 + 3 = 8 \times 4 = 32$ to express the two steps when they are asked to add 5 to 3 and then multiply the result by 4. The correct solution to the problem has been found, but the written statement is incorrect, since 5 + 3 is clearly not equal to 32. In algebraic contexts it is common to see erroneous statements like:

$$3x - 5 = 7 = 3x = 12 = x = 4 \text{ and } \cos\theta = \tfrac{3}{5} = 0.6 = \theta = 53.1°$$

This is an extension of the 'something to do' interpretation where the equals sign is used to link the steps of an argument. The idea that the equals sign should only be used to indicate that two expressions are equivalent is not difficult to understand, but errors in its use are frequent even when the written statements of teachers and text books consistently provide good models for students to follow.

These illustrations show all too clearly the considerable confusion about simple algebraic ideas that many students display when their understanding is probed. It is not just that they forget rules of procedure, but that they lack an adequate and secure underlying meaning for the symbols they are working with and a basis for deciding for themselves what makes sense. The problem is not restricted to groups of poorly motivated or poorly performing students, because even some of those who have achieved success in algebra, indeed even those training as mathematics teachers, can still display serious misunderstandings. The response should be much more than one of correcting errors: research suggests that misconceptions can 'remain hidden unless the teacher makes specific efforts to uncover them' and, for effective learning, they need to be 'addressed, exposed and discussed', Askew and Wiliam (1995, p. 12).

UNKNOWNS AND VARIABLES

Küchemann (1981a, p. 104), as part of the *Concepts in Secondary Mathematics and Science (CSMS)* project reported in Hart (1981), investigated the different interpretations that students gave to letters and produced a six-part categorization which he described as:

- letter evaluated;
- letter not used;
- letter as object;
- letter as specific unknown;
- letter as generalized number;
- letter as variable.

In the first case – *letter evaluated* – a number is immediately assigned to a letter, as in stating that $a = 3$ when given $a + 5 = 8$. No rearrangement or operations are required to see the answer, because $3 + 5 = 8$ is so familiar. In the second case, letters are ignored, as when asked for the value of $a + b + 2$ given that $a + b = 43$. Attention here is focused on the fact that 2 has to be added on so the letters can be ignored. In both these cases there is some sense that the letters stand for numbers, but there is no idea that the letters can be operated on in any way other than by replacing them with numbers. Wayne's interpretation of $5y$, discussed earlier, is an example of a misunderstanding that is clearly related to these categories.

The third category, *letter as object*, refers to the common misinterpretation of a letter as shorthand for an object, rather than as a number. Using b and c to stand for bananas and carrots and m and k as miles and kilometres are typical examples of this phenomenon. In this case it may well be possible to operate on expressions involving letters, but often the results will be erroneous or meaningless, as earlier examples have demonstrated. It is clearly useful to use the first letter of the name of an object in many algebraic situations, but it has to be clear that the letter refers to a number which is in some way linked to that object, not the object itself. This misinterpretation is clearly remarkably persistent and, sadly, it is often to be found in either explicit or implicit forms in many school text books.

Letter as a *specific unknown* is the interpretation linked with equation solving, and in that context it is a perfectly valid one. However, conflict may arise when students meet equations which have more than one solution and there is evidence that when different letters are used to represent the same equation students do not realize that the solutions will be the same. For example, Wagner (1981) found that significant numbers of twelve- to seventeen-year-old students did not immediately see that the equations $7w + 22 = 109$ and $7n + 22 = 109$ had identical solutions.

Letter as *generalized number* extends the idea of a specific unknown to the letter taking more than one value, which might be seen as a step towards the more subtle concept of letter as variable where the sense of the letter varying across a whole range of values is involved. Küchemann (1981a, p. 109) used the question: 'What can you say about c if $c + d = 10$ and c is less than d?' The most common response was to give a single value, usually 4, but others gave a systematic list – 1, 2, 3, 4 – which indicates the notion of the letter as a generalized number. A more sophisticated response was $c < 5$, which possibly suggests a greater understanding of the idea of variable, although it cannot be clear whether it was intended to say 'any number less than 5' or was seen as a property of a few specific numbers. A less common response was $c = 10 - d$, which again may imply some sense that more than a few numbers could be involved, but it does not take account of the requirement that $c < d$.

The distinction between generalized number and variable seems less clear and less important than that between specific unknown and variable. In some algebraic contexts the idea of a letter as a specific unknown is sufficient, but if that is the only interpretation available to the student it will clearly act as a barrier to working meaningfully with expressions and functions. However, for many students, there is an earlier barrier that is created by the first three categories, particularly that of letter as object. This needs to be addressed both in the early stages of learning the subject and constantly reinforced thereafter by emphasizing the idea of letter as number, whether it be unknown or variable.

EXPRESSIONS

I have referred previously to the difficulties created by an expression like $3k + 4$. Tall and Thomas (1991), in an important study that used computers with students to improve their understanding of algebra, suggest that there are four obstacles to making sense of algebraic expressions:

- the parsing obstacle;
- the expected answer obstacle;
- the lack of closure obstacle;
- the process-product obstacle.

The *parsing obstacle* arises because of the way in which we read from left to right. It leads, for example, to students reading ab as 'a and b', thereby thinking it has the same meaning as $a + b$. In the same way it is natural to interpret as $3 + 4k$ as $7k$, because $3 + 4$, which is 7, is read before the k. The thinking that leads from $3k + 4$ to $7k$ involves the same element, but also involves the other obstacles. All their early experience of simple arithmetic requires students to do some calculation when they see an operation sign like +, so they expect to produce an answer when they see an expression like $3k + 4$ – the *expected answer obstacle*. Related to this they are uncomfortable with $3k + 4$ as an answer, because it looks incomplete – the *lack of closure obstacle*.

The underlying difficulty here resides in the nature of an expression like $3k + 4$ that represents both a *process* and a *product*. It gives both the instructions for a calculation and it represents the result of that calculation in the absence of a specific value for the variable. That result, or product, can be manipulated mentally as though it was an object in its own right. The *process-product obstacle* is the failure to appreciate this dual nature of algebraic expressions.

Elsewhere, in Tall (1991), Gray and Tall (1993) and Tall (1995), an entity that is represented symbolically and has these two characteristics is referred to as a *procept*. It is hypothesized that for all mathematical learning 'the difference between success and failure lies in the difference between procept and procedure'. Many students come to regard mathematics, and algebra in particular, as procedures (or processes) to be remembered and carried out, rather than ideas to be understood, whereas Gray and Tall argue that the great power of mathematics lies in the 'flexibility provided by using the ambiguity of notation as process or product'. If an algebraic expression is just viewed as a process or a recipe, then the powerful way in which it can be manipulated and linked to other expressions makes little sense and failure with algebra becomes inevitable. Gray and Tall suggest that this is true for all mathematical entities and assert that it provides the reason why 'mathematics is known chiefly as a subject in which people fail, fail badly and fail often'.

FLUENCY

Much time has traditionally been spent in school algebra lessons practising routine skills like substitution, simplification and equation solving through the medium of repetitive exercises. For those who make little sense of the ideas being practised any immediate gains in fluency are rapidly lost and, for those who already understand, further repetitive practice does little to deepen understanding or to sense the power conferred by an ability to manipulate and transform expressions and equations. Concern about lack of fluency in algebraic skills among students in higher education in the UK has been expressed in recent years by mathematics and engineering lecturers. For example, the report *Tackling the Mathematics Problem*, (LMS/IMA/RSS, 1995, p. 2), speaks of 'a serious lack of essential technical fluency – the inability to undertake numerical and algebraic calculation with fluency and accuracy'. These concerns are a reflection of the long-standing difficulties we have in effective teaching mathematics in general, and algebra in particular. Some attempts to make algebra more accessible and attractive to all students have resulted in less time being devoted to practising skills to the detriment particularly of those who in the past might have acquired a high degree of fluency, and without any obvious gains in other aspects of learning the subject.

However, a more thoughtful response to justifiable concerns is needed than a renewed emphasis on repetitive exercises to practise skills in isolation from solving problems, not least because another element of concern in LMS/IMA/RSS (1995, p. 2) is 'a marked decline in analytical powers when faced with simple problems requiring more than one step'. Fluency with skills means that they can be used without conscious attention so that the mind is released for the higher order thinking required to solve problems. If the routine details in an algebraic argument are problematic for students, it is difficult to focus attention on the overall strategy, purpose and logic and on any new ideas that might be involved. Practice is certainly necessary to achieve fluency, but it should not be divorced from the purposes it is intended to serve.

Hewitt (1996) draws attention to the 'impressive learning' that takes place when a young child learns to walk and notes that this entails a considerable amount of practice, but it is largely practice that occurs whilst trying to achieve other objectives, such as retrieving a toy from the other side of the room or exploring in a park or playground. As Hewitt says, the practice is 'subordinate' to the main objective: the child is becoming a fluent walker whilst giving their attention to achieving something else. Another feature of walking is that once it has been learnt it is not forgotten, whereas much mathematical learning is at best temporary. This suggests that effective practice is acquired when the focus of attention is on achieving something else which is significant to the student. Another analogy that I find useful is that of learning to ride a bicycle, where fluency is achieved as a by-product in trying to achieve other objectives. In fact, like walking, the skill of riding a bicycle involves a host of sub-skills – balancing, pedalling, steering, braking and so on. We do not have lengthy separate lessons in each sub-skill before attempting to ride the bike: we learn them by riding the bicycle, and we do not forget the skills.

In contrast, algebra lessons commonly focus on manipulating expressions and solving equations. To the student, the skills do not enable them to do anything that they recognize as significant. As a consequence, they forget them and then have to go through an endless cycle of re-teaching and revision. The lesson for algebra teaching would seem to be that skills are best learnt in the pursuit of wider objectives, where the focus of attention is on solving significant problems and exploring interesting numerical and geometrical properties. The next section looks at the question of providing suitable contexts for learning algebra; particular aspects of developing skills are considered in greater detail in Chapter 4.

PROVIDING A CONTEXT

One of the reasons why mathematics is so powerful is that it can be divorced from immediate contexts and its elements manipulated and transformed in an abstract fashion without making any direct reference to the interpretation of the symbols. As Stewart (1987, p. 320) observes: 'Its very abstraction – which many people admittedly find repelling – gives it a unity and a universality that would be lost if it were made more concrete or specialised'. However, since abstraction can act as a considerable barrier to many learners it is important both to link ideas to things that seem real and concrete and to provide reasons for choosing to represent the world in an algebraic form. Algebra needs to be seen as a way of solving problems that have significance for the learner.

Students often sense that algebra is not 'about anything', a phrase used in Cockcroft (1982, p. 141), in the sense that they see no purpose for the procedures being rehearsed. A common response is to suggest that algebra, and indeed the whole of school mathematics, should be presented in the context of 'real world problems'. I would argue that this is too limited an interpretation of what can make an idea or a problem significant and that it can often lead to trivial or contrived situations. What matters is whether the ideas and problems relate to something that is concrete and familiar to the student and that something can often come from within mathematics. Nemirovsky (1996, p. 313) speaks of 'contextualised and decontextualised problems' and notes that problems are often described as 'being decontextualised because they are just about numbers (as opposed to quantities or measures of specific things), as if all the rich background of ideas and experiences that students develop around numbers could not offer a context'.

All students bring to their algebra lessons some familiarity with both numbers and geometrical objects and can be stimulated by problems and puzzles which build on that familiarity without having any obvious or immediate application to the real world in a utilitarian sense. In the early stages of learning algebra it is difficult to find genuine examples from the 'real world' that either could not be more readily solved without algebra or else cause difficulty by introducing complexities apart from those arising from the algebra. That is not to say that we should ignore the real world, but rather that we should not restrict our sources of examples or imagine that students will necessarily find real-world applications more motivating or comprehensible than problems that are entertaining and enlightening in themselves. Solving a numerical or geometrical problem or explaining a surprising number property can be just as motivating and meaningful as applying mathematical ideas to a financial or travel problem.

I recall a lesson many years ago when a class of twelve-year-olds were working on the problem of finding a relationship between the number of diagonals and the number of sides in a polygon. The students drew their polygons and tabulated their results as shown in Figure 2.3.

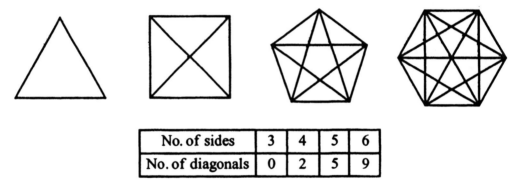

No. of sides	3	4	5	6
No. of diagonals	0	2	5	9

Figure 2.3 *How many diagonals in a polygon?*

The challenge I posed for the lesson was to find a way of determining how many diagonals there are in a 20-sided polygon. The students quickly realized that it would take a long time to draw all the diagonals in the 20-sided case, and that counting might be a bit unreliable. They did spot the pattern in the differences between the numbers of diagonals, but realized that it would involve a lot of adding up to get to the result they wanted. So, we focused on the simpler case of the hexagon and considered the number of diagonals from one of its vertices. There are 3 diagonals from each of the 6 vertices so it looked as though there should be 6 × 3 diagonals altogether, but the table said 9, not 18, so, what was wrong? Further discussion, including a look at some of the other cases, led them to point out that each diagonal had been counted twice and 18 had therefore to be halved.

We were now in a position to solve the problem of the polygon with 20 sides, but we needed to know how many diagonals there are from each vertex. By looking at the cases we had, and realizing that a diagonal cannot go to the 2 adjacent vertices or to the point it starts from, it was clear that the number of diagonals was 3 less than the number of vertices, which is the same as number of sides. We now had a formula for any polygon:

Number of diagonals for an *n*-sided polygon $= \frac{1}{2}n(n-3)$

The number of diagonals for a 20-sided polygon is then $\frac{1}{2}$ of $20 \times 17 = 170$. The polygons provided a meaningful context that was understood by the students and the power of the algebraic result was evident, because they could now work out the number of diagonals for *any* polygon. At the end of the lesson I remarked casually that if they wanted to they could always check that the answer was correct by drawing the polygon and counting its diagonals. I was delighted next day to be met by one of the students who had produced a hand-drawn diagram of a polygon with 20 sides and all the 170 diagonals! Whilst this may not have been the most mathematically fruitful way of spending an evening, it does suggest that students are not always best motivated by appeals to the utility of mathematics or to the need to prepare for tests and examinations.

LINKS AND CONNECTIONS

It is all too easy for algebra to be associated in the student's mind with a set of procedures such as simplification, substitution and finding factors, and a set of topics, such as simultaneous equations, graphs, quadratic equations and algebraic fractions, each of which appears to sit in a separate compartment. Apart from some common language and symbols, the procedures and topics often seem to have little connection either with each other or with other areas of mathematics. Labels for processes and topics have a powerful effect in compartmentalizing knowledge and tend to set up barriers in the student's mind if explicit links between ideas are not made.

Askew *et al.* (1997) looked at the characteristics displayed by teachers who were 'effective' in teaching numeracy to young children. Their research identified three orientations based on the beliefs that the teachers they investigated held about mathematics teaching. These 'ideal types' were described as 'connectionist', 'transmission' and 'discovery', although no individual teacher fitted precisely into one of the categories since all combined some elements of each. However, a number of individual teachers did display the characteristics of one of the orientations more strongly in their talk and their classroom behaviour. In brief, 'discovery' teachers emphasized practical activities designed to enable students to discover methods for themselves, 'transmission' teachers gave verbal explanations so that students could learn to use standard procedures and 'connectionist' teachers saw teaching as a 'dialogue between teacher and pupils to explore understandings' with an emphasis on drawing out links and connections. Six of the sixteen teachers in the study were rated as 'highly effective' and five of those were ones whose orientation was described as 'strongly connectionist'.

Whilst we should be cautious in extrapolating the results of a small study with teachers of numeracy to young students, to the teaching of algebra at a later stage, it is significant that teachers who emphasized connections were apparently particularly effective, because a failure to make connections of all kinds is a common problem in learning algebra. I would argue that reinforcing the connection between numbers and algebra and the links to pictorial representations through graphs and diagrams are of crucial importance.

Elementary algebra is often referred to as generalized arithmetic and has its roots in solving what are essentially numerical problems and in representing and explaining relationships between numbers. Numbers are relatively familiar and accessible to students and thus provide a valuable reference point when helping them to make sense of algebraic expressions. It is important to maintain this link so that students are constantly aware of the numerical back-drop to algebraic ideas, because it serves as a way of reinforcing the meaning of symbols and checking that results make sense.

$$2a + 3a = 5a$$

$$2 \times 7 + 3 \times 7 = 14 + 21 = 35 = 5 \times 7$$

$$2 \times 143 + 3 \times 143 = 5 \times 143$$

$$2 \times 0.25 + 3 \times 0.25 = 5 \times 0.25$$

$$n^2 + n = n(n+1)$$

$$3^2 + 3 = 12 = 3 \times 4$$

$$19^2 + 19 = 380 = 19 \times 20$$

$$40^2 + 40 = 1640 = 40 \times 41$$

Figure 2.4 *Reinforcing the links between numbers and algebra*

Two algebraic identities with some related numerical examples are shown in Figure 2.4. The symbolic form is a succinct way of representing the general property displayed in the numerical statements, but equally the special cases obtained by substituting particular values is a powerful way of helping students make sense of the symbolic form. Mason (1988), in his excellent book *Learning and Doing Mathematics*, argues very powerfully that the interplay between these two ideas of generalization and specialization is a vital element in making sense of a new piece of mathematics and in solving mathematical problems. If a general idea does not make sense then looking at a special case is a good strategy, but, equally, within any special case there is always the possibility of generalization.

A simple example that illustrates this is the observation that the answers $8 \times 8 = 64$ and $7 \times 9 = 63$ differ by one. This may simply be dismissed as a coincidence until other cases are considered to display the emerging pattern shown in Figure 2.5, which can be expressed as $x^2 - 1 = (x - 1)(x + 1)$. Equally though if the starting point is the algebraic identity, the numerical results are one way of helping it to make sense.

$2 \times 2 = 4$	$1 \times 3 = 3$
$3 \times 3 = 9$	$2 \times 4 = 8$
$4 \times 4 = 16$	$3 \times 5 = 15$
$5 \times 5 = 25$	$4 \times 6 = 24$
$6 \times 6 = 36$	$5 \times 7 = 35$
$7 \times 7 = 49$	$6 \times 8 = 48$
$8 \times 8 = 64$	$7 \times 9 = 63$
$9 \times 9 = 81$	$8 \times 10 = 80$

Figure 2.5 *An emerging pattern*

Pictures are also a powerful way of representing and communicating ideas and whilst a picture always shows a particular case it contains within it the idea of generality. Figure 2.6 uses squares to illustrate the identity $x^2 - 1 = (x - 1)(x + 1)$ in the case where $x = 5$. The left hand diagram shows a big square with one little square missing. The top row of shaded squares in the diagram has been removed and placed at one end to make the rectangle on the right. The pictures display neatly the relationship for any positive value of x and, indeed, to generalize further by considering $x^2 - y^2$, the difference of two squares which is considered at length in Chapter 5.

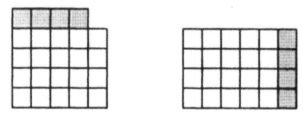

Figure 2.6 *Linking an identity to a picture:* $x^2 - 1 = (x - 1)(x + 1)$

Graphs are a specialized form of picture that have a key role in algebra, but their potential in providing links and developing understanding is not always fully exploited. The graph of $y = x^2 - 1$, shown in Figure 2.7, can be seen as translating the graph of $y = x^2$ one unit downwards. Expressing $x^2 - 1$ as $(x - 1)(x + 1)$ gives an equivalent form, which shows readily that the curve intersects the x axis at $x = 1$ and $x = -1$. Having plotted the graph of $y = x^2 - 1$ it is instructive to ask students what they think the graph of $y = (x - 1)(x + 1)$ will look like. In my experience, their response is often not immediate, even though they are familiar with the identity relating the two.

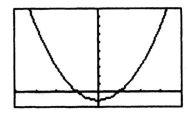

Figure 2.7 *Picturing an identity with a graph:* $y = x^2 - 1$ *and* $y = (x - 1)(x + 1)$

Standard algebraic procedures involving multiplying two linear expressions or finding the factors of quadratic expressions can be both enlivened and set in a wider context by drawing out the links with numerical factors and graphical and other pictorial representations, but the same is true of all other aspects of algebra where students' understanding can be enhanced by emphasizing links and connections and different ways of viewing the same idea.

THE ROLE OF TECHNOLOGY

Over the 30-year period that calculators have been available there has been, and continues to be, much controversy about the role that they should play in the learning of arithmetic. The same is likely to be increasingly the case in the coming years over the impact of advanced calculators, like the TI-89 and TI-92, and computer-based algebra systems, like Derive, and the graph- plotting capabilities of graphic calculators and graph-plotting software. Some of the range of problems and possibilities, with a diversity of approaches to them, will be found in publications such as Berry and Monaghan (1997), Kutzler (1996), NCET (1995) and NCTM (1992). As with simple calculators, concerns are focused on the influence of such technology on students' understanding and skills and the extent to which the curriculum should change to take account of the power that these tools provide. It is important, however, to make a clear distinction between using technological devices as a fast and accurate labour-saving tool, which can be used when applying algebra to problems, and as a versatile tool with a whole range of capabilities that can be used to enhance the way in which students learn algebra.

Hergel *et al.* (2001, p. 3) usefully distinguish between the goals of performing an operation, for which it may be appropriate to use a calculator, and choosing a strategy when solving a problem, which cannot be done by a calculator. The ability to choose a strategy will be influenced by familiarity with algebraic ideas and processes and experience of using them in solving problems. Although an ability to perform operations by hand may not be essential when actually solving a problem, substantial experience of doing so, at least with simple examples, is likely to be necessary to ensure the familiarity and understanding of ideas required in making choices of strategy. Familiarity with both the purpose and the process of factor-ization is needed in order to be able to make a decision that it would be a sensible strategy to factorize an expression as a step towards solving a problem. Some will argue that this familiarization should take place before students are allowed to use a calculator, whereas I would argue that the calculator has a valuable role in contributing to this learning by using it as a *learning tool* rather than just as an *applications tool*.

One valuable feature of the debate about the role of simple calculators has been the way that it has highlighted the important role that mental calculation has as an appropriate cal-culation strategy when numbers are simple or an estimate is required, and as a means of developing students'understanding of numerical operations and their general fluency. A wide variety of calculator-based tasks and activities have been developed which are aimed at enhancing numerical understanding and exploring numerical conjectures and patterns, although, as suggested earlier in this chapter, such use of patterns is not always used to good effect in extending algebraic ideas.

In different ways, these possibilities apply to the algebraic capabilities of calculators and computer software when they are thought of as learning tools. It is important to make a distinction between algebraic skills applied to simple examples that should be done mentally, or at least written down with little or no intermediate working, and more complicated examples where using a calculator might be appropriate. Thus we would expect a student to factorize $x^2 - 1$ or $x^2 - 3x + 2$ mentally, but a calculator would be much more appropriate in dealing with $6x^3 - 17x^2 - 5x + 6$. Mastering examples like the first two is part of coming to understand the nature of algebraic factors, but the second is a complex task in manipulation which does not necessarily add anything to understanding or to the ability to use the idea of factorization. More time spent on developing mental algebra skills with *simple* examples, and much reduced emphasis on complicated manipulations, might well be beneficial quite apart from the issue of calculator use.

The screen from a TI-89 calculator in Figure 2.8 could be used as a focus for an intro-ductory discussion about the ideas involving algebraic fractions. Substituting the values 1 to 5 for x in the first case gives the fractions $\frac{6}{8}$, $\frac{8}{10}$, $\frac{10}{12}$, $\frac{12}{14}$ and $\frac{14}{16}$. It is immediately evident that numerator and denominator have a common factor of 2, so the fractions can be simplified and this simplification can be related to the corresponding algebraic procedure. The second example can be discussed in a similar way and the fact that numerical fractions obtained for the third case cannot always be simplified explains why the algebraic fraction does not have a simpler form. The calculator is used here to provoke discussion about understanding the procedures involved in simplifying algebraic fractions.

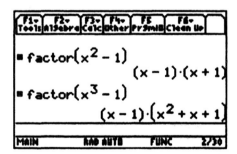

Figure 2.8 *Simplifying fractions with a TI-89 calculator*

The left hand screen in Figure 2.9 displays a pattern in the factors of two expressions to encourage explanation and generalization. Whilst the factors of $x^2 - 1$ should be familiar, those of $x^3 - 1$ are less likely to be so. Expanding the brackets in the second case is therefore instructive to see why they are equivalent to $x^3 - 1$. An obvious further question is to consider $x^4 - 1$ and is likely to lead to a suggestion, in line with the two previous examples, that the factors are $(x - 1)(x^3 + x^2 + x + 1)$. Reference to the right hand screen in Figure 2.9 shows that there are further considerations! When these are resolved it is worth looking at $x^5 - 1$ and $x^6 - 1$ to generalize further.

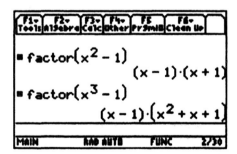
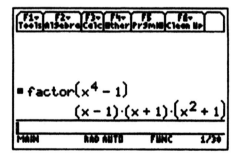

Figure 2.9 *Patterns in factors*

Calculators which carry out algebraic operations are a potentially rich resource when they are exploited in this way to promote understanding by exploring the significance of the results they can generate, but they do not replace the need for students to be fluent in handling simple algebraic procedures independently of the machine.

CONCLUSION

Every teacher of mathematics is all too familiar with the difficulties that students have in making sense of algebra and their common view that it is a rather purposeless pursuit. In this chapter I have reviewed some of the factors that act as barriers to making sense of algebra and some strategies that are important in teaching and learning it more effectively. These are summarized below:

- Algebra often seems to students to lack meaning and purpose.
- Much current algebra teaching at all levels, encouraged by many textbook tasks and assessment items, leads to rote learning aimed at instrumental understanding. Rote learning places too high a reliance on memorizing facts and skills rather than understanding and using them. Meaningful learning, associated with relational understanding, reduces memory load by placing ideas in a coherent framework and enables students to think flexibly about problems for themselves.
- Understanding and fluency in performing operations with number, including negative numbers and fractions at an appropriate stage, is an essential prerequisite for learning algebra successfully and can be enhanced by emphasizing mental calculation.
- Students often interpret letters erroneously as objects rather than as unknowns or variables which can take numerical values. They also have difficulty in interpreting the juxtaposition of symbols and the role of the equals sign to denote equivalence.
- Misconceptions and errors need to be confronted and discussed, and used as growth points for learning. Cognitive conflict is an important element in helping students to see that their current thinking is inadequate and to promote relational understanding of algebra.
- Expressions need to be understood as having a dual role as a process and as a product. They encapsulate a process as instructions to calculate a numerical value, but they are also a product as objects which can be manipulated in their own right. Failure to appreciate this dual nature of expressions is a major barrier to success with algebra.
- Fluency in the skills of manipulating algebraic expressions is essential and requires practice through frequent repetition. Practice should largely arise through using the skills in solving significant problems and exploring interesting numerical and geometrical properties. Skills practised in isolation from meaningful applications tend to be forgotten.
- Whilst algebra is powerful because it can be divorced from immediate contexts most learners need to link ideas to things that are real to them. This does not necessarily require 'real world contexts', because surprising number properties and problems and puzzles of all kinds can be just as real to students and they provide a rich field for using algebraic ideas.
- Algebra is a way of representing generality, but special cases help in generating and making sense of general ideas. The interplay between generalizing and specializing is an important element in making sense of new ideas and in solving problems.
- Algebraic topics often become compartmentalized and divorced from each other and from other mathematical topics. It is important to draw out the links and connections between ideas and topics by using a variety of numerical and pictorial representations to enhance understanding.
- Technology in the form of calculators of all kinds and computer software has a valuable role, if used appropriately, in promoting algebraic understanding, as well as being a means for doing complex calculations and plotting graphs. None the less, fluency in operating with simple algebraic expressions will inevitably continue to be an essential component of understanding and using algebra effectively.

The way in which algebra is introduced is crucial. It is only when students make sense of it at the start that they have any real chance of subsequent success. Two quotations from Tall and Thomas (1991, p. 127) juxtapose the stark choice between success and failure.

> When algebra is taught as an essentially manipulative activity, following a sequence of mechanistic rules, it is only to be expected that a poor understanding of the subject prevails.
> ... the beginning of the subject – giving meaning to the variable concept and devising ways of overcoming the cognitive obstacles – is fundamental to laying a foundation for meaningful algebraic thinking.

It is therefore to this all important subject of beginnings that we turn in Chapter 3 to show that algebra can be meaningful, purposeful and even exciting, when it is introduced thoughtfully and imaginatively.

Chapter 3

Beginnings

Julie, aged 14 years, was asked about the expression $3x + 8y + 2x$:
  I: 'Do the x and y mean anything there, do they stand for anything?'
  J: '*No*, they're just letters, you have them in algebra.'

(Booth, 1984, p. 13)

MEANING AND PURPOSE FOR LETTERS

For many students, the whole subject of algebra frequently becomes associated at a very early stage with tasks which appear to lack any meaning or serve any obvious useful purpose. This naturally leads to failure and distaste. However, even many of those who achieve some success, in the sense that they are able to produce 'right answers' to routine exercises, commonly come to feel that the subject is obscure and unrelated to anything that is real or of interest to them.

The use of letters and the expressions and equations built up with them in mathematics lessons rapidly become linked in students' minds to a rather arbitrary set of routines which have to be endured rather than enjoyed. For the majority of students assurances that algebra is important and useful in the real world, and that this connection will become clearer as their studies progress, does not accord either with their own experience or with the reactions and attitudes they find in older siblings and most adults. Whilst most people will readily acknowledge the importance of using and making sense of numbers in a wide variety of situations, they do not believe that the same is true of algebra, unless they belong to that small minority who see themselves as future scientists or engineers. The widespread use of computers in society might be expected to highlight the importance of algebraic understanding, but for most computer users the only obviously relevant mathematics is again that which relates directly to number.

The way in which algebra is introduced to students is inevitably very significant in determining both their success and their attitudes towards the subject. Providing meaning and purpose is essential from the very first introduction to the use of letters in expressions and equations. An expression like $2n$ has to be seen initially as meaning '2 times a number' or 'a number doubled' giving the set of even numbers when n is a natural number. Thinking of it as two objects mysteriously referred to as n may make it easy to produce a correct response to a request to simplify $2n + 3n$, but may leave students perplexed by $2n + 3$. Meaning can only be imparted alongside purpose: this strange new language needs to explain things and to solve problems that are significant to the learner. Students need to see it as helping to make some tasks simpler rather than complicating simple tasks that they can already do in other ways. Much current practice, sadly encouraged by the style of many text books and the influence of tests and examinations, concentrates on practising technical skills divorced from situations which could provide them with meaning and purpose. As noted in Chapter 2, understanding is often hindered by examples which lead students to identify letters with objects rather than numbers and to fail to develop the key idea of a letter representing a variable. Initially simple expressions arising from linear sequences, equations of straight line graphs and formulae for perimeters provide plenty of examples which can help students understand the nature of algebraic ideas, as they begin to develop a necessary fluency with technical skills and an ability to use algebra successfully in solving a wide range of problems.

A review of most current school text books will reveal a combination of some or all of four introductory approaches to algebra:

- expressions and rules for operations;
- equation solving;
- formulae;
- patterns leading to functions.

These are considered in the next four sections of this chapter and pursued in greater detail in subsequent chapters.

EXPRESSIONS AND RULES FOR OPERATIONS

In Chapter 2 I have discussed at length the important issue of the interpretation that students give to letters and the common misinterpretations that arise. At its worst, starting with expressions and rules leads to students interpreting an expression like $2a + 5a$ as an instruction to add 2 apples and 5 apples to give 7 apples written as $7a$ and leaving the simplification of $2a + 3b + 5a + 6b$ as $7a + 9b$ because 'you cannot add apples and bananas together'. Such an approach can be made more mathematically acceptable by linking the letters to numbers by relating an expression like $2a + 5a$ to $2 \times 8 + 5 \times 8 = 7 \times 8$ or $2 \times 99 + 5 \times 99 = 7 \times 99$. Then the second expression above can be seen to arise from generalizing examples of the form $2 \times 4 + 3 \times 7 + 5 \times 4 + 6 \times 7 = 7 \times 4 + 9 \times 7$. However, it is difficult to see that this on its own offers a strong motivation for spending a lot of time learning how to manipulate algebraic expressions.

The difficulty with introducing algebra using an expressions and rules approach is that it can lead to the inappropriate interpretation of letters as objects, like the apples, bananas and carrots referred to in Chapter 2, rather than as numbers. This can happen even when it is not explicitly encouraged by the teacher. Moreover, students are likely to see it as using strange language and procedures to solve trivial problems that can easily be done without recourse to symbols, leading to a rejection of algebra. This approach, which continues to be very dominant in text books, was referred to as using the 'Four Rules' and dismissed very bluntly a long time ago in a report on algebra teaching by the Mathematical Association (1934, p. 12):

The Four Rules method is unsatisfactory, not because it is difficult, but because it is uninteresting and leaves the boy [*sic*] in a very bad position for further progress. He will have learnt to regard the new subject as meaningless and artificial, and this is the most difficult of all defects to remedy.

Nothing said here is intended to detract from the importance of students becoming fluent in using the technical skills of algebra, but it is intended to question teaching strategies which give this too dominant a place in the introductory stages. Chapter 4 takes a detailed look at the important skills of substituting, simplifying, expanding and finding factors whilst Chapter 7 considers equation solving, which clearly has a central role in any course in algebra because the formulation and solution of equations lies at the heart of much mathematical problem solving.

EQUATION SOLVING

Equation solving is often advocated as a good way of introducing students to algebra, often at a very early age, in the guise of 'find the missing number' or 'I am thinking of a number' problems.

> *T*: I am thinking of a number and I double it. Then I take 5 away and the answer is 7. What was my number?
> *A*: 6
> *T*: Is that right?
> *B*: *Yes. It's 2 times 6 and that's 12 and then take 5 to get 7.*
> *T*: So, A, how did you work it out?
> *A*: *Well, 12 take 5 is 7, so you halve 12 and get 6.*
> *T*: Did anybody think about it differently?
> *C*: *You took 5 away so I added it back on to 7 to get 12. Then I halved it, like A.*
> *T*: Good. Now D, you think of a number and multiply it by 5 and then add 7.
> *D*: *That makes 52.*
> *T*: So, what is D's number?

It is a short step from this sort of dialogue to representing the equations algebraically as $2x - 5 = 7$ or $5x + 7 = 52$ and then to consider more formal methods of solution. Representing such puzzles as equations is a valuable task because it involves translating a verbal statement into a mathematical form and the reverse process of interpreting the mathematical statement is similarly important. Helping students to make this translation in each direction is often neglected because greater emphasis is given to the process of solution.

Unfortunately, learning formal procedures at too early a stage can lead to confusion through students failing to understand how the procedure mirrors the mental method. It can also lead to students thinking that algebra is a harder way to do on paper something that they can easily work out in their head, which encourages them to think that algebra is of little use because they have other ways of solving the teacher's problems. It should be clear that formal procedures are only useful when it becomes difficult to see the way to a solution without a systematic method which may involve written steps. Textbook exercises commonly require lengthy formal 'working' to solve equations that can be done mentally, which some students will feel is an inappropriate complication and others will find confusing. It would be much more motivating to use these methods when the solution is less immediately obvious, either because the numbers involved are not so simple or because the number of operations is greater, as in the following two examples:

$$2.7x - 5.9 = 7.6 \qquad \frac{5(x+2)-7}{3} = 6$$

Another significant objection to emphasizing equations in the early stages is that it encourages the view that letters stand for a specific unknown number and, whilst this may be the case in many problem solving contexts, it may hinder the development of the important idea that letters are used to represent variables. This point is made in characteristic blunt fashion in the previously quoted Mathematical Association report (1934, p. 13) in arguing the case for the formula method:

> ... there is danger that the boy [sic] may learn at first to regard the idea of x as representing an unknown in an equation as more important than the idea of x as a variable. In the formula method the idea of x as a variable is in the forefront from the start.

FORMULAE

Formulae can be presented as a useful, short and memorable way of summarizing a procedure for calculating a variety of quantities in a range of applications which arise both within mathematics and elsewhere. Figure 3.1 illustrates this by showing a wide variety of formulae that will arise in some form in a school algebra course.

$$P = 2l + 2w \qquad A = lw$$
$$C = 2\pi r \qquad A = \pi r^2$$
$$P = A(1 + 0.01r)^n$$
$$v = u + gt \qquad s = \tfrac{1}{2}gt^2$$
$$r = \sqrt{x^2 + y^2} \qquad y = x\tan\theta$$

Figure 3.1 *A variety of mathematical formulae*

The perimeter of a rectangle is a simple example where the link with numerical calculation is strong and easy to understand. The three equivalent forms of the formula shown below represent increasing levels of sophistication in the procedure used to calculate a perimeter.

$$P = l + w + l + w \quad P = 2l + 2w \quad P = 2(l + w)$$

The first case does little more than define perimeter as adding together the lengths of the four sides in turn. The second case puts in an algebraic form the doubling that is required because a rectangle has two pairs of equal sides. It does serve to emphasize the meaning of the expressions $2l$ and $2w$ as two times a number, in this case representing length or width, together with the requirement to double each dimension and then add. The third form may be prompted by asking students for an alternative way to do a particular numerical calculation, leading to the suggestion that the two dimensions can be added first and then the result doubled. This serves to introduce both the way in which brackets are used to indicate priority in an algebraic formula and the important idea that algebraic expressions may have different equivalent forms.

The algebra report of the Mathematical Association (1934) follows the emphasis given in an earlier book on teaching algebra by Nunn (1919), who suggested that it is important 'to cultivate the formula as an instrument of mathematical statement and investigation' (p. 63) and that should be given priority over rules for manipulating expressions and equation solving in the initial stages. Clearly, formulae are important and the skill of substituting values for the variables needs to be developed from an early stage, but these recommendations have not prevented manipulation and equation solving from dominating the way in which the early stages of algebra have been treated in many school text books over the past century and that this is still the case to a large extent today.

An approach to algebra through formulae has the advantage that the meaning of letters can be linked to obvious quantities like length and time that take varying numerical values. Thus the letters are clearly linked to numbers and the idea of variable is very evident. It is easy to point to the wide application in the real world of formulae as a way of writing a calculation procedure in a succinct form. There is, however, a danger that the necessarily simple examples used in the early stages of algebra are seen by students as trivial, because using a formula does not immediately appear to be a necessary step, for example, in doing calculations concerning the perimeter of a rectangle.

Length	Width	Perimeter
5	3	16
8	6	28
10	5	30
24	17	82

F1▼ Tools	F2▼ A13ebra	F3▼ Calc	F4▼ Bther	F5 Pr9mI0	F6▼ Clean Up	

■ Define p = 2·l + 2·w   Done
■ 5 → l   5
■ 3 → w   3
■ p   16

p
| MAIN | RAD AUTO | FUNC | 4/30 |

Figure 3.2 *Using a formula for the perimeter of a rectangle*

A greater sense of purpose can be given to an introduction to algebra through formulae by using a spreadsheet or a graphical calculator. Figure 3.2 shows a spreadsheet and a calculator display. Both use the rectangle perimeter formula to generate results, although the formula in the spreadsheet display is hidden from view. The question becomes how to program the computer or calculator to give the perimeter when length and width are entered. Whatever medium is used, the heart of the problem is to devise and use an appropriate formula.

PATTERNS LEADING TO FUNCTIONS

As I have noted, the three approaches to introducing algebra considered so far have, with varying degrees of relative emphasis, commonly played a major part in school algebra courses over the last 100 years and more. Number patterns and the idea of function, which might be seen as an extension of approaches involving formulae, have a more recent history at school level with origins in 'modern mathematics' in a variety of different forms which influenced mathematics curricula in many countries from the 1950s.

At its simplest level, students can be prompted to look for the pattern in a simple linear sequence like 1, 4, 7, 10, ... and asked to predict subsequent terms. This leads initially to an inductive definition of the sequence as 'start with 1, add on 3', but the problem of finding a term a long way through the sequence leads to the general expression for the nth term in the form $3n - 2$. Driscoll (1999, p. 90) notes that work like this with patterns can help students to develop:

- an understanding of the concept of a function;
- the habit of seeking generalizations as something that 'always works'.

Although the study of students' work on pattern by Orton (1999) points to some difficulties that can arise from this approach, these often reflect some of the misconceptions discussed in the previous chapter and they arise in the context of much current practice which has a tendency, noted below, to trivialize tasks rather than develop their full potential. Orton's study is very valuable in alerting us to the difficulties that students may have, but also in showing the very rich range of possibilities that exist for introducing and developing algebraic ideas.

Finding functional relationships has much in common with an approach through formulae, but the appeal to pattern and the wide range of potentially attractive examples may have advantages in helping students to see meaning and purpose in algebraic ideas in the initial stages as a way of expressing generalizations. The simple expressions involved are less trivial than simple formulae like that for the perimeter of a rectangle and they have a predictive power which is lacking in a situation where you already know how to solve the immediate calculation problem without recourse to algebra. Moreover they can be linked to work involving co-ordinates and graphs which, besides being an important topic in itself, provides an attractive visual representation of algebraic ideas.

The essence of algebra is clearly the power that symbolic representation gives. In order to develop the understanding and facility to capitalize on that power, the links between symbolic forms, numbers and pictures (both graphs and other diagrams) need to be established and constantly reinforced. These different ways of viewing algebraic ideas are referred to as multiple representations by Driscoll (1999) and the links between them are emphasized by the diagram of Figure 3.3.

However, the path to learning algebra is never simple and pattern spotting has its dangers when 'finding the formula' becomes an end in itself. Hewitt (1992) speaks of the limiting way in which this can confine attention to the behaviour of the numbers alone and ignore the greater mathematical richness that may be present in the situation. Mason (1996, p. 76) notes also the way in which such activity can be trivialized: 'Unfortunately there is already an established practice of making a table, guessing a formula, checking that it works on one or two more examples, and then moving on to the next question.' Both these writers seem to imply that more time spent developing the rich mathematical possibilities of a few situations might be more advantageous than superficial work on a large number of unrelated tasks.

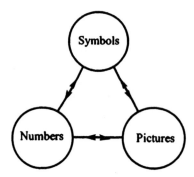

Figure 3.3 *Multiple representations*

I pursue this idea of developing a few situations in some depth in the rest of this chapter. The classroom tasks I describe draw particularly on number patterns and the idea of function and are characterized by three features. First of all, the intention is that they should precede any time devoted to formalizing and practising manipulation of algebraic expressions. Inevitably, some consideration of simplification, substitution and equation solving is required, but these are only developed in an almost incidental way when the need for them arises. Manipulative skills certainly do need to be formalized and practised, but this should only happen after reasons for developing them have been established. Secondly, the tasks should involve situations where the introduction of algebraic expressions is for a clear purpose which enables something to be attained which would be difficult without recourse to algebra. Thirdly, sufficient time should be devoted to any one example so that it may be explored thoroughly and extended to questions that students will see as significant and interesting.

ODD AND EVEN NUMBERS

The sequence of odd numbers is familiar to almost all eleven-year-old students and provides a useful starting point for an introduction to linear sequences. Their algebraic representation is easily derived from their link to even numbers. Moreover they have interesting properties which can be used to provoke curiosity and stimulate discussion. Here is a typical initial dialogue between a teacher and some students:

T: What is an odd number?
A: A number that is not even.
T: So, what is an even number?
B: It's in the 2 times table.
C: It divides by 2 exactly.
T: So, is 53 486 293 an odd number?
D: Yes, because it ends in 3, which is odd.

Some interesting work by Frobisher (1999, pp. 46–47) looked at students' ability to recognize numbers with varying numbers of digits as odd or even. His work suggested that, whilst as many as 15 per cent of eleven-year-olds could not reliably make this distinction with single digit numbers, about two thirds of eleven-year-olds, could safely be assumed to have no difficulty in deciding whether any two digit number was even or odd, and presumably many of these would cope readily with more than two digits. However, Frobisher's work does alert us to the fact that there are some children who may think that 72 is odd because they look at the tens digit and some may have stranger ideas like that of Kurt who suggested that 63 was both even and odd because '60 is even and 3 is odd'!

Clearly, initial discussion with a class does need to check that they are familiar with the nature of odd numbers. Three key ideas are essential to make any sense of their use as a starting point in learning about their algebraic representation:

- the sequence of natural numbers alternates between odd and even;
- the units digit identifies whether a number is odd or even;
- divisibility by two is the essential defining feature.

If asked to tell you the 10th odd number, students will usually respond with 19, because they can easily count up on their fingers, or write down the sequence of numbers if the answer is not immediately obvious to them. Asking them for the 20th odd number commonly brings forth a few responses of 41, the occasional 38 ('double it'), as well as 39, the correct number. Requests for the 100th increases the likelihood of errors with 99, 101 and 201 competing with the correct answer of 199. Errors are always instructive: invariably the answers offered have either 1 or 9 as units digit, suggesting that students are either looking for a number that is 1 above or below a multiple of 10 or, in the case of 9, they may be thinking of each block of five odd numbers having 1, 3, 5, 7 and 9 successively as units digit. Asking for the 100th even number invariably produces a correct response and readily leads to agreement that the corresponding odd number is one less and hence to the general result that any odd number is one less than the corresponding even number.

Here we have a way of interpreting the expression $2n - 1$ for the nth odd number with the $2n$ identified as the nth even number. The expressions are given a meaning which is linked firmly to their numerical interpretation and their purpose is clear because students can do some impressive things with this simple result.

T: What is the 324th odd number?
A: 647, because 648 is the 324th even number and it is one less.
T: Which odd number is 283?
B: The 142nd, because the corresponding even number is 284 and you halve it.

The first question is in effect using simple substitution into $2n - 1$ to find a given odd number, whilst the second provides an informal approach to solving the linear equation $2n - 1 = 283$. Substitution and solving linear equations are important skills that students need to acquire – they can first be encountered informally in interesting contexts like this, where meaning and purpose are clear and curiosity is stimulated, before attempts are made to formalize and practise procedures.

Another example uses the odd number result to illustrate further the explanatory power of algebra. Here students are asked to think of a pair of consecutive odd numbers and add them. It is so easy to assume that students are familiar with our meanings: I once met a ten-year-old student who insisted that odd numbers cannot be consecutive because they are not 'next to each other', presumably in contrast to natural numbers. Looking at results like those in Figure 3.4, students will readily conclude that the answers are not only even but that they seem always to be multiples of 4.

$$3 + 5 = 8 \qquad 9 + 11 = 20 \qquad 7 + 9 = 16$$
$$15 + 17 = 32 \qquad 1 + 3 = 4 \qquad 21 + 23 = 44$$

Figure 3.4 *Adding consecutive odd numbers*

This prompts some obvious questions:

- Why should this be so?
- How can we represent the situation algebraically?
- If an odd number is given by $2n - 1$, what is the next odd number?

With $2n + 1$ representing the next odd number, some simplification gives the answer to our problem: $(2n - 1) + (2n + 1) = 4n$. However, it would be easy to underestimate the level of algebraic understanding involved in making sense of this argument. Figure 3.5 illustrates some results with a table as a step in helping students to understand the justification provided by representing the problem algebraically.

n	$2n - 1$	$2n + 1$	$4n$
1	1	3	4
2	3	5	8
3	5	7	12
4	7	9	16
5	9	11	20

Figure 3.5 *Why multiples of four?*

The fact that $2n + 1$ is the next odd number may be thought of as '2 more' or '1 more than the even number' or the $(n + 1)$th odd number which is $2(n + 1) - 1 = 2n + 2 - 1 = 2n + 1$ and the simplification to arrive at $4n$ involves an understanding of the 'cancelling' of the 1s.

Interesting extensions arise if we consider sums of 3 or 4 or more consecutive odd numbers.

Successive sums of consecutive odd numbers suggest the surprising property that the sum of the first n odd numbers is n^2, the nth square number. Figure 3.6 makes it strikingly clear why this is so.

In the classroom, the teacher can build up the picture as each additional odd number is added to the sum. Thus the nine crosses in the right hand column and the bottom row increase the square from four by four to five by five and eleven more zeros are needed to make it six by six. The arrangement of nine crosses for the fifth odd number can also reinforce the idea of an odd number as one less than the corresponding even number by noting that the column and the row both contain five crosses, but one cross is common to both so the total is $2 \times 5 - 1$, and in the general case $2n - 1$.

The 'sum of odd numbers as a square number' property is an example of the sum of an arithmetic series, a topic which is discussed at length in Chapter 11. At a more sophisticated

$$1 = 1$$
$$1 + 3 = 4$$
$$1 + 3 + 5 = 9$$
$$1 + 3 + 5 + 7 = 16$$
$$1 + 3 + 5 + 7 + 9 = 25$$

×	o	×	o	×
o	o	×	o	×
×	×	×	o	×
o	o	o	o	×
×	×	×	×	×

Figure 3.6 *Sums of consecutive odd numbers*

level, it can be proved by letting S be the sum of the first n consecutive odd numbers and adding corresponding pairs as follows:

$$S = 1 + 3 + 5 + \ldots + 2n - 3 + 2n - 1$$
$$S = 2n - 1 + 2n - 3 + 2n + 5 + \ldots + 3 + 1$$
$$2S = 2n + 2n + 2n + \ldots + 2n + 2n$$

This gives $2S = n \times 2n = 2n^2$, and so $S = n^2$ as required.

TRIANGLE NUMBERS

Triangle numbers are named after the characteristic patterns of dots used to represent them, as shown in Figure 3.7. Finding a formula to generate the numbers provides a good focus for an early lesson to show the power of algebra.

Looking at the dot patterns it becomes clear that each triangle number is the sum of a series of consecutive natural numbers, since each row has one more dot than the previous row. Having counted up the dots in the first few triangle numbers, we can pose a challenging question:

What is the 100th triangle number?

This problem can either be approached by looking directly at the numbers or by working from a pictorial representation. Thinking about it in terms of the numbers, the problem is to calculate the sum:

$$1 + 2 + 3 + 4 + \ldots + 97 + 98 + 99 + 100$$

When students are asked to think about this they come up with a variety of strategies some of which are successful and others of which are either incorrect or too complicated to be useful. One common tactic is to add together the numbers from 1 to 10 and then use that result to calculate the sum of each succeeding set of 10 terms. Another frequent idea arises from noticing that successive pairs of terms like 1 with 99 and 2 with 98 have a sum of 100, but careful thought is needed here to see what happens in the middle – 50 does not have a number to pair up with – and there is the final 100 that must not be forgotten. The real breakthrough comes when somebody suggests pairing up 1 with 100, 2 with 99 and so on to get 50 pairs each

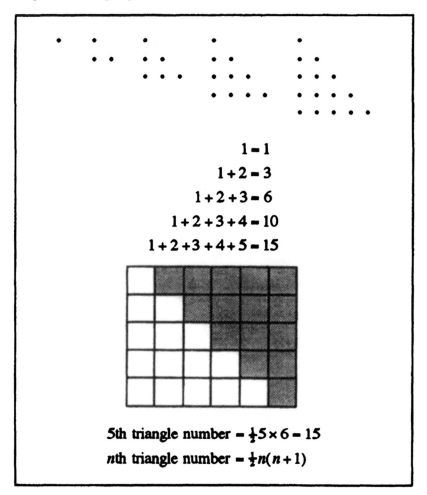

1 = 1

1 + 2 = 3

1 + 2 + 3 = 6

1 + 2 + 3 + 4 = 10

1 + 2 + 3 + 4 + 5 = 15

5th triangle number = $\frac{1}{2}$5 × 6 = 15

nth triangle number = $\frac{1}{2}n(n+1)$

Figure 3.7 *Triangle numbers*

with a sum of 101. The sum of the first 100 numbers, which gives us the 100th triangle number, is then easily calculated as 50 × 101 to give a value of 5050.

Looking back at the product 50 × 101, students see readily that the 50 is half of 100, the number of numbers and 101 is the sum of each pair, in particular, the sum of the first and the last or one more than the number of numbers. Thinking of the result as $\frac{1}{2}$ 50 × 101 makes it easy to calculate other triangle numbers such as $\frac{1}{2}$ 5 × 6 to give 15 for the 5th triangle number. It is then a short step to the general formula $\frac{1}{2}$ $n(n + 1)$.

For a pictorial approach I like to make a staircase with cubes to represent a triangle number. Two of these staircases fit together very neatly to form a rectangle whose length is one unit greater than its width, as shown in Figure 3.7. The particular and general results follow immediately, with each row in the staircase corresponding to the pairs of numbers that were added in the numerical approach, and with an obvious reason for finding a half.

The problem of finding the 100th triangle number can be linked to the result in the previous section about adding consecutive odd numbers. The first 100 natural numbers consist of 50 odd numbers and 50 even numbers. The 50 odd numbers have a sum of $50^2 = 2500$. Since each even number is one more than the corresponding odd number, the sum of the 50 even numbers is $50^2 + 50 = 2550$. So, the sum of the first 100 natural numbers is $2500 + 2550 = 5050$, the result we have obtained in a more direct way above.

This problem and the approaches above have much in common with finding the number of diagonals in a polygon which was discussed in Chapter 2, and there are many other problems which give rise to the triangle numbers. The handshake problem, described in Billington and Evans (1987), provides a particularly impressive example of the wide range of approaches used by students in arriving at and justifying their results. The general formula for triangle numbers, $\frac{1}{2}n(n + 1)$, is an important algebraic result, because it is the sum of the first n natural numbers, the simplest example of an arithmetic series. The sum is often denoted by Σi, which is discussed in Chapter 11 in conjunction with the use of sigma notation to denote series of all kinds.

CO-ORDINATES AND STRAIGHT LINE GRAPHS

When students meet co-ordinates to describe points in the positive quadrant it is useful to distinguish between the two numbers by referring to them at an early stage as x and y co-ordinates, and to name the axes as the x axis and the y axis. Initially, the letters are being used as a convenient label with the particular letters chosen as an agreed convention so that 'we all do the same thing'. However, from the start the letters are taking on the role of a variable, because they can take a range of numerical values. It is natural to observe the patterns in sets of points that lie on a straight line and to see how this leads to a way of labelling straight lines.

One starting point would be to plot the points (0,0), (1,1), (2,2), (3,3) and so on, and then ask what can be said about them. This leads readily to the equations $x = y$ or $y = x$. The parallel line through (0,3), (1,4), (2,5), (3,6) then allows a focus on the key question: 'How can we find the y co-ordinate from the x co-ordinate?' Asking what happens when x is 4 and then 10 and then 50, and so on, will focus attention on the '3 more' relationship rather than counting on in ones. The equation $y = x + 3$ provides a succinct way of representing the idea that the y co-ordinate is always 3 more than the corresponding x co-ordinate.

Alternatively, we could start with a slightly less obvious example like $y = 2x - 1$, as shown in Figure 3.8, and challenge students to find the relationship by looking at the co-ordinates of a few points. There is a clear link in this case to the previous discussion of odd numbers, which it would be entirely appropriate to make explicit at some point. The thinking that leads to the equation can be encouraged in a similar way by making the link to even numbers and by comparing the graph of $y = 2x$ at an appropriate moment.

It may be argued that determining an equation from a set of points on a line is a harder task to start with than using a given equation to find points to plot a line, which is the approach adopted by many school text books. It is certainly necessary to acquire this skill in due course, but at the early stages of learning algebra it is more important that students come to find meaning in algebraic symbols, expressions and equations and that they see purpose in what they are doing. Once an equation has been found they are able to find the co-ordinates of any point on the particular straight line, although it may be prudent to delay considerations of negative numbers at the introductory stage. The equation is a powerful generalization because it not only enables them to find points when x takes large values, but it also extends to fractional values. We can ask, for example, what happens when $x = 1\frac{1}{2}$ or $x = 3\frac{1}{4}$. This adds a dimension that is not present when odd numbers and other linear sequences which relate to

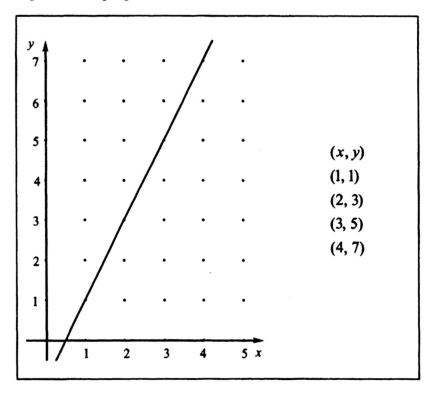

Figure 3.8 *What is the equation of the straight line?*

counting discrete objects are considered, although it may not be something to emphasize for all students in a first encounter with straight line graphs.

The emphasis here has been on the equation of a straight line as a way of expressing a relationship between numbers algebraically and the predictive power that this confers. There are obviously many other important aspects of straight line graphs and these will be considered together with the graphs of other functions in much greater detail in Chapter 6.

MAGIC NUMBERS

In the early stages activities should be designed to establish meaning and purpose for algebra by looking at a variety of situations where the use of letters arises naturally out of a numerical context and where the power of algebra is used to predict and to explain. Some conventions of algebraic notation and some simplification will arise through discussion at this stage, but these do not need to be reinforced immediately by exercises divorced from more motivating problems, because this rapidly leads to the unfortunate notion acquired by many students that algebra is all about meaningless manipulation. They need to understand right from the start what simple algebraic expressions mean and why they are useful in numerical contexts that make sense to them.

A student is asked to suggest a set of four randomly chosen, distinct, single digit numbers. The teacher writes the numbers down and successively adds pairs of numbers to generate a

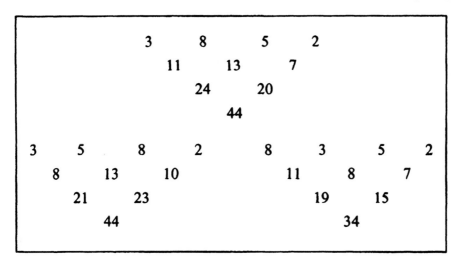

Figure 3.9 *Three examples from the magic number problem*

single 'magic number', as shown in the examples of Figure 3.9. Discussion then focuses on the effect on the magic number of changing the order of the initial four numbers:

- When will the magic number be the same?
- How many magic numbers are possible with a given set of four numbers?
- How can you predict what the magic number will be?

Having established, perhaps by systematically listing the possibilities, that there are 24 ways of arranging four distinct numbers, students can be asked to find the magic number for each arrangement and then to work on these three questions. They will find that there are, at most six magic numbers for any set of four distinct numbers. Sets of four arrangements have a common answer, although in some situations more than one set of four can give the same answer. Typically, students will note that swapping either the outer or the inner pairs of numbers does not alter the magic number which leads to an explanation why each magic number arises from four different arrangements. Some will find a way to predict the magic number.

After students have spent some time working on the problem the teacher can build on their results and explanations by introducing some algebra by proposing that the four numbers are represented by *a*, *b*, *c* and *d*. Even if the students have not met algebraic notation before, they can contribute to and begin to make sense of the algebraic representation shown in Figure 3.10.

The problem offers a lot of scope for students to generate results and then to make predictions and seek explanations. Familiarity with the numerical task helps to make a simple algebraic analysis make sense – the letters are clearly related to numbers, simplification arises naturally and the final result provides a way both to predict the magic number and to explain why swapping the middle or outer number pairs leaves it unchanged. In addition, alternative ways of predicting the magic number can arise by asking students how the calculation can be made simpler. 'Add the middle numbers, multiply the answer by 3 and then add on the other 2 numbers' can be denoted by $3(b + c) + a + d$, drawing attention to the equivalence of

$$
\begin{array}{cccc}
a & b & c & d \\
a+b & b+c & c+d \\
a+2b+c & b+2c+d \\
a+3b+3c+d
\end{array}
$$

Figure 3.10 *Algebraic representation of the magic number problem*

algebraic expressions which look very different, but making that link in a context where the numerical significance is clear.

A simpler version of the problem would be to use only three numbers, whilst an obvious extension lies in considering a set of five or more numbers and noting the links to Pascal's Triangle. Alternative versions of the problem can be created by changing the rules for generating the magic number. For example, adding each number to twice the number on its right gives a magic number of $a + 4b + 5c + d$.

At a later stage in the students' study of algebra, the same idea can be used with the operations of subtraction, multiplication or even division. Subtraction naturally brings in negative numbers at the numerical stage and, then, simplification involving subtraction and brackets to show, for instance, that $(a - b) - (b - c) = a - 2b + c$. Multiplication involves operations with powers with the magic number given by the expression ab^3c^3d. Division can lead to further ideas, both numerical and algebraic.

Generating these magic numbers is rich in possibilities because the simple situation provokes curiosity and encourages students to make predictions and search for explanations. Magic numbers provide a simple numerical context which gives a clear meaning to letters and simple algebraic expressions and a clear purpose for simplification. Students can thus begin to appreciate the power of algebra as a tool for solving problems and providing explanations.

LINEAR SEQUENCES

Figure 3.11 shows a task for students which is designed to help them find the linear function relating the number of pins to the number of cards. This is the same type of exercise as the one we have discussed earlier concerning odd numbers. It moves from counting through the sequence to determining terms where counting is not a sensible strategy, and then on to the generalization as $3n + 1$.

The pictorial presentation of the problem means that the relationship between the numbers can be related back to the picture, something that students often seem reluctant to do. The two questions asking 'why?' focus on explaining the two parameters 3 and 1 in terms of the pins in the picture – the fact that 3 extra pins are required for each card and that there is 1 extra pin required for the first card. The research reviewed in Orton (1999) makes clear that students have little difficulty in spotting and explaining the common difference of 3 in an example like this, but find it much more difficult to relate that to an expression for a general term.

With the odd numbers problem the link to even numbers as multiples of 2 provides a useful starting point, so with the cards problem the idea of 3 pins for each card suggests multiples of

Display cards are pinned to a board as shown in the picture on the left.

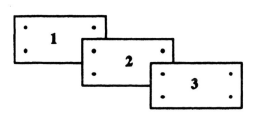

No. of cards	No. of pins
1	4
2	7
3	
4	
5	

- Complete the table for 3, 4 and 5 cards.

- Why does the number of pins go up by 3 each time?

- How many pins for 10 and for 20 cards?

- Why do these two answers end in 1?

- How many pins for 100 and for 200 cards?

- How many pins for *n* cards?

- If there are 1000 pins, how many cards are there?

Figure 3.11 *How many pins?*

3. In the case of 10 cards, 3 pins per card gives 30, but counting through the sequence gives 31, so where has the extra 1 come from? When it comes to 20 cards some may decide that it is 60 by multiplying 20 by 3, some may use a false proportionality argument to suggest 62 – 'double the answer for 10' – and yet others will either count through the sequence or reason in some appropriate way to find 61.

Talking about the various suggestions – both the right ones and the wrong ones – is an essential part of the process of helping students to understand. It may even be useful for the teacher to interject a wrong answer if one does not arise naturally, so that students are challenged to see why it is wrong and resolve the conflict between different results from different lines of reasoning. The step to the general result and its simple symbolic form is dependent on establishing a clear understanding in verbal terms along the lines of '3 times the number of cards and 1 more'. If the purpose of the exercise is to help students understand linear expressions and to generate, interpret and use them successfully, then finding an expression to represent a sequence should not be the end point when considering a particular task like this. Having established the general result, its meaning and application needs to be reinforced through further questions and discussion:

- How many pins for 50, 80 or 120 cards?
- How many cards if we had 91 or 901 pins?
- Can we generate any term of the sequence on a spreadsheet?
- What will a graph of number of cards against number of pins look like?
- What would the corresponding result be for triangular or hexagonal cards?

There are many similar examples which generate linear sequences: for example, Orton (1999, pp. 128–134) discusses students' responses to a range of problems involving match sticks and a variety of problems involving coloured tiles characterizes the introductory approach to algebra in the text books of the School Mathematics Project (SMP, 2000). Figure 3.12 shows some typical examples with questions that move from a small number, through a large number to a generalization and then ask a question that requires an inverse process or the solution of an equation.

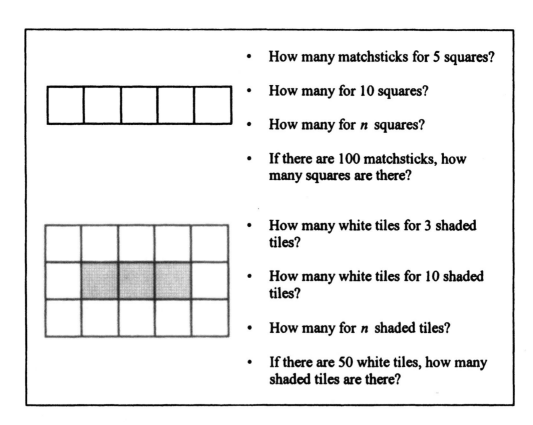

Figure 3.12 *Examples leading to linear sequences*

NUMBER PUZZLES

Puzzles which involve an element of surprise are a good way to stimulate students' curiosity. Algebraic skills and understanding can be developed through arriving at a surprising result and then seeking an explanation for it. Students then have the means to construct their own similar puzzles.

A teacher might ask a group of students to write down their result at each stage as a set of instructions is given:

- Think of a number
- Add 7
- Double
- Multiply by 5
- Subtract 20
- Divide by 10
- Subtract the original number

Asking round the group most students find to their surprise that they have the same final number of 5. The teacher asks several students for their starting number to show that they did not all choose the same number. Any students with a final number which differs from 5 will rapidly check to find their error. Curiosity has been aroused and students are more receptive to seeking an explanation.

> *T*: Let the number we start with be x. We added 7. How can we write that?
> *A*: $x + 7$
> *T*: We then doubled, so what shall we write next?
> *B*: $2x + 7$
> *T*: C. What number did you start with?
> *C*: 3
> *T*: So, what is $x + 7$ if $x = 3$?
> *C*: 10
> *T*: D, what is $2x + 7$ with $x = 3$?
> *D*: 13, *but that's not double*.
> *T*: So, what should double $x + 7$ be?
> *D*: 2x + 14

The discussion can continue with the algebraic representation of each step being written down and comparisons made with some of the students' numerical results. A table like that shown in Figure 3.13 illustrates the steps in the problem using several different starting numbers.

Establishing a correct expression at each stage requires discussion about appropriate algebraic procedures and conventions together with verification through numerical checks. Asking students to create their own puzzles of the same form which they can then try out on their peers is a motivating activity which provides much reinforcement of simple skills applied to a situation where both the meaning and purpose of what they are doing is clear.

The task can be readily extended by increasing the number of steps, by introducing other operations, such as subtracting from a given number and powers and roots, and by extending the range of numbers which are used. Using fractions and negative numbers or larger numbers, with a calculator used to aid calculation, reinforces the generality of a procedure described by the same set of algebraic expressions.

x	3	8	5	2
x + 7	10	15	12	9
2x + 14	20	30	24	18
10x + 70	100	150	120	90
10x + 50	80	130	100	70
x + 5	8	13	10	7
5	5	5	5	5

Figure 3.13 *Surprise – 5 every time!*

CONCLUSION

The initial encounters that students have with algebra are crucially important in establishing both their attitudes towards the subject and the foundations on which to build their subsequent study of the subject together with its links to the rest of mathematics. I have argued that it is essential for students to see algebra as both meaningful and purposeful from the earliest stages. There are two questions that students may quite legitimately ask about any piece of algebra:

- What does this mean?
- What is the use of it?

They are more likely to respond positively to these questions if they are introduced to problems and tasks which show algebra as a powerful tool which enables them to explain and do things that would be difficult without. They are much less likely to respond positively if they are required to spend a lot of time practising procedures whose meaning is not clear and whose purpose will only become apparent at some unspecified later time. Practising skills only makes sense when meaning and purpose are clear. The reason for practising skills is very apparent when learning to play a musical instrument or to drive a car, but it is much more difficult to impart the same sense of immediate purpose when learning algebra. Since algebra is a powerful explaining and problem solving tool, these two roles should be in evidence at every stage in learning the subject. Situations that generate a variety of problems to solve and results to explain should be used as a vehicle to introduce appropriate symbolic conventions and procedures as the need for them becomes apparent.

One of the key features of algebra is its use of symbols as a succinct and memorable way of expressing procedures and relationships. In particular, letters are used to denote variables whose essential characteristic is that they can take a range of numerical values. It is important that the idea of letter as variable is constantly reinforced in the early stages by giving a dominant role to contexts which involve relationships between sets of numbers rather than those where the letter is a specific unknown number. Letters are one of the building blocks of algebraic expressions which have the two key features of procedure and concept encapsulated in the word 'procept' coined by Gray and Tall (1993, p. 6) and discussed in Chapter 2. Students have to learn to treat an expression like $2n - 1$ as a meaningful element in its own right as well as seeing it as a procedure to carry out when a value is assigned to the number n.

Odd and even numbers and other linear sequences arising in a variety of ways have provided contexts in which a general property of a set of positive whole numbers is observed for small numbers, extended to larger numbers and then expressed in a conventional symbolic form. Similarly triangle numbers, the equations of straight line graphs, predicting magic numbers and explaining and devising number puzzles all provide ways of introducing algebraic expressions meaningfully and using them for a clear purpose. The link between an expression and numbers is kept to the forefront in all these examples, but additionally expressions act as a label for a set of numbers and as an entity that can be operated on itself, when used as part of a proof or explanatory process. The power of algebra is demonstrated when any term in a sequence can be determined and relationships and properties can be deduced or conjectured and then shown to be generally true.

An urge to let students 'do lots of examples' or 'practise the sort of questions that they will get in examinations' may result in formula spotting activities which regard finding the formula as the end point. Likewise an emphasis on learning skills without using them to solve significant problems does little to give algebra meaning and purpose. Developing these very necessary skills in appropriate ways is the subject of Chapter 4, but looking for patterns should be the starting point for a rich mathematical experience which draws on the full possibilities of situations and introduces algebra in a way that seems comprehensible, exciting and relevant.

Chapter 4

Developing Algebraic Skills

Practice can take place without the need for what is to be practised to become the focus of attention. (Hewitt, 1996, p. 34)

MENTAL ALGEBRA

Substituting values, simplifying expressions, expanding and finding factors, equation solving and graphing are all important skills where fluency and understanding are needed if a student is to make progress with algebra. Fluency with an algebraic skill means being able to carry it out readily and accurately as an immediately available response in an appropriate situation. Learning such skills is not an end in itself, but one of the key requirements in being able to use and apply algebra successfully. When simple skills have become automatic the student can concentrate on the higher order thinking that is required to apply ideas to interesting problems. Unfortunately, the common emphasis in textbooks and tests is just on acquiring the skills, without using them in ways which are meaningful to the student or promoting the relational understanding advocated by Skemp (1976), discussed in Chapter 2. Such an emphasis has the effect of reinforcing the common impression that algebra is an obscure and irrelevant activity.

I argued in Chapter 3 that students need to encounter algebra as an activity for exploring and solving significant problems that are difficult to resolve without such a powerful tool. There is clearly a dilemma here, because the skills are needed in order to solve the problems which provide the motivation for learning them. Which comes first: the problems or the skills? My argument in Chapter 3 was that this is a false dichotomy: the skills should be developed alongside their applications, so that their meaning and purpose are reinforced constantly and motivation is enhanced.

However, it will rightly be said that skills have to be practised in order to develop the necessary fluency. The need to practise scales and arpeggios when learning to play the piano is often advanced as an analogy, but there is an important difference. The ultimate aim is clear with piano playing, namely to be able to play beautiful music, but when students start learning algebra the perception of an algebraic equivalent of beautiful music is rarely clear to them. As a consequence, motivation is often limited and diminishes as any purpose seems ever more distant and obscure. The need to practise skills is obvious; the ways in which it is done need to be much more imaginative and stimulating than what is offered by the average school text-book. This chapter seeks to show how skills can be developed through talk and tasks which reinforce meaning and purpose.

A proper understanding of algebraic processes is inevitably very dependent on a corresponding understanding and facility with arithmetical operations. Helping students to do calculations mentally is particularly valuable in this respect because simple numbers are involved and underlying principles have to be secure for success. Practice with mental methods constantly reinforces the distributive law through examples like 7×17 calculated as $7 \times 10 + 7 \times 7$ and 8×98 calculated as $8 \times 100 - 8 \times 2$. Seemingly awkward looking examples like $7 \times 3.5 + 3 \times 3.5$ and $7 \times 237 + 3 \times 237$ also reinforce the distributive law and give appropriate meanings to an algebraic simplification like $7a + 3a = 10a$. Mental arithmetic skills are best developed by asking students to perform simple calculations with a minimum of written working and then, most importantly, to engage in discussion about the methods used. Short, orally-given, questions where students write down their answers provide one way of reviewing frequently and quickly a variety of types of calculation and of discussing those areas where difficulties continue to arise.

Algebraic skills can be reviewed and practised by using the same technique as with mental arithmetic – short and simple algebra questions with key information written on the board. For want of a better phrase I refer to this as mental algebra. The emphasis should be on identifying errors and discussing them as they arise. Students then have immediate feedback, something which they do not get with a timed test where attention tends to focus on right answers and the total marks obtained. Questions should be short and simple because fluency and understanding are best developed and reinforced when attention is focused on the key idea involved with no distraction from awkward numbers or complicated expressions. It is also important to ensure that the skills that have already been developed are constantly reviewed and reinforced in this way. The typical text book review or revision exercise is designed for this purpose, but use of such exercises can be time-consuming and too infrequent to serve a useful purpose.

Figure 4.1 shows a set of ten skill-related questions linked to three of the introductory activities discussed in Chapter 3. Substitution is required for questions 1, 7, 8 and 9 and the identical results to questions 7 and 8 provide a useful point for discussion. Questions 3, 4 and 6 involve simplification and question 5 explores an aspect of the meaning of the expression $2n + 3$ with a link back to question 3. Questions 2 and 10 require the student to solve a simple linear equation, but in each case the equation arises from a situation which gives some meaning to the task – odd numbers and straight line graphs. Besides giving necessary practice in important skills as one means of developing fluency, well-designed short questions like this also provide an opportunity to discuss errors, to make links and to reinforce understanding. Such questions should not be seen as a test where invariably the emphasis is only on getting right answers, but as an opportunity for students to learn more from the questions and the discussion that follows.

SUBSTITUTING VALUES

When the key idea that letters are used to represent numbers is constantly emphasized, substitution arises all the time as a natural part of algebraic activity. Prematurely divorcing

1. Find the 12th odd number by evaluating $2n-1$ when $n = 12$.

2. Find n if $2n-1 = 19$.

3. What is the next odd number after $2n+1$?

4. Add the two consecutive numbers $n+1$ and $n+2$.

5. Is the answer to question 4 odd or even?

6. Add $a+b$ and $b+c$.

7. Evaluate $a+2b+c$ when $a = 4$, $b = 2$ and $c = 1$.

8. Evaluate $a+2b+c$ when $a = 1$, $b = 2$ and $c = 4$.

9. What is the y co-ordinate of the point on the straight line $y = 3x+1$ where $x = 4$?

10. What is the x co-ordinate of the point on the straight line $y = 3x+1$ where $y = 16$?

Figure 4.1 *Ten mental algebra questions*

algebra from its underlying numerical basis is one source of many of the misconceptions discussed in Chapter two. Being able to move between a symbolic expression or equation and the numerical pattern or relationship that it represents is a vital part of a proper understanding of algebra. The ability to substitute values and evaluate expressions should develop naturally as meaning is given to those expressions.

Exercises designed to practice substitution are generally more effective if they arise as a means to an end rather than as an end in themselves, although there are particular situations which require a specific focus. For instance, many students have difficulty in substituting values into expressions of the form $5t^2$. The common error, which the notational convention tends to encourage, is to multiply the value of t by 5 and then square the result, rather than to square first and then multiply. Discussion can easily be provoked by asking students to evaluate 5×2^2 mentally. Invariably some will give the answer 100 and some will say 20 – a clear case of cognitive conflict! This gives a valuable opportunity to discuss the need for agreement about a common meaning. Using a calculator to do the calculation with a more awkward number can lead to the same conflict. Figure 4.2 shows the different results depending on whether or not the enter or equals key is pressed before squaring.

Two contrasting short classroom exercises related to this substitution problem are shown in Figure 4.3. The first is designed to reinforce the rule by a set of routine substitution tasks, whereas the second provides a simple context where it is clear why the squaring must be performed first. Tasks of the first type tend to encourage teacher and students to concentrate on how to get answers, whereas the second task is designed to reinforce understanding by linking the formula to the familiar idea of area which can be represented pictorially.

It would be simplistic to suggest either that the second task provides a model for successful algebra teaching or that exercises of the first type are of no value, but exclusive reliance on

■ 5·3.7	18.5
■ $(18.5)^2$	342.25

■ $5·(3.7)^2$	68.45

Figure 4.2 *Multiply and square or square and multiply?*

Remember that $5t^2$ means:

Square first, then multiply by 5.

Example:

$t = 3: \ 5t^2 = 5 \times 3^2 = 5 \times 9 = 45$

Evaluate the following:

1. $5t^2$ with $t = 3$.

2. $5t^2$ with $t = 7$.

3. $2a^2$ with $a = 4$.

4. $6y^2$ with $y = 2$.

5. $\frac{1}{2}x^2$ with $x = 6$.

6. $2p^2 + 3q^2$ with $p = 3$ and $q = 5$.

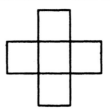

The diagram shows the net for an open topped cube.

1. Evaluate the area of the outer surface of the cube if the edge length is 3 cm.

2. With the length of the edge of the cube in cm given by d, explain why the surface area is given by $5d^2$.

3. Calculate the area if $d = 10$.

4. Find the value of d if the area is $180 \, \text{cm}^2$.

Figure 4.3 *Two contrasting exercises*

practising skills through tasks of the first type is an inadequate response both to the difficulties students have with algebra and to their frequent lack of motivation.

Substituting values into an expression of the form $a + bc$ is a another example where the question of priority in carrying out operations arises. As with the earlier example, a request to evaluate $3 + 2 \times 4$ is likely to produce two different responses, in this case 20 and 11. The conflict is reinforced if the same calculation is attempted on two different calculators, where one is a simple four-function calculator that does not respect the usual algebraic conventions.

This helps to undermine the blind faith that students often have in the output of calculators and the conflict provokes discussion about the need for the convention which gives priority to multiplication and division over addition and subtraction. Students usually have little difficulty in correctly interpreting brackets indicating priority of operations in a given expression. However, they often omit brackets when they construct their own expressions, for example by writing $2a + b$ when they mean $2(a + b)$.

Calculators and software like graph plotters where algebraic expressions can be entered are particularly useful as a way of drawing attention to the role of brackets because it is necessary to enter rational expressions along a single line. It is therefore necessary to distinguish clearly between a pair of expressions like $a/b + c$ and $a/(b + c)$ and to see that a/bc is potentially very ambiguous. A calculator will calculate $3/2 \times 5$ as $(3/2) \times 5$ to give 7.5 and that is not the same as $3/(2 \times 5)$ which is equivalent to $3/2/5$ with a value of 0.3. The distinctions can be summarized in algebraic terms as follows:

$$\tfrac{a}{b} \div c = a \div b \div c = a \div (b \times c) = \tfrac{a}{bc} \text{ and } \tfrac{a}{b} \times c = a \div b \times c = a \times b \div c = \tfrac{ac}{b}$$

However, reference to particular cases as they arise is likely to be much more effective in helping students than showing them a summary like this!

In the early stages of learning algebra, coming to terms with the meaning of letters and the conventions associated with symbolic representation is a major hurdle. Complications which take attention away from that major focus of attention should therefore be avoided. It is sensible to base a lot of work on small whole numbers with occasional reference to large numbers to illustrate the power of the ideas. Introducing fractions and negative numbers before students are completely fluent in their use can make algebra seem hard when the difficulty actually stems from problems in handling these types of numbers correctly and fluently. For example, some of the problems associated with learning about simultaneous equations, which are considered in Chapter 7, could be avoided in the initial stages if work was limited to equations involving addition only with solutions restricted to positive whole numbers. Once the general principles have been established and students have gained some confidence in solving simple equations, it is much easier to extend to others which involve fractions and negative numbers.

Failure to develop understanding and fluency with negative numbers and fractions is often a major barrier to later success with algebra, although there is much that can and should be done before the need for them becomes crucial. Negative numbers have an immediate relevance to simplification so they must come next with some discussion of fractions towards the end of the chapter.

NEGATIVE NUMBERS

Students normally first encounter negative numbers as a way of denoting positions below zero on a number line through considering practical examples like temperature and mathematical situations involving co-ordinates. As labels on a line, negative numbers present few problems to students. Conceptual difficulties arise when operations with negative numbers are introduced. Addition is often considered as a movement along a number line, although the numbers are then being used in two different ways: to denote position and to denote a movement in terms of length and direction. None the less students usually have little difficulty with addition presented in this way. Küchemann (1981b, p. 82) found that items involving addition of positive and negative numbers were 'generally answered correctly by well over 80 per cent of fourteen-year-old pupils', but performance on subtraction items was very much weaker. Subtraction is less amenable to an approach through movements along a number line. Finding a difference on a number line gives the magnitude easily, but it is not intuitively obvious whether it should be positive or negative. Furthermore, students are much more familiar with subtraction as taking away than they are with the idea of difference.

Notation and the way things are said are a further source of difficulty. Many textbooks write $5 - -3$ or $5 -(-3)$, which are both read as 'five minus minus three'. The repeated minus sounds confusing and using the same word to describe both the operation and the type of number does not help to distinguish clearly the two ideas. Writing $5 - {}^-3$, which is read as 'five minus negative three' has the advantage of making the necessary distinction in both the written and the spoken form. Although most everyday usage uses the form 'minus three' rather than 'negative three', it is not evident from my own experience that this is of itself a source of confusion.

An alternative to the number line approach is to appeal to a pattern like that shown in Figure 4.4, which leads to the useful idea of subtraction as 'addition of the opposite kind of number' or 'addition of the inverse'. However, it does not obviously suggest to students that something has been taken away and can lead to a 'two minuses make a plus' rule. Like all rules, this may be applied inappropriately – for instance, to obtain a positive answer when adding two negative numbers. Appealing to pattern is certainly useful, both with addition and subtraction, but it may not be sufficient to provide a good intuitive feel which can be drawn upon when a particular calculation arises in isolation.

$$3 - 2 = 1$$
$$3 - 1 = 2$$
$$3 - 0 = 3$$
$$3 - {}^-1 = 4$$
$$3 - {}^-2 = 5$$
$$3 - {}^-3 = 6$$

Figure 4.4 *Subtracting negative numbers*

Küchemann (1981b, p. 87) suggests that 'the number line should be abandoned, despite its proven effectiveness for addition' and replaced by an approach where 'the integers are regarded as distinct entities or objects, constructed in such a way that the positive integers cancel out the negative integers', although he does not give an example of such an approach. Building on this idea, students' intuitive feel for subtraction as taking away can be invoked through seeing positive or negative numbers actually being physically removed. A negative number is an additive inverse so that, for instance, $^-1$ is defined as the number which satisfies the equation $^-1 + 1 = 0$. I originally came across an approach based on this idea in Kaner (1964), whose approach I have adapted in what follows. If some small squares marked with 1 and ⁻1 are displayed in pairs, as shown in Figure 4.5, students will immediately accept the defining property and agree that the sum of all the numbers displayed is zero.

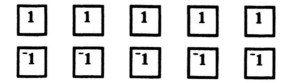

Figure 4.5 *Negative numbers as additive inverses:* ⁻1 + 1 = 0

To calculate 4 −⁻3, four extra 1s are added to the display as shown in Figure 4.6 and then three ⁻1s are removed making it immediately clear that 4 − ⁻3 = 7. Seeing ⁻3 physically removed shows immediately that adding positive 3 is equivalent, which is a very powerful reinforcement of the idea of subtraction as addition of the inverse.

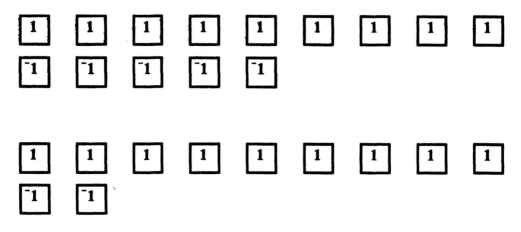

Figure 4.6 *Subtracting a negative number: 4 − ⁻3*

Although this approach is particularly useful for subtraction, it has the considerable virtue that it works equally well for addition. Figure 4.7 shows the two steps involved in calculating ⁻3 + 2 = ⁻1.

Initially, each student can be equipped with a set of small card or paper squares each depicting either 1 or ⁻1 and an envelope to store them in for subsequent use. After a time, I have found that many students internalize the procedure and do it in their heads, whilst others are happy to jot down rapidly some 1s and ⁻1s and do some crossing out to do their calculations. The big advantage of this method is that it provides a simple concrete representation, which is remembered and can be referred back to, rather than a set of rules, which are often forgotten or misused.

Multiplication of two negative numbers is conceptually a very difficult idea and I am not aware of a really simple and satisfying concrete way of representing it, or an obvious everyday example where it makes sense and is seen to be useful. Many ideas will be found in textbooks, but they do not have the same simple appeal as the representation of addition and subtraction that has just been described. The result of multiplying a positive number by a negative number

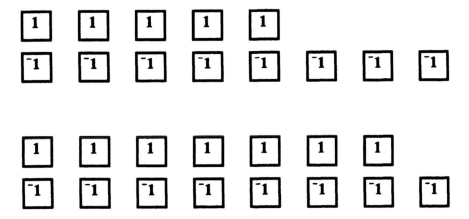

Figure 4.7 *Adding a negative number:* ⁻3 + 2 = ⁻1

is intuitively obvious and provides a starting point for the multiplication table for negative three, shown in Figure 4.8. An appeal to pattern does make the positive result for multiplying two negative numbers seem very plausible. It is not much to remember, but it is very difficult to understand, so it is perhaps not surprising that students are frequently confused by multiplication.

$$3 \times {}^-3 = {}^-9$$
$$2 \times {}^-3 = {}^-6$$
$$1 \times {}^-3 = {}^-3$$
$$0 \times {}^-3 = 0$$
$${}^-1 \times {}^-3 = 3$$
$${}^-2 \times {}^-3 = 6$$
$${}^-3 \times {}^-3 = 9$$

Figure 4.8 *The negative three times table*

This plausibility can be further reinforced at different times by comparing the graphs of $y = 3x$ and $y = {}^-3x$ and by looking at the effect of enlargements with a negative scale factor centred at the origin on the vertices of a shape some of whose co-ordinates are negative.

Furthermore, it is possible to prove that multiplying two negative numbers gives a positive result in a simple way. One of the numbers is denoted by the subtraction of two positive numbers and the resulting expression is multiplied out and simplified. Here, for example, are two ways of showing that ⁻2 × ⁻3 = 6:

$$^-2 \times {}^-3 = {}^- 2 \times (1 - 4) = {}^- 2 \times 1 - {}^- 2 \times 4 = {}^- 2 - {}^- 8 = 6$$
$$^-2 \times {}^-3 = {}^- 2 \times (0 - 3) = {}^- 2 \times 0 - {}^- 2 \times 3 = 0 - {}^- 6 = 6$$

Being able to perform operations successfully with negative numbers is an essential pre-requisite for many algebraic ideas beyond the introductory stage. It is vital that students spend sufficient time acquiring and maintaining a fluency based on a feel for what they are doing, rather than being compelled to place too much reliance on remembering seemingly arbitrary rules.

SIMPLIFYING

Simplification can too easily become an end in itself whose purpose is even more obscure than that of substitution. In Chapter 3 I argued that it is not sensible to introduce too much formal simplification in the early stages of learning algebra, because it is very difficult to justify when presented in isolation other than by saying that it is a skill that will be useful later. Students are better motivated if they can see a purpose in what they are doing when they are doing it. The necessary skills of simplification should be developed and practised alongside tasks which use them in interesting ways.

Many of the misconceptions related to treating letters as objects arise because textbooks fail to present simplification as in any way linked to the number relationships that the equivalent forms represent. Being able to operate with symbols without making frequent reference to the numbers they represent is an essential aim, but failing to make that numerical link frequently in the early stages inhibits understanding and does not give students any means of checking whether their results make sense.

The approach in so many school textbooks results in pupils spending a lot of time sim-plifying expressions like $3n + 2n - 1$ without developing any sense of where such things come from or what an answer like $5n - 1$ might mean. It would help their understanding greatly if the numerical links were emphasized much more. This particular example could be approached by asking students to write down the first five multiples of 3 and alongside them the first five odd numbers. Adding corresponding pairs of numbers, as shown on the left in Figure 4.9, gives an interesting set of results where the units digits alternate between 4 and 9. The question to pose then is why this should be so. If the results are tabulated as shown on the right, and a column is included to number the terms in each sequence, the headings on the columns effectively illustrate the identity $3n + 2n - 1 = 5n - 1$. The units digit pattern in the last column is explained by each term being of the form $5n - 1$, one less than a multiple of 5.

Figure 4.10 provides another pair of examples which show the interesting results which arise when adding and subtracting simple expressions. The pattern in the right hand column is explained in each case by simplifying the expression at the top:

$$(n - 2) + (n + 1) = 2n - 1 \text{ and } (n + 3) - (n - 1) = 4.$$

These examples are designed to forge a strong link between simplification and the numerical sequences arising from the expressions involved. In each case there is an obvious pattern in the third column which stimulates curiosity. Does the pattern continue and if so how can we be sure? Simplification serves a useful purpose by providing an explanation for what is observed and confirming a general result.

When adding expressions we know that the brackets are not essential. It would then appear

$$3 + 1 = 4$$
$$6 + 3 = 9$$
$$9 + 5 = 14$$
$$12 + 7 = 19$$
$$15 + 9 = 24$$

n	$3n$	$2n-1$	$3n+2n-1$
1	3	1	4
2	6	3	9
3	9	5	14
4	12	7	19
5	15	9	24

Figure 4.9 *Alternating units digits*

n	$n-2$	$n+1$	$(n-2)+(n+1)$
1	‾1	2	1
2	0	3	3
3	1	4	5
4	2	5	7
5	3	6	9

n	$n+3$	$n-1$	$(n+3)-(n-1)$
1	4	0	4
2	5	1	4
3	6	2	4
4	7	3	4
5	8	4	4

Figure 4.10 *Simplification through number patterns*

to be a simple matter for students to simplify $n - 2 + n + 1$ to get $2n - 1$, but errors can arise from the way students read and interpret the expression. One difficulty with expressions of this type is that students attach the subtraction sign to the wrong term and subtract the second n from the first n because they think that the 2 cannot be subtracted from the n. Thus, no term in n remains, leaving the 2 and the 1 to give a final result of 3. Tabulating several numerical cases for the two expressions shows clearly that such a result is wrong. Looking more closely at a numerical case also shows that attaching the sign to the term that follows is not such an unfamiliar notion. For example, with $n = 5$, the complete calculation is $5 - 2 + 5 + 1$, with no temptation to subtract the second 5 from the first.

The subtraction example, $(n + 3) - (n - 1)$, raises different issues because ignoring the brackets gives $n + 3 - n - 1$, which clearly gives 2 if the signs are attached to the correct terms. That conflicts with the tabulated results and gives students a motivation for examining the role of brackets more carefully in the case of subtraction. Discussing a variety of numerical examples like $8 - (5 + 2)$ and $8 - (5 - 2)$ helps students to see that $a - (b + c) = a - b - c$ and $a - (b - c) = a - b + c$. It is then clear that $(n + 3) - (n - 1) = n + 3 - n + 1 = 4$, as required.

For most students, a single explanation on one occasion will not suffice to ensure understanding and fluency with these technical points of simplification. Time spent looking at a few examples in detail is needed so that students see that simplification does have a purpose and that recourse to numbers is always a useful check as well as a way to enhance understanding. It is obviously important to develop fluency using a wide variety of examples so that expressions can be simplified accurately and rapidly, but practice to attain that desirable state will be more effective if it takes a variety of forms and students have a means of seeing that their answers make sense.

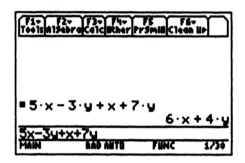

Figure 4.11 *Simplification with an advanced calculator*

An advanced calculator like the TI-89 or TI-92 that does symbolic algebra simplifies expressions where possible when they are entered, as shown by Figure 4.11. Of course, the calculator gives all the right answers, so it would be fruitless to ask students to do an exercise asking them to enter expressions like this and record the answers. However, an alternative form of exercise, like that shown in Figure 4.12, where the result is given but the signs have been deleted from each expression that was simplified, offers much more scope. Students have to try different possibilities to find the given result. They use the calculator to check, so that they keep trying until they have it right. After overcoming an initial tendency to guess wildly, they begin to think carefully about what signs to insert to give a correct answer. This reinforces their understanding of the simplification process by drawing attention to the fact that the operation sign refers to the immediately succeeding term and to the effect of placing a minus sign before a bracketed expression.

Some of the examples in Chapter 3 provide situations where the need to simplify arises in a meaningful context:

- $(2n - 1) + (2n + 1) = 4n$ to show that the sum of two consecutive odd numbers is a multiple of 4.
- $(a + 2b + c) + (b + 2c + d) = a + 3b + 3c + d$ in the 'magic number' problem.
- $l + w + l + w = 2l + 2w$ for the perimeter of a rectangle.
- Doubling $x + 7$ and subtracting 20 from $10x + 50$ in the number puzzle.

Each of these examples suggest a variety of related possibilities that provide opportunities for simplification with nothing more complicated than simple linear expressions. The sum of two consecutive odd numbers is another example of the idea of adding corresponding terms from a pair of sequences considered in the first part of this section. The magic number problem can be developed in a variety of ways by varying the rules for combining the numbers leading to different expressions whose predictive power can be tested.

Perimeters of a variety of shapes lead to simple formulae with length providing a clear association between letters and numbers. Figure 4.13 shows a pattern created by a set of

$5x$ $3y$ $2x$ $2y = 7x + 5y$ $(a \quad b) \ (a \quad b) = 2a$

$5x$ $3y$ $2x$ $2y = 7x + y$ $(a \quad b) \ (a \quad b) = 2a + 2b$

$5x$ $3y$ $2x$ $2y = 3x + 5y$ $(a \quad b) \ (a \quad b) = 2b$

$5x$ $3y$ $2x$ $2y = 3x - 5y$ $(a \quad b) \ (a \quad b) = 0$

$5x$ $3y$ $2x$ $2y = 7x - y$ $(a \quad b) \ (a \quad b) = -2b$

$5x$ $3y$ $2x$ $2y = 3x - y$ $(a \quad b) \ (a \quad b) = 2a - 2b$

Figure 4.12 *Find the missing signs*

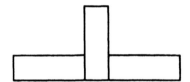

Figure 4.13 *Find the perimeter*

rectangles. With the length and width of each rectangle denoted by l and w, the perimeter consists of four edges of length l and four edges of width w together with two edges of length $l - w$. Adding these gives a perimeter of:

$$4l + 4w + 2(l - w) = 6l + 2w$$

An alternative approach would be to say that there are three rectangles each with a perimeter of $2l + 2w$, but at the two places where the rectangles touch $2w$ is eliminated, so the total is:

$$3(2l + 2w) - 2 \times 2w = 6l + 6w - 4w = 6l + 2w$$

Students can be asked to find the perimeter in their own way and results can be compared and discussed. The task can be extended by looking at the expressions which arise when additional rectangles are added to the diagram creating examples like that shown in Figure 4.14. This can lead to an expression for the perimeter when there are n rectangles and the surprising fact that the perimeter is unchanged if the rectangles are placed end to end:

$$n(2l + 2w) - 2w(n - 1) = 2nl + 2w$$

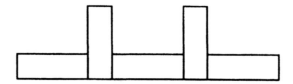

Figure 4.14 *Another perimeter to find*

Number puzzles are a powerful source of motivation for students and simplification lies at the heart of both creating and explaining them. As a final example in this section, let us look at the effect of reversing the digits of a number. Adding some pairs of two digit numbers to their 'reverses' always seems to produce a multiple of 11:

$$31 + 13 = 44 \quad 53 + 35 = 88 \quad 75 + 57 = 132$$

If a two digit number has tens digit a and units digit b, then it can be represented as $10a + b$. Reversing the digits then gives the number represented by $10b + a$. The result about multiples of 11 can then be proved by using a little simplification to give:

$$(10a + b) + (10b + a) = 10a + b + 10b + a = 11a + 11b = 11(a + b)$$

There is the added bonus here that $a + b$ in the simplified form tells you which multiple it is. In a similar fashion, the difference between a two digit number and its 'reverse' gives a multiple of 9 and $a - b$ indicates which multiple it is:

$$(10a + b) - (10b + a) = 10a + b - 10b - a = 9a - 9b = 9(a - b)$$

An obvious extension here is to explore to what extent there are similar results for numbers with three or more digits.

The primary purpose of simplification is obviously to make an expression look simpler and thereby to explain some simple property or enable the result to be used in a manageable form for some further purpose. Often though there is more than one form that might be deemed to be simple. Recognizing the equivalence of these forms, the different information they convey and when each is appropriate is an important aspect of making sense of algebra.

EXPANDING AND FINDING FACTORS

The perimeter of a rectangle can be expressed either as $2l + 2w$ or as $2(l + w)$. Students will understand this as two different ways of calculating the perimeter and readily understand the equivalence with the aid of some simple numerical examples. However, this sense of the equivalence of expressions is all too easily lost when students are presented with lots of unrelated expressions to expand or to factorize. It is important therefore to present these skills in ways which emphasize the equivalence between the pairs of expressions considered and help the student appreciate the utility of different forms.

Tall and Thomas (1991) designed software called the 'algebraic maths machine' which accepted numerical inputs for several variables from which two expressions could be constructed so that the results of evaluating them could be compared. Their empirical evidence from studies with students suggested that such an approach using the 'machine' significantly improved algebraic understanding. In a similar way, a spreadsheet, as shown in Figure 4.15, provides a good medium for demonstrating and exploring the equivalence (or non-equivalence) of expressions.

a	b	2a+6b	2(a+3b)
2	3	22	22
5	2	22	22
4	7	50	50
6	6	48	48
37	59	428	428

Figure 4.15 *Equivalent algebraic expressions on a spreadsheet*

Let us look at the possibilities that arise through exploring two simple equivalent expressions in different ways. Adding a number and its square always seems to produce an even number:

$$3^2 + 3 = 12 \qquad 8^2 + 8 = 72 \qquad 99^2 + 99 = 9900$$

A simple explanation for this is that either two even numbers are added or else two odd numbers, so in either case the result will be even. An algebraic approach opens up a different perspective: using the fact that $n^2 + n = n(n + 1)$ it is clear that the sum of a number and its square is equivalent to the product of two consecutive numbers, n and $n + 1$. Clearly one of any such pair is always even and so the result is proved. Incidentally, the identity also provides a simple way of approaching mentally a rather hard looking calculation like $99^2 + 99$ which can be thought of verbally as 99 lots of 99 and then an additional 99 to make 100 lots of 99 altogether.

Another way of looking at the identity is to think of it as an area with a square and an additional strip of unit width at one end, as shown in Figure 4.16. Using a for the length of the edge of the square, the two parts have areas of a^2 and a, and they form a rectangle with width a and length $a + 1$, providing a useful illustration of the identity $a^2 + a = a(a + 1)$.

In a different context, students may consider the graph given by the equation $y = x^2 + x$, shown in Figure 4.17. Here the alternative form $y = x(x + 1)$ is useful because it shows where the curve intersects the x axis. Often students do not immediately sense that the two different looking equations will give the same graph, so a demonstration with a graph plotter does serve as another way of illustrating the equivalence of the two forms.

At a more sophisticated level, the equivalent completed squares form $y = (x + \frac{1}{2})^2 - \frac{1}{4}$ shows that the curve is obtained by translating $y = x^2$ through a $\frac{1}{2}$ unit to the left and a $\frac{1}{4}$ unit downwards or, equivalently moving the minimum point to the point $(-\frac{1}{2}, -\frac{1}{4})$. The graphs of quadratic functions are discussed fully in Chapter 6.

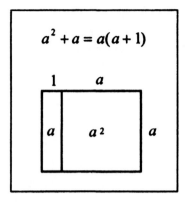

Figure 4.16 *Adding a number and its square*

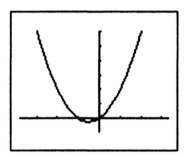

Figure 4.17 *The graph of $y = x^2 + x$*

FUNCTION NOTATION

The idea of a mathematical function as an input–output device, shown as a flow chart in Figure 4.18, can be introduced at an early stage. It is easy, for instance, to set up a spreadsheet as a function machine with two cells, one for input and one for output. Typically this can be used to explore different functions by playing the game of 'guess the function', where students are invited to determine the form of a function by looking at the outputs generated by different inputs.

The next step is to introduce the notation, whereby an input of x gives an output of $f(x)$, as shown in the lower part of figure 4.18. We can then describe the function with an algebraic expression so that $f(x) = x^2 + 1$, for instance, is the 'square and add one' function. The big advantage of function notation at an elementary level is that it provides a simple way of indicating the value of a function for a particular value of the variable by writing statements like $f(0) = 1$, $f(1) = 2$ and $f(3) = 5$ in the case of $f(x) = x^2 + 1$.

The TI-89 and TI-92 calculators have a very useful facility for defining a function, illustrated in Figure 4.19 with a simple linear function, that provides a powerful way of making the notation more familiar.

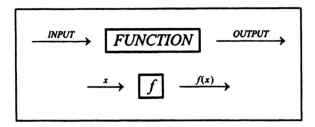

Figure 4.18 *Function machines*

```
 F1▾    F2▾   F3▾  F4▾   F5    F6▾
Tools Algebra Calc Other PrSmIO Clean Up

■ Define f(x) =3·x - 2      Done
■ f(1)                         1
■ f(2)                         4
■ f(3)                         7
■ f(4)                        10

MAIN          RAD AUTO      FUNC      5/30
```

Figure 4.19 *Function notation on a TI-89 calculator*

FRACTIONS

Equivalence is one the most fundamental ideas with fractions: different forms like $\frac{3}{4}$, $\frac{9}{12}$ and $\frac{15}{20}$ all have the same value. Understanding this idea and the relationship between proper and improper fractions are essential in order to add and subtract fractions and to simplify results:

$$\tfrac{5}{6} + \tfrac{5}{12} = \tfrac{10}{12} + \tfrac{5}{12} = \tfrac{15}{12} = \tfrac{5}{4} = 1\tfrac{1}{4}.$$

Facility with the steps involved in such calculations is necessary before algebraic fractions can make any sense. When that facility has been acquired it can be used together with procedures for manipulating algebraic expressions to carry out similar calculations with algebraic fractions. Particular difficulties arise with simplifying algebraic fractions – a fraction like $\frac{x+2}{x+4}$ is often erroneously simplified to $\frac{x+1}{x+2}$ by cancelling out an apparent common factor of 2. Worse still, it is sometimes reduced to either $\frac{2}{3}$ or $\frac{1}{2}$ by inappropriately eliminating the x in both numerator and denominator. Such errors arise through a failure to see that it is only possible to cancel factors that are common to the complete expression in each place. Substituting simple numbers into such fractions is one way of highlighting the error. Figure 4.20 shows the effect of substituting numbers into the sort of fractions that commonly give rise to simplification errors. Students can be asked to complete a table like this, simplifying the numerical fractions where possible. Discussion can then focus on how the results indicate which of the algebraic forms simplify and how that is achieved by seeking genuine common factors.

Adding and subtracting algebraic fractions clearly needs practice to develop the necessary skills and the ability to apply them to problem situations. There are many ways in which this

	1	2	3	4	5
$\dfrac{x+1}{x+2}$	$\dfrac{2}{3}$	$\dfrac{3}{4}$	$\dfrac{4}{5}$	$\dfrac{5}{6}$	$\dfrac{6}{7}$
$\dfrac{x+2}{x+4}$	$\dfrac{3}{5}$	$\dfrac{4}{6}=\dfrac{2}{3}$	$\dfrac{5}{7}$	$\dfrac{6}{8}=\dfrac{3}{4}$	$\dfrac{7}{9}$
$\dfrac{2x+2}{2x+4}$	$\dfrac{4}{6}=\dfrac{2}{3}$	$\dfrac{6}{8}=\dfrac{3}{4}$	$\dfrac{8}{10}=\dfrac{4}{5}$	$\dfrac{10}{12}=\dfrac{5}{6}$	$\dfrac{12}{14}=\dfrac{6}{7}$
$\dfrac{2x+4}{3x+6}$	$\dfrac{6}{9}=\dfrac{2}{3}$	$\dfrac{8}{12}=\dfrac{2}{3}$	$\dfrac{10}{15}=\dfrac{2}{3}$	$\dfrac{12}{18}=\dfrac{2}{3}$	$\dfrac{14}{21}=\dfrac{2}{3}$

Figure 4.20 *Simplifying algebraic fractions*

task can be made both more meaningful and more congenial. For example, adding a sequence of fractions to their reciprocals provides practice with a purpose. If the numerator and denominator differ by 1, the intriguing pattern of 'two and a bit', shown in Figure 4.21, appears in the results. This is represented in a generalized form by the algebraic identity which appears below the calculations.

$$\frac{1}{2}+\frac{2}{1}=2\frac{1}{2} \qquad \frac{2}{3}+\frac{3}{2}=2\frac{1}{6} \qquad \frac{3}{4}+\frac{4}{3}=2\frac{1}{12} \qquad \frac{4}{5}+\frac{5}{4}=2\frac{1}{20} \qquad \frac{5}{6}+\frac{6}{5}=2\frac{1}{30}$$

$$\frac{n}{n+1}+\frac{n+1}{n}=2+\frac{1}{n(n+1)}$$

Figure 4.21 *Two and a bit*

Showing that an identity like this is true provides a meaningful context for learning how to manipulate algebraic fractions. Understanding the steps involved in transforming one side of the identity into the other, in either direction, is enhanced by comparing the corresponding steps taken with numerical fractions as illustrated in Figure 4.22

$$\frac{3}{4}+\frac{4}{3}=\frac{9+16}{12}=\frac{25}{12}=\frac{24+1}{12}=2\frac{1}{12}$$

$$\frac{n}{n+1}+\frac{n+1}{n}=\frac{n^2+(n+1)^2}{n(n+1)}=\frac{2n^2+2n+1}{n(n+1)}=\frac{2n(n+1)+1}{n(n+1)}=2+\frac{1}{n(n+1)}$$

Figure 4.22 *Adding algebraic fractions*

This particular task, which I have discussed in French (1995), can readily be extended by considering pairs of fractions where the denominators differ by more than 1. Exploring this provides abundant opportunity for practice with adding both numerical and algebraic fractions. The identities that arise then point interestingly to a further generalization:

$$\frac{n}{n+p}+\frac{n+p}{n}=2+\frac{p^2}{n(n+1)}$$

CONCLUSION

Algebraic ideas are a direct extension of numerical operations and relationships and are therefore totally dependent on understanding and fluency with number. Skill with mental arithmetic, and the understanding and fluency that should accompany it, is thus a key requisite for success with algebra. Beyond the initial stages, where the positive integers provide a sufficient numerical background, negative numbers and fractions become increasingly important. Failure to understand them adequately and to acquire sufficient mastery of operations involving them commonly acts as a barrier to success with algebra.

Developing students' capacity to perform standard algebraic manipulations with fluency requires more than frequent practice with routine tasks. To be effective, the development of skills needs to be presented in meaningful contexts that enable students to see the underlying purpose in what they are doing. Students should increasingly come to appreciate:

● the meaning of algebraic symbols and expressions
● the importance of arithmetical skills and understanding, particularly with reference to negative numbers and fractions;
● how algebraic results relate to numerical patterns and calculations;
● ways of checking for errors;
● the importance of fluency with mental algebra using simple examples as a basis for understanding more complex written algebraic manipulation;
● the role of algebra as a powerful tool for explaining and problem solving.

Acquiring skills with substitution, simplification and the ability to convert expressions into different forms by expanding, factorizing and manipulating algebraic fractions are all essential requirements for students to apply algebra successfully to a wide variety of mathematical situations. Quadratic functions are particularly important in elementary algebra and they are considered at length together with the related technical skills in Chapter 5. Equation solving and graphs have only been given brief mention in this chapter, leaving a detailed treatment to Chapters 6 and 7.

It often appears to students that school algebra is only about learning skills and techniques that seem to have little obvious purpose. Improved motivation and greater success is more likely to come through learning these skills alongside the many interesting and powerful ways in which algebra can be used to explain surprising results and solve intriguing problems.

Chapter 5

Patterns with Squares: Explaining and Proving

$$0 \quad 1 \quad 4 \quad 9 \quad 16 \quad 25 \quad 36 \quad 49 \quad 64 \quad 81 \quad 100$$
$$1 \quad 3 \quad 5 \quad 7 \quad 9 \quad 11 \quad 13 \quad 15 \quad 17 \quad 19$$

PATTERNS WITH SQUARES

A simple numerical challenge for students with little or no knowledge of appropriate algebraic identities, is to ask how 21^2 can be found starting from the fact that $20^2 = 400$. A typical response would be to look at a sequence of three products:

$$20 \times 20 = 400 \qquad 21 \times 20 = 420 \qquad 21 \times 21 = 441$$

Examining what has happened here at each step, we see that first 20 is added and then 21. The reason for this should be clear and the idea can be applied generally. So, knowing that $50^2 = 2500$, it follows that $51^2 = 2500 + 50 + 51 = 2601$ and, using the same argument precisely, that $(n + 1)^2 = n^2 + n + n + 1 = n^2 + 2n + 1$. This is a familiar and important result which among other things explains why the differences between consecutive square numbers are given by the odd numbers.

This may not be the most obvious way to introduce this important identity, but it certainly offers an interesting alternative way of looking at it at some stage, besides making a useful link between numerical results and algebraic expressions. As I have said in previous chapters, algebraic identities are often best introduced through patterns in numbers or through pictorial representations. In this case, a good way to begin would be to ask students to find squares of numbers like 11, 21, 31 and so on with a calculator, as shown in Figure 5.1, and ask them to look for a general result.

The pattern in the units, tens and hundred digits is particularly clear here and it is therefore not difficult to see how it should continue in the next few terms of the sequence: 2601, 3721, 5041 and so on. This again leads to the identity in the familiar form $(n + 1)^2 = n^2 + 2n + 1$ or, possibly, as $(10n + 1)^2 = 100n^2 + 20n + 1$. Similar investigations with $19^2, 29^2, 39^2$ and so on give either $(n + 9)^2 = n^2 + 18n + 81$ or, much more usefully, $(n - 1)^2 = n^2 - 2n + 1$. Generalizing further we have the two important identities:

$$(a + b)^2 = a^2 + 2ab + b^2 \text{ and } (a - b)^2 = a^2 - 2ab + b^2.$$

$\blacksquare 11^2$	121
$\blacksquare 21^2$	441
$\blacksquare 31^2$	961
$\blacksquare 41^2$	1681

Figure 5.1 *A pattern with squares*

Pictures are always valuable as a way of illustrating algebraic identities. Patterns with dots, squares or interlocking coloured cubes like Multilink are very useful for this as a variant on the standard diagram of Figure 5.2, where a square is subdivided into four parts. The diagram leads readily to $(a+b)^2 = a^2 + 2ab + b^2$. If the right hand rectangle and square are folded in and the bottom part is folded up, the corresponding result with subtraction, $(a-b)^2 = a^2 - 2ab + b^2$, can be pictured, although careful thought is needed to justify the b^2 term.

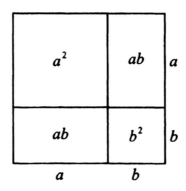

Figure 5.2 $(a+b)^2 = a^2 + 2ab + b^2$

Another task linked to the same identity is to ask students to calculate a sequence of values for 'something-and-a-half squared': $1\frac{1}{2}^2$, $2\frac{1}{2}^2$, $3\frac{1}{2}^2$ and so on. This can also lead to discussion of errors and of appropriate mental methods. Students commonly make the error of supposing, for reasons that are very obvious, that $3\frac{1}{2}^2$ is equal to $9\frac{1}{4}$. Rather than immediately pronouncing that to be wrong, a good follow-up question is to ask them to calculate $3 \times 3\frac{1}{2}$, which they are likely to state correctly as $10\frac{1}{2}$. This conflicts with the previous answer: they can see for themselves that something is wrong because the first answer should be greater than the second. An additional $\frac{1}{2} \times 3\frac{1}{2}$, which is $1\frac{3}{4}$, is needed to give the correct result that $3\frac{1}{2}^2 = 12\frac{1}{4}$. Some students may choose to calculate $3\frac{1}{2}$ as $\frac{7}{2}^2 = \frac{49}{4} = 12\frac{1}{4}$, which is fine when the numbers are small, but may cause some difficulty with a larger number like $8\frac{1}{2}^2$. Once students have a reliable way of doing the calculation they can calculate the values shown in Figure 5.3 and note any patterns that would help them to calculate something more ambitious like $30\frac{1}{2}^2$ or $100\frac{1}{2}^2$.

Students commonly suggest two alternative methods for calculating the whole number part of these products:

- multiply the whole number by the next number;
- add the whole number to its square.

$$1\tfrac{1}{2}^2 = 2\tfrac{1}{4} \qquad 5\tfrac{1}{2}^2 = 30\tfrac{1}{4}$$

$$2\tfrac{1}{2}^2 = 6\tfrac{1}{4} \qquad 6\tfrac{1}{2}^2 = 42\tfrac{1}{4}$$

$$3\tfrac{1}{2}^2 = 12\tfrac{1}{4} \qquad 7\tfrac{1}{2}^2 = 56\tfrac{1}{4}$$

$$4\tfrac{1}{2}^2 = 20\tfrac{1}{4} \qquad 8\tfrac{1}{2}^2 = 72\tfrac{1}{4}$$

Figure 5.3 *Something-and-a-half squared*

These give the two alternative ways of calculating $30\tfrac{1}{2}^2$ of Figure 5.4 shown with the two corresponding alternative algebraic forms for $(n + \tfrac{1}{2})^2$. The link between the two procedures is provided by the identity $n(n + 1) = n^2 + n$, which was discussed in Chapter 4, and the right-hand form is directly linked to the standard identity $(a + b)^2 = a^2 + 2ab + b^2$ discussed above.

$$30\tfrac{1}{2}^2 = 30 \times 31 + \tfrac{1}{4} = 930\tfrac{1}{4} \qquad 30\tfrac{1}{2}^2 = 30^2 + 30 + \tfrac{1}{4} = 930\tfrac{1}{4}$$

$$(n + \tfrac{1}{2})^2 = n(n + 1) + \tfrac{1}{4} \qquad (n + \tfrac{1}{2})^2 = n^2 + n + \tfrac{1}{4}$$

Figure 5.4 *Linking two alternatives*

This last example illustrated the common error where students assume that $(a + b)^2$ is equivalent to $a^2 + b^2$, which can be expressed in words as: 'adding two numbers and then squaring the result is the same as squaring two numbers and then adding'. This is a remarkably tenacious error which seems to arise for a long time after students appear to have mastered the art of multiplying out brackets. I even recall an occasion where a student who had to simplify $(\cos\theta + \sin\theta)^2$ proceeded by writing down $\cos^2\theta + \sin^2\theta = 1$! It is important when students make these errors for them to see by substituting some simple numbers that their answer makes no sense, before pointing them yet again to the correct procedure.

Figure 5.5 shows a short task which highlights this particular error. Students are asked to try their own pairs of numbers in the first two columns, calculate values for the third and fourth columns and then include the difference between these two in the last column. They are then asked to establish a suitable heading for the last column, as another way of reinforcing the correct identity.

The preceding discussion has been concerned with ways of introducing the two identities $(a + b)^2 = a^2 + 2ab + b^2$ and $(a - b)^2 = a^2 - 2ab + b^2$ and the frequent misconceptions related to the first of them. It is common practice in textbooks for the first encounter with these identities to arise in conjunction with the topic of multiplying pairs of binomial expressions. There are, however, advantages in looking at the two identities, and the difference of two squares which is considered next, before introducing the more general procedure. The identities can be closely linked to arithmetical procedures, as we have seen above, and that provides

a	b	$(a+b)^2$	a^2+b^2	
2	3	25	13	12
3	5	64	34	30
1	4	25	17	8
3	3	36	18	18
5	7	144	74	70

Figure 5.5 *Add and square or square and add?*

an interesting context in which to introduce them and some useful procedures for doing mental calculations. Furthermore, each identity can be applied to a range of problems so that algebraic ideas can be developed alongside applications. As an example, the dissection of the square array of dots in Figure 5.6 suggests that the square of an odd number is one more than a multiple of 8. Successive numerical cases display a pattern and an algebraic proof for the square of any odd number is shown alongside. In addition, it is worth noting that the multiples of 8 are actually multiples of the triangle numbers, a fact that is easily demonstrated by adding lines subdividing the dot patterns in the four rectangles.

Besides applications, which do in themselves act as a way of reminding students about important results and practising their use, other ways are needed to provide practice and reinforcement. Mental algebra was discussed in Chapter 4: frequent use of short, simple questions, often given orally, is a valuable way of developing fluency and a useful complement to more traditional written text book exercises. In this particular case there is a close link between mental arithmetic and mental algebra because the identities provide useful ways of calculating the squares of some numbers mentally. Figure 5.7 shows a variety of question forms involving the two identities that can provide frequent practice alongside those related to other algebraic skills.

THE DIFFERENCE OF TWO SQUARES

The difference of two squares is another important, and ubiquitous, identity that students should encounter initially as a result of doing numerical calculations. They can become fluent in its use with numbers alongside as they are developing algebraic skill and understanding. Figure 5.8 shows a useful introductory task which enables students to establish the result for themselves.

Besides being odd numbers, the results in the first column: 3, 5, 7, 9, 11, are readily seen to be the sum of the two numbers that have been squared in each case. With the second column, that sum has been doubled and in the third column multiplied by 3. Using this pattern students can evaluate the other examples, which can be checked with a calculator as necessary. Students do not find it difficult to propose a rule in the form 'add the numbers, subtract them and then multiply the two answers' and can then be helped to express that in an algebraic form:

$$a^2 - b^2 = (a - b)(a + b)$$

At some stage, the identity needs to be placed in the context of expanding brackets and

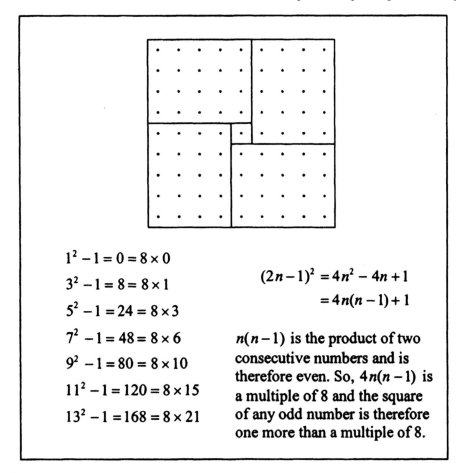

$$1^2 - 1 = 0 = 8 \times 0$$

$$3^2 - 1 = 8 = 8 \times 1$$

$$5^2 - 1 = 24 = 8 \times 3$$

$$7^2 - 1 = 48 = 8 \times 6$$

$$9^2 - 1 = 80 = 8 \times 10$$

$$11^2 - 1 = 120 = 8 \times 15$$

$$13^2 - 1 = 168 = 8 \times 21$$

$$(2n - 1)^2 = 4n^2 - 4n + 1$$
$$= 4n(n - 1) + 1$$

$n(n - 1)$ is the product of two consecutive numbers and is therefore even. So, $4n(n - 1)$ is a multiple of 8 and the square of any odd number is therefore one more than a multiple of 8.

Figure 5.6 *Squaring an odd number*

factorizing and this, of course, provides a ready formal explanation of why the result is true. However, at the introductory stage the pictorial demonstration of Figure 5.9 is a particularly instructive and memorable way of seeing the result. Coloured cubes like Multilink provide a particularly good medium with which to construct the picture.

Important mathematical results and procedures need constant reinforcement in a variety of ways and in a variety of contexts if students are to acquire an appropriate level of familiarity and fluency to enable them to use the ideas effectively. The examples in Figure 5.10 present the difference of two squares at different levels to illustrate the range of forms that should eventually become familiar, and to indicate something of the variety of contexts in which it arises, a feature that I have discussed at length in French (1997).

Besides providing necessary practice in algebraic skills, many questions like those shown in Figure 5.10 offer further possibilities. I give three examples;

- $(2n + 1)^2 - (2n - 1)^2 = 8n$ shows that the difference of the squares of two consecutive odd

Evaluate $4\frac{1}{2}^2$.

Use this to find 45^2.

Evaluate 21^2, given that $20^2 = 400$

Use this to find 2.1^2.

Calculate 19^2 given that $20^2 = 400$

Calculate 26^2 given that $25^2 = 625$

Evaluate $(p+3)^2$ with $p = 3$ and $q = 5$.

Evaluate $p^2 + q^2$ with $p = 3$ and $q = 5$.

Expand $(p+3)^2$

Expand $(2n+1)^2$

Expand $(x-y)^2$

Simplify $(x+y)^2 + (x-y)^2$

Figure 5.7 *Fluency with squaring in arithmetic and algebra*

numbers is a multiple of 8, a fact which is also a consequence of the result noted previously that the square of any odd number is one more than a multiple of 8.

- $(2 + \frac{1}{2})(2 - \frac{1}{2})$ shows that $2\frac{1}{2} \times 1\frac{1}{2} = 4 - \frac{1}{4} = 3\frac{3}{4}$, giving a neat way to multiply a pair of numbers that are the same fraction above and below a given number.
- $(\sqrt{3} + \sqrt{2})(\sqrt{3} - \sqrt{2}) = 1$ is a striking exact result, particularly when students see that their calculators produce an answer that is only approximately equal to one. Finding and working with other similar examples is a useful task and students should certainly see and appreciate the related results:

$$\frac{1}{\sqrt{3} - \sqrt{2}} = \sqrt{3} + \sqrt{2} \text{ and } \frac{1}{\sqrt{3} + \sqrt{2}} = \sqrt{3} - \sqrt{2}$$

As an extension to this, try using the same kind of approaches to investigate the sum and the difference of two cubes:

$$a^3 - b^3 = (a - b)(a^2 + ab + b^2) \text{ and } a^3 + b^3 = (a - b)(a^2 - ab + b^2)$$

EXPANDING AND FACTORIZING

Multiplying a pair of binomial expressions, or expanding, and the reverse process of finding factors, or factorizing, are both essential procedures used in constructing algebraic arguments. Students need to understand the equivalence between the two forms and to develop some skill in being able to carry out the two procedures. Multiplication of algebraic expressions obviously has direct parallels with methods used for multiplying numbers. Figure 5.11 compares two common textbook approaches with a numerical illustration followed by the corresponding algebraic approach. One method uses a table and the other in a more formal manner expands 'along the line' in two stages.

Students need to develop sufficient skill in multiplying such pairs of expressions so that they can write down an expansion for simple cases without a table or intermediate lines of working.

Calculate the following:

$2^2 - 1^2$	$3^2 - 1^2$	$4^2 - 1^2$
$3^2 - 2^2$	$4^2 - 2^2$	$5^2 - 2^2$
$4^2 - 3^2$	$5^2 - 3^2$	$6^2 - 3^2$
$5^2 - 4^2$	$6^2 - 4^2$	$7^2 - 4^2$
$6^2 - 5^2$	$7^2 - 5^2$	$8^2 - 5^2$

Extend each column of results further.

What patterns do you notice in the answers?

Use the patterns to work out:

$21^2 - 20^2$	$31^2 - 29^2$	$22^2 - 19^2$

Extend the idea to work out:

$18^2 - 14^2$	$7.5^2 - 2.5^2$	$37^2 - 27^2$
$32^2 - 28^2$	$1.7^2 - 1.5^2$	$55^2 - 45^2$

Can you suggest a general formula?

Figure 5.8 *Investigating the difference of two squares*

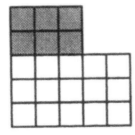 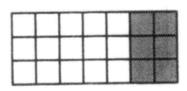

Figure 5.9 *Demonstrating the difference of two squares:* $5^2 - 2^2 = (5 - 2)(5 + 2)$

One of the barriers to success here, and with factorizing which I discuss next, is the common difficulty experienced doing operations with negative numbers; the remarks made in Chapter 4 about developing this prerequisite skill are equally pertinent to this situation.

Like other identities in this chapter, efforts to make links with numbers are useful in the early stages of developing the skill of finding factors. A simple quadratic function like $x^2 + 4x + 3$, shown in Figure 5.12, can be evaluated for some consecutive values of x and students can then be asked to consider the patterns in the results.

Factorize:	Expand:
$101^2 - 99^2$	$(p+1)(p-1)$
$a^2 - 4$	$(2a+b)(2a-b)$
$2.8^2 - 2.2^2$	$29 \times 31 = (30+1)(30-1)$
$9x^2 - 4y^2$	$(2 + \frac{1}{2})(2 - \frac{1}{2})$
$1\frac{1}{4}^2 - \frac{3}{4}^2$	$(\sqrt{3} + \sqrt{2})(\sqrt{3} - \sqrt{2})$
$(2n+1)^2 - (2n-1)^2$	$(1 + \cos\theta)(1 - \cos\theta)$
$\cos^2\theta - \sin^2\theta$	$(2+i)(2-i)$

Figure 5.10 *Fluency with the difference of two squares*

$$
\begin{array}{c|cc}
 & 30 & 2 \\
\hline
30 & 900 & 60 \\
3 & 90 & 6 \\
\end{array}
$$

$32 \times 33 = 30 \times 33 + 2 \times 33$
$= 990 + 66$
$= 1056$

$$
\begin{array}{c|cc}
 & x & 2 \\
\hline
x & x^2 & 2x \\
3 & 3x & 6 \\
\end{array}
$$

$(x+2)(x+3) = x(x+3) + 2(x+3)$
$= x^2 + 3x + 2x + 6$
$= x^2 + 5x + 6$

Figure 5.11 *Expanding algebraic expressions*

T: What do you notice about the numbers in the right hand column?
A: *They go up 7, 9, 11, 13, . . .*
T: So, what about $x = 7$?
B: *It will be 17 more – that's 80.*
T: What about $x = 19$?
A: *That's hard!*
T: Anything else you notice about the numbers?
B: *4 is 35 and that's 5 × 7.*
A: *And 5 is 48 which is 6 × 8.*
T: Can you do $x = 19$?
B: *20 × 22 which is 440.*
T: Why is it that?
A: *Because it's 1 more and 3 more.*
T: How then can we write $x^2 + 4x + 3$ as 2 factors multiplied together?
B: $(x + 1)(x + 3)$.
T: And how can you check that is right?
A: *Multiply out the brackets.*

x	$x^2 + 4x + 3$
1	8
2	15
3	24
4	35
5	48
6	63

Figure 5.12 *Evaluating a quadratic function*

A useful follow up task is to ask students to look in the same way at the functions $x^2 + 4x + 4$, $x^2 + 4x$ and $x^2 + 4x + 2$, which I have discussed at some length in French (1999). Each expression gives rise to further points for discussion, not least the fact that quadratic functions do not always have factors. The dialogue above brings out the connection between algebraic factors and numerical factors and the inverse relationship between expanding and factorizing summarized by Figure 5.13.

Acquiring technical skill in factorizing quadratic functions is totally dependent on fluency with the reverse process of expanding and is helped by concentrating on simple examples where the coefficient of x^2 is 1. Examples that cannot be factorized should be included in practice exercises so that students learn to recognize when the process cannot be carried out. An alternative introductory approach utilizes the table approach mentioned above for expanding, so that students start from the secure ground of expanding and move to finding missing numbers for different cells in the table, as illustrated by the sequence of examples in Figure 5.14.

However, it is important not to lose sight of the ultimate objective which is an ability to factorize such simple expressions mentally as an automatic process without the aid of a device

EXPAND

$$\longrightarrow$$

$$(x+1)(x+3) \quad = \quad x^2+4x+3$$

$$\longleftarrow$$

FACTORIZE

Figure 5.13 *Expand and factorize*

	x	2
x	x^2	
3		

$$(x+2)(x+3)$$
$$= x^2 + \quad\quad +$$

	x	
x	x^2	
2	$2x$	8

$$(x+\quad)(x+2)$$
$$= x^2+6x+8$$

	x	
x	x^2	
		12

$$(x+\quad)(x+\quad)$$
$$= x^2+7x+12$$

Figure 5.14 *Factorizing with tables*

like a table or an intermediate line of working, to recognize simple cases related to the standard identities and to identify those cases where factorizing is not possible. When the principles are understood and fluency is achieved with simple examples, it is not a big step to deal with more complicated expressions.

EXPLAINING AND PROVING

As students develop these technical skills they should have opportunities to use them to solve problems by formulating equations and as a tool for generating proofs of conjectures arising from number patterns and in other ways. Quadratic functions offer a rich field in this respect. Problems and the equations which they generate are considered in Chapter 7, but here we look at some examples which use algebraic reasoning to explain and extend ideas arising from numerical situations.

> *T*: Think of four consecutive numbers. Multiply the middle pair and the outer pair and subtract the results. What answer do you get?
> *A*: *2*
> *B*: *I get 2 as well!*

C: And I do!
T: What numbers did you start with?
A: 5, 6, 7 and 8.
B: 2, 3, 4 and 5.
C: 1, 2, 3 and 4.
T: Strange! So, you started with different sets of numbers, but you all had the same result. How can we explain this? If the first number is denoted by n, what do we write for the other numbers?
A: n + 1, n + 2 and n + 3.
T: How do we write the product of the middle pair?
B: (n + 1)(n + 2).
T: Now see if you can prove why the answer must always be 2.

This leads readily to a simple chain of reasoning which utilizes the skills of expanding and simplifying to prove that the answer is indeed always 2:

$$(n + 1)(n + 2) - n(n + 3) = (n^2 + 3n + 2) - (n^2 + 3n) = 2$$

A range of related similar tasks can be generated by considering sets of consecutive even or odd numbers or other sets of numbers forming an arithmetic sequence. Other possibilities involve subtracting different pairs of products drawn from the set of four numbers or generating examples of the same type using sets of three or five consecutive numbers. Students should also be asked to consider whether the same results arise for sets of negative numbers or numbers involving fractions. It is certainly not always obvious to them that a result that has arisen with positive integers is also true for a wider set of numbers, even though they have seen an algebraic argument which applies generally.

The next short dialogue introduces a situation where factorizing provides a key to explaining an interesting result.

T: Think of a small number and work out its cube. Now subtract the number from its cube. What do you get?
A: 60
B: 24
C: 120
D: 6

These and other results obtained from the students are written up for all to see. When asked what they notice they will usually spot quickly that all the numbers are multiples of 6. Any rogue answers stand out and can be re-calculated. So, why are the results multiples of 6? Some simple algebraic manipulation makes the reason clear:

$$n^3 - n = n(n^2 - 1) = n(n - 1)(n + 1)$$

The difference between a number and its cube is equivalent to the product of three consecutive numbers so that both 2 and 3, and hence 6, are factors of the product.

The identity is illustrated neatly by Figure 5.15. When the line of shaded cubes is removed from the large cube, the remaining cubes can be rearranged to form a cuboid, whose dimensions are three consecutive numbers. A more detailed discussion of this particular example will be found in French (1992). Illustrating algebraic ideas with pictures like this and through the corresponding number patterns enhances the meaning that students give to algebraic expressions and to the operations of expanding and factorizing, besides making their study of these important operations more interesting and purposeful.

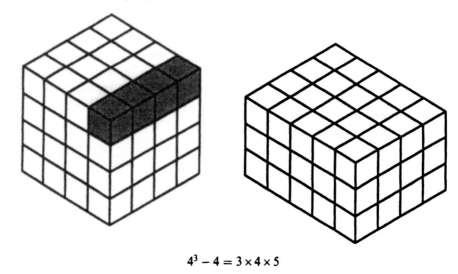

$$4^3 - 4 = 3 \times 4 \times 5$$

Figure 5.15 *The difference between a number and its cube*

PASCAL'S TRIANGLE AND THE BINOMIAL THEOREM

Whilst factorizing polynomials of degree higher than two may be less straightforward, multiplying out more than two bracketed expressions, although sometimes arduous, is not particularly difficult. It does, however, offer some fruitful possibilities, because the coefficients form Pascal's triangle, displayed alongside the expansions in Figure 5.16, which has many interesting applications and extensions.

$$
\begin{aligned}
(a+b)^0 &= 1 \\
(a+b)^1 &= a+b \\
(a+b)^2 &= a^2 + 2ab + b^2 \\
(a+b)^3 &= a^3 + 3a^2b + 3ab^2 + b^3 \\
(a+b)^4 &= a^4 + 4a^3b + 6a^2b^2 + 4ab^3 + b^4 \\
(a+b)^5 &= a^5 + 5a^4b + 10a^3b^2 + 10a^2b^3 + 5ab^4 + b^5
\end{aligned}
$$

```
           1
          1  1
         1  2  1
        1  3  3  1
       1  4  6  4  1
      1  5 10 10  5  1
```

Figure 5.16 *Pascal's triangle*

The additive property, whereby each coefficient is the sum of a consecutive pair of coefficients in the line above, is easy to spot and provides an obvious means of generating successive lines of the triangle. When the multiplication by $x + 1$ is set out in a formal way, as shown in Figure 5.17, it becomes clear how this property arises.

$$a^4 + 4a^3b + 6a^2b^2 + 4ab^3 + b^4$$
$$a + b$$
$$\overline{a^5 + 4a^4b + 6a^3b^2 + 4a^2b^3 + ab^4}$$
$$a^4b + 4a^3b^2 + 6a^2b^3 + 4ab^4 + b^5$$
$$\overline{a^5 + 5a^4b + 10a^3b^2 + 10a^2b^3 + 5ab^4 + b^5}$$

Figure 5.17 *Explaining the additive property*

Several interesting properties can be explored and explained:

- Why do the powers of 11 up to 11^4 generate lines of Pascal's triangle and what goes wrong with 11^5?
- Why does the sum of each line give successive powers of 2?
- What are the corresponding expansions with $a - b$ and how do they behave when $a = 10$ and $b = 1$, and when $a = b$?
- How can the result be generalized further?

To generalize further, we need a way of finding any line of Pascal's triangle independently of the previous lines. Asking how we could find, say, the 80th line provides an interesting challenge for students. Clearly, the first two terms are 1 and 80, but it is not immediately obvious how to work out subsequent terms. However, seeking a multiplicative link between successive terms in the earlier lines yields a simple and amazing pattern. This is shown in Figure 5.18 for the case of the fourth line, which then leads to a way of calculating the terms in the 80th line and to a general procedure.

Once this general procedure to find the nth line is established, we can derive the formula for the rth term:

$$^nC_r = \frac{n!}{r!(n-r)!}$$

This can easily become just another formula to be remembered, whereas if it is linked clearly to Pascal's triangle, and the associated difficulties and connections are discussed with students, it becomes much more meaningful:

- The formula will make better sense to students if it is approached through a particular numerical case such as

$$^5C_2 = \frac{5!}{2!3!} = \frac{5 \times 4}{2 \times 1}$$

where $\frac{5!}{3!}$ is a convenient way of expressing 5×4 that extends readily to larger numbers.

$$1 \xrightarrow{\times\frac{4}{1}} 4 \xrightarrow{\times\frac{3}{2}} 6 \xrightarrow{\times\frac{2}{3}} 4 \xrightarrow{\times\frac{1}{4}} 1$$

$$1 \xrightarrow{\times\frac{80}{1}} 80 \xrightarrow{\times\frac{79}{2}} 3160 \xrightarrow{\times\frac{78}{3}} 82160 \xrightarrow{\times\frac{77}{4}} \ldots$$

$$1 \xrightarrow{\times\frac{n}{1}} n \xrightarrow{\times\frac{n-1}{2}} \frac{n(n-1)}{2} \xrightarrow{\times\frac{n-2}{3}} \frac{n(n-1)(n-2)}{6} \xrightarrow{\times\frac{n-3}{4}} \ldots$$

Figure 5.18 *The amazing pattern in a line of Pascal's triangle*

- It is important for students to be aware that both the lines and the terms are numbered starting with zero rather than one. The line number is then the same as *n* in the corresponding binomial expression $(a + b)^n$ and the term number corresponds to the appropriate power of *b*.
- Since the value of ^nC_r is 1 both when *r* is zero and when $r = n$, the value of 0! has to be defined as 1. This always seems a little strange to students, because 0! looks as though it should have a value of zero. However, the pattern in the factorials shown below helps to make it seem more reasonable:

$$4! = 24 \xrightarrow{\div 4} 3! = 6 \xrightarrow{\div 3} 2! = 2 \xrightarrow{\div 2} 1! = 1 \xrightarrow{\div 1} 0! = 1$$

- The symmetry in each line arises because

$$^nC_r = \frac{n!}{r!(n - r)!} = {}^nC_{n-r}$$

- The formula for ^nC_r also gives the number of ways of choosing a set of *r* items from *n* items and this interpretation applies also to the binomial coefficients. $^5C_2$ is the coefficient of the b^2 term in the expansion of $(a + b)^5$ because it is the number of ways of choosing the variable *b* from two of the five repetitions of the expression $a + b$ in the product.

The binomial theorem, which summarizes this way of evaluating the expansion of powers of binomial expressions, is often given more simply as an expansion of $(1 + x)^n$ with each coefficient, derived from the corresponding value of ^nC_r, given in terms of *n* as follows:

$$(1 + x)^n = 1 + nx + \frac{n(n - 1)}{2!}x^2 + \frac{n(n - 1)(n - 3)}{3!}x^2 + \ldots$$

Newton had the remarkable insight that the binomial theorem is not only true for positive integers, but also for negative and fractional values of *n*, with the proviso that the numerical value of *x* is less than one. The resulting series is infinite and the proviso is necessary if it is to converge. Whilst Pascal's triangle is not a very useful way of looking at the extension to fractional values for *n*, it does extend to negative integers very readily. By including zeros on each line corresponding to the positive integers and using the additive property, lines corre-

1	⁻2	3	⁻4	5	⁻6
1	⁻1	1	⁻1	1	⁻1
1	0	0	0	0	0
1	1	0	0	0	0
1	2	1	0	0	0
1	3	3	1	0	0
1	4	6	4	1	0
1	5	10	10	5	1

$$\frac{1}{1+x} = (1+x)^{-1} = 1 - x + x^2 - x^3 + x^4 - \ldots$$

$$\frac{1}{(1+x)^2} = (1+x)^{-2} = 1 - 2x + 3x^2 - 4x^3 + 5x^4 - \ldots$$

Figure 5.19 *Extending Pascal's triangle*

sponding to negative integers and the corresponding expansions can be deduced, as shown in Figure 5.19.

Providing an awareness of the numerical pattern that underlies a symbolic result is a powerful way of helping it make sense to students, but it is also important to draw attention to smaller details that can cause difficulty. Zero can be a source of confusion in making sense of ^nC_r, with the need to give 0! a somewhat counter intuitive definition and to number the lines and the terms in each line from zero. However, even these small points do have their intrinsic interest!

CONCLUSION

Quadratic expressions, together with the operations of expanding and factorizing, are of fundamental importance, because they constantly arise in various forms in the study of algebra and in its varied applications. The three identities involving squares provide a valuable starting point:

- $(a + b)^2 = a^2 + 2ab + b^2$
- $(a - b)^2 = a^2 - 2ab + b^2$
- $(a + b)(a - b) = a^2 - b^2$

It is vital that students develop understanding and fluency with quadratic expressions through a judiciously integrated balance between appropriate practice of essential skills and applications to proving and problem solving. They need frequent opportunities to use the identities in doing mental calculations with numbers and to become proficient in expanding and factorizing with simple algebraic expressions. The emphasis should be on simplicity, because complication can obscure the essential purpose of developing both understanding and fluency, and on frequency, because many brief encounters are likely to be more effective than an occasional long session devoted to practising a particular routine. Number patterns, area diagrams and models with cubes all have an obvious and valuable role in the introductory stages, but they should also be used frequently to re-emphasize the underlying meaning of expressions and operations and to aid their application to problems. It is all too easy for students to reach a point where they regard algebra as a set of meaningless routines that serve no useful purpose, so the teacher should strive constantly to present, reinforce and develop ideas in ways which stimulate curiosity and interest as their meaning and mathematical purpose are made clear.

It is only by using algebraic ideas to explain and prove interesting results and to solve problems that students will come to see that there is any real purpose in learning algebra. Application should not be an optional extra that follows the development of algebraic skills. Proving and problem solving are an integral part of learning algebra, both as a source of new ideas and as a motivating context for developing fluency with routines. It may be objected that this introduces the very complication that I have argued against, but a proof or a problem need not be complicated. If aptly chosen it may only require a brief argument using simple expressions. Of course, some proofs and problems are very challenging and we should not underestimate what students might be able to achieve, but the confidence to cope with complication comes through appreciating the underlying nature and simplicity of algebraic ideas.

Nowhere is this underlying simplicity made more clear than with Pascal's triangle as it appears in expanding the powers of binomial expressions, something which makes a seemingly complicated task much more comprehensible and manageable. Pascal's triangle is a rich source of mathematical ideas that students should encounter at an early stage. Determining a general form for any term in the triangle and extending the binomial theorem beyond the powers of positive whole numbers are both challenging problems. Helping students to make sense of them needs clarity about potential sources of difficulty and care in developing the arguments.

Making links between different aspects of mathematics is an important part of the process of giving meaning and purpose to algebra. Pascal's triangle is a very good example of a mathematical idea that has links to a wide range of topics, but that is even more true of quadratic functions, which again feature strongly in Chapters 6 and 7 to discuss graphs and equation solving with their wide-ranging applications, both within mathematics and beyond.

Chapter 6

Functions and Graphs

Harnessing this new power [of computer technology] within mathematics and school mathematics is the challenge for the 21st century. (RS/JMC, 1997, p. 6)

STRAIGHT-LINE GRAPHS

Straight-line graphs were discussed in Chapter 3 as one of a number of ways of introducing algebraic ideas and symbols. They are particularly attractive in this respect because they provide a ready link between numbers, symbols and pictures. An equation provides a way of encapsulating the patterns in the co-ordinates of a set of points that lie on a straight line by acting as a unique label which highlights key properties. Although a graph is an abstract representation it has a visual appeal and looks interesting, particularly when a family of related graphs is depicted.

Students need to understand the links between the equation, the table of values or set of co-ordinates and the graph, and to be able to move fluently between these different representations. In Chapter 3 it was suggested that introductory work on straight-line graphs should be confined to positive whole numbers and should begin by looking at a set of points on a straight line, using the pattern in the numbers to determine the equation of the line. This builds on the idea of representing the terms of a linear sequence algebraically and makes clear from the start where the equation comes from and what it means.

Text books often start with equations and show students how to produce a table of values and then plot the corresponding lines. Whilst this may seem simpler as it is a more routine task, it starts from something that is unfamiliar, namely the equation, which can set up an immediate barrier because it looks strange and new and seems to have appeared for no apparent reason. Co-ordinates and their graphical representation should already be familiar and therefore provide a more reassuring start to a new idea. Once the idea of equations has been established as a way of describing straight lines and curves it is perfectly legitimate to explore the graphical representations of new functions as they arise, often using graphical calculators or graph-plotting software as a powerful tool, but in the beginning the major priority is to establish the meaning of equations and to develop the skills involved in moving between equation, table of values and graph.

Figure 6.1 displays three examples with the different starting points: equation, table of values or graph. In the early stages students will move between equation and graph via the table of values, but once that skill has been established the next major task is to establish direct links between them through recognition of the gradient and the intercept on the y axis. At this point, a graph plotter, either a graphical calculator or on a computer, becomes a valuable tool when combined with appropriate written tasks. A graph plotter enables the student to obtain an accurate plot of a graph and is therefore helpful in identifying the common properties of a set of related graphs.

Although the availability of graph plotters may diminish the need to plot accurate graphs by hand it does not reduce the importance of being able to make quick sketches of graphs by hand. Indeed experiences with graph plotters should be designed to enhance the skills of graph sketching and the related task of recognizing the sort of equation that fits a given graph. A graph plotter can provide far more examples from which to draw out common features and links with equations than is possible using hand-drawn graphs alone and can thus enhance understanding and improve retention of ideas.

EXPLORING GRAPHS WITH A GRAPH PLOTTER

To the novice, a graph plotter may look somewhat forbidding because there are such a wide variety of facilities. It is important therefore to make it clear to students that only a very small subset of these are needed to do a lot of very useful things. Enthusiasts tend to want to explain all the complications from the start, which is very off-putting for most novices. Most features of a graph plotter are best learnt once the essential simple features have become familiar and can be used with ease. It is important that the technicalities of using calculators and computers are not allowed to obscure the mathematical ideas, a point that is as crucial for the teacher as it is for students. There is always a temptation to use sophisticated features which are quicker or neater, but this can often be at the expense of clarity and the confidence of students. In fact students only need to know *three* things in order to begin using a graph plotter productively:

- how to *enter and plot* a function;
- how to *modify the scales* on the axes;
- how to *delete graphs* that are incorrect or no longer required.

The way in which these three operations are carried out will vary between different calculators and software packages, but the teacher must ensure that each student can carry them out readily with the graph plotter they are using, so that attention can focus quickly on learning about graphs and their equations.

The great virtue of a graph plotter is that it allows the student to see the effect of varying the parameters in an equation. In the case of straight lines with equations in the form $y = mx + c$, this means varying the values of c and m and observing how they relate to the intercept on the y axis and the gradient, as shown in Figure 6.2.

The equation does not need to be referred to initially as $y = mx + c$: the important point is that students should be learning to recognize the role that the two numbers play in a given equation like $y = 2x + 3$, with the number 2 as the common feature of the equations of a set of parallel lines. To develop this understanding, students can be asked, either in the course of class discussion or when working individually, to find equations which satisfy particular conditions. Three typical examples would be to find equations for:

<table>
<tr><th>Equation</th><th>Table of values</th><th>Graph</th></tr>
<tr><td>$y =$</td><td><table><tr><th>x</th><th>y</th></tr><tr><td>0</td><td>3</td></tr><tr><td>1</td><td>4</td></tr><tr><td>2</td><td>5</td></tr><tr><td>3</td><td>6</td></tr><tr><td>4</td><td>7</td></tr></table></td><td>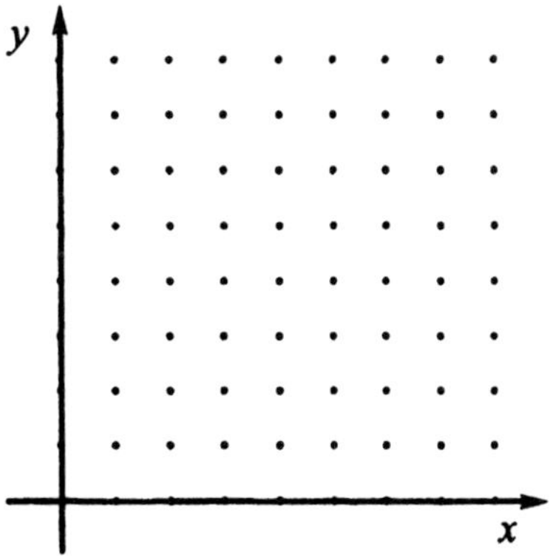
</td></tr>
<tr><td>$y = 2x - 1$</td><td><table><tr><th>x</th><th>y</th></tr><tr><td>0</td><td></td></tr><tr><td>1</td><td></td></tr><tr><td>2</td><td></td></tr><tr><td>3</td><td></td></tr><tr><td>4</td><td></td></tr></table></td><td>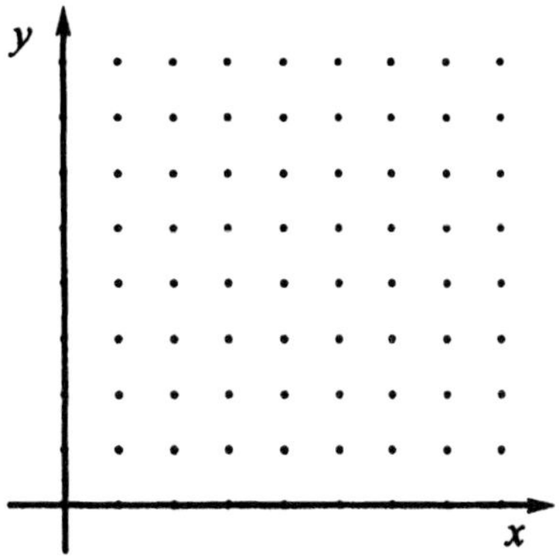
</td></tr>
<tr><td>$y =$</td><td><table><tr><th>x</th><th>y</th></tr><tr><td>0</td><td></td></tr><tr><td>1</td><td></td></tr><tr><td>2</td><td></td></tr><tr><td>3</td><td></td></tr><tr><td>4</td><td></td></tr></table></td><td>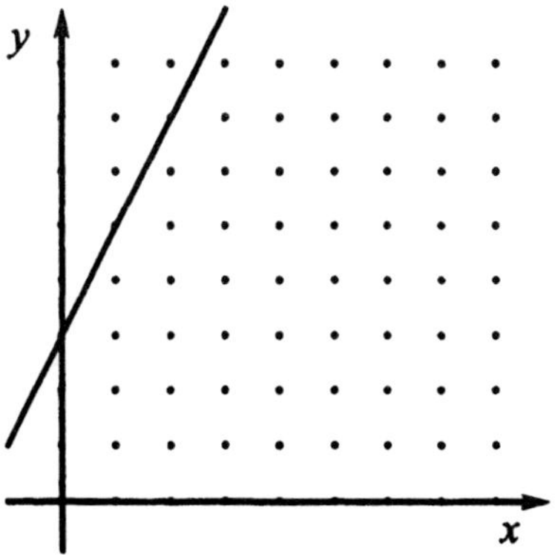
</td></tr>
</table>

Figure 6.1 *Understanding straight-line graphs*

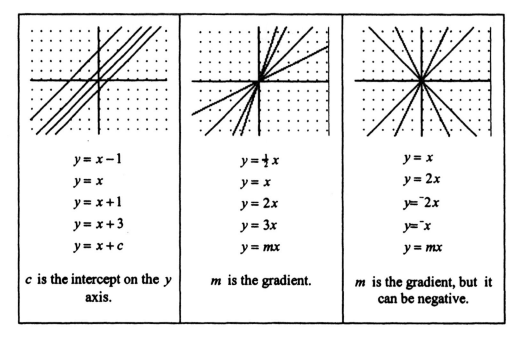

$y = x - 1$	$y = \frac{1}{2}x$	$y = x$
$y = x$	$y = x$	$y = 2x$
$y = x + 1$	$y = 2x$	$y = {}^-2x$
$y = x + 3$	$y = 3x$	$y = {}^-x$
$y = x + c$	$y = mx$	$y = mx$
c is the intercept on the y axis.	m is the gradient.	m is the gradient, but it can be negative.

Figure 6.2 *Key properties of straight-line graphs*

- some lines which are parallel to the line $y = 2x + 3$;
- some lines which pass through the point (0, 3);
- some lines which pass through the point (1, 5).

Tasks like this give students some freedom to choose for themselves, something which often engenders greater enthusiasm and effort than more closely structured tasks. The use of a graph plotter ensures that they can work at the task until they have found several correct solutions rather than wait for the teacher to check their work. The machine provides instant feedback and an incentive to get things right. This does not reduce the teacher's role because student activity needs to be interspersed with class discussion both to introduce new ideas and to draw threads together by highlighting key ideas, and individual students always need to be encouraged, helped and challenged to think further when they are working on tasks.

GRADIENT: A KEY CONCEPT

The gradient of a straight line and its extension to the gradient of a curve at different points is a key mathematical concept with its links to rates of change and turning points and its central role in the differential calculus. It is the crucial qualitative feature of any graph because it describes the way in which the variables are changing. Students need to appreciate this qualitative aspect as well as being able to give a numerical measure to gradient or rate of change.

Graphs related to straight-line motion are particularly useful for developing this qualitative

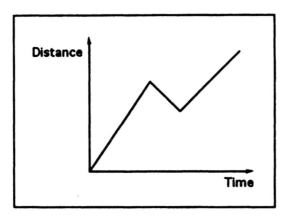

Figure 6.3 *A distance–time graph*

feel and yet research evidence suggest that students commonly have considerable difficulty interpreting distance time graphs. Kerslake (1981) indicates that only about a quarter of fifteen-year-olds could give a correct interpretation to a graph like that shown in Figure 6.3.

Common misinterpretations referred to 'climbing a mountain' and 'going up, going down, then up again'. In other cases, a graph is viewed like a map of a journey: in another of Kerslake's examples a child speaks of 'going along, then turning left'. Many students interpret the visual clues of such graphs wrongly by seeing them as a literal picture of what is happening rather than as a more abstract picture whose meaning has to be interpreted.

Data-logging devices are widely used in science classrooms. They have considerable potential for helping students to make sense of distance–time graphs, but they do not seem to have been adopted by mathematics teachers very widely. The screen shown in Figure 6.4 has been obtained using a motion-sensing device, the Calculator-Based Ranger (CBR), on a TI-92 calculator.

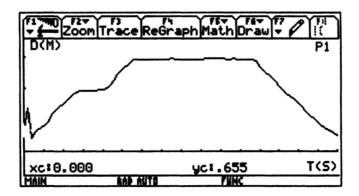

Figure 6.4 *A distance–time graph using a calculator-based ranger (CBR)*

When students see a graph being generated directly by a moving person it gives them a good qualitative feel for the link between speed and direction and the slope of the corresponding graph. This is illustrated below by a sample of work, shown in Figure 6.5, which was done by a typical twelve-year-old student in a class with a wide range of ability.

She walks slowly. Then stops. Then goes on faster. Stops, turns round, and comes back fast.

Figure 6.5 *A student's interpretation of a distance–time graph*

The writing shows clearly how the student has grasped the essential ideas linking gradient to speed, direction and standing still. The teacher had asked different pupils to move in front of the sensor in different ways and discussed the resulting graphs. The class were then given a number of sketch graphs and asked to write sets of instructions to generate each graph on the screen. Finally, individual pupils were invited to see whether their instructions did indeed produce the desired result. The ability to relate the abstract graph to the reality of the motion was impressive and does suggest that skilful use of technological tools can have very beneficial effects on students' understanding of a key concept like gradient.

Although distance–time graphs will quite rightly initially be considered independently of work on equations of straight-line graphs, the two can readily be linked. For instance, how long would it take a car travelling at 80 km/h to catch up with another car travelling at 50km/h which is 1 kilometre ahead? Obviously this could be approached in a variety of ways, but one possibility would be to represent the situation using two distance–time graphs. Using s for distance in kilometres and t for time in hours, the equations of the two graphs are $s = 80t$ and $s = 50t + 1$, but the form of the equations is the same as when the more familiar x and y are used and the link between gradient and speed can be duly emphasized. Other examples involving cars moving in opposite directions help students to appreciate the meaning of a negative gradient and relate it to the form of equations of straight lines.

At a later stage when velocity–time graphs are introduced the parallel can be drawn between the equation $v = u + at$, relating initial and final velocity when acceleration is constant, and the straight line equation $y = mx + c$.

Distance–time graphs provide a natural way of prompting consideration of the gradient of a curve because students readily appreciate that bodies do not always move with constant velocity and yet they do have a measurable velocity at any particular instant. Whilst precise calculations require the calculus, which must wait until Chapter 12, students can begin to appreciate how the changing gradient of a curve can be interpreted in qualitative terms. For instance, the graph of distance travelled by a falling body against time is given by $s = 5t^2$ with s as the distance in metres and t the time in seconds. The graph, shown in Figure 6.6, is the same parabolic shape as the familiar $y = x^2$ and the increasing gradient in the positive quadrant corresponds to the increasing speed of a falling body.

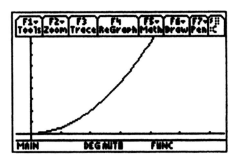

Figure 6.6 *Distance–time graph for a falling body*

TRANSFORMING GRAPHS: TRANSLATING AND STRETCHING

The graphs of quadratic functions are the natural next step to take once students have developed some familiarity with straight-line graphs. The graph of $y = x^2$ is worth discussing when square roots of numbers which are not perfect squares are introduced, because it provides a simple example of using a graph to provide an approximate solution to an equation. Graphs should also be introduced in conjunction with factorizing quadratic expressions, discussed in Chapter 5, and linked to solving quadratic equations, considered in Chapter 7. The link between the factorized form of a quadratic function, the solution of the corresponding equation and the intersection of the curve and the x axis are all fairly straightforward ideas, although students do not always immediately realize why a pair of very different looking functions like $y = x^2 - 4x + 3$ and $y = (x - 1)(x - 3)$ must have identical graphs.

The translations which link the position of the graph of a quadratic function of the form $y = x^2 + bx + c$ and the graph of $y = x^2$ require much more extensive consideration for which a graph plotter is an invaluable tool. Students have little difficulty in seeing that the graph of $y = x^2$ can be translated vertically up and down by adding or subtracting a constant. Moreover, a simple example like $y = x^2 - 4$, shown in Figure 6.7, can be linked readily to the factorized form, $y = (x - 2)(x + 2)$, and to its intersections with the x axis at 2 and -2 and the y axis at -4.

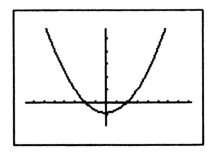

Figure 6.7 *The graph of $y = x^2 - 4$*

The problem of translating $y = x^2$ to left or right is much more interesting and is a good focus for class discussion with the graph displayed on a graph plotter screen for all to see.

T: How can we move the graph of $y = x^2$ three units to the right? What form will the equation take?

A: It's $y = x^2 + 3$. [Without comment, T displays this on the screen.] *Oh no, that moves it up.*

B: Try $y = (x + 3)^2$. [Again without comment, T deletes the previous graph and displays the new one on the screen.] *Oh dear, it has moved the wrong way.*

T: So, what should it be?

B: It must be $y = (x - 3)^2$. [Retaining the previous graph, T displays the new graph on the screen, which now looks like Figure 6.8.] *Yes, it's right now.*

T: Why must it be $y = (x - 3)^2$?

C: Because it has to be zero when $x = 3$ to move it to the right.

T: What happens with $y = (x + 3)^2$?

D: It is zero when $x = {}^-3$, so it moves to the left.

T: How could we move $y = (x - 3)^2$ four units downwards?

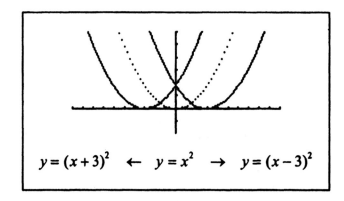

$$y = (x+3)^2 \quad \leftarrow \quad y = x^2 \quad \rightarrow \quad y = (x-3)^2$$

Figure 6.8 *Translating $y = x^2$ to left and right*

Obviously, a real discussion will not be as tidy as the idealized dialogue presented here, but it serves to illustrate some important teaching points:

- Ideas are accepted by the teacher and displayed without comment so that the students can see for themselves whether what they suggest gives what they want: the teacher is not acting as the authority in deciding what is right or wrong.
- Incorrect graphs are not condemned, but accepted as useful suggestions which may act as pointers to the right answer. Since $y = (x + 3)^2$ moves the curve to the left, it is then easy to see that $y = (x - 3)^2$ is likely to move it to the right. The teacher can sometimes use the tactic of writing all suggestions from the students on the board before trying them out on the screen. It is then possible to engineer the situation so that some incorrect graphs are viewed first!
- The students are asked to explain what they observe to help them develop ways of reasoning about the behaviour of graphs.

Having established how to translate the graph of $y = x^2$ independently in either the x or the y direction, it is easy to combine the two. In Figure 6.9 the graph has been translated by 3 in the x direction and by $^-4$ in the y direction by using the equation $y = (x - 3)^2 - 4$.

At this point students need to develop fluency with two operations:

- Finding an equation for a given graph either when a translation is specified or from diagrams like those in Figure 6.10. A graph plotter is a useful check here -- finding an equation

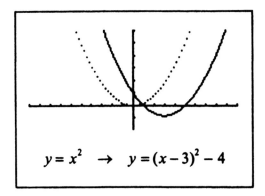

$$y = x^2 \quad \rightarrow \quad y = (x-3)^2 - 4$$

Figure 6.9 *A general translation of* $y = x^2$

for a graph requires some thought, whereas plotting a graph from a given equation is a routine task.
- Making sketch graphs from equations without using a graph plotter.

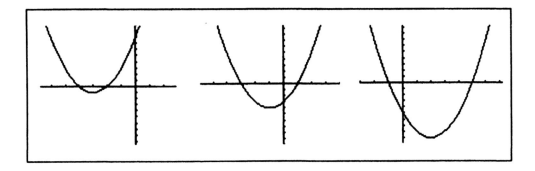

Figure 6.10 *Find equations for these graphs*

The completed squares form has arisen here as a way of translating the graph of $y = x^2$, but it is worth noting that it provides a way of determining the minimum point of the curve and a way of finding the points of intersection with the x axis, and also that it takes the familiar form $y = x^2 + bx + c$ when multiplied out. The links between the different forms and the solution of quadratic equations is discussed at length in Chapter 7.

Varying the coefficient of x^2 has the effect of stretching the graph of $y = x^2$ in the y direction and reflecting in the x axis as well when the coefficient is negative. Stretching in the x direction, however, introduces difficulties. For example, since $(\frac{1}{2}x)^2 = \frac{1}{4}x^2$, a stretch by a factor 2 in the x direction is the same as a stretch by a factor of $\frac{1}{4}$ in the y direction. Most students will find this confusing and it is therefore better with quadratic functions only to consider stretches in the y direction.

Quadratic functions and the parabolic form of their graphs have many applications to real world problems. The path of a projectile and the shape of a reflecting mirror are two obvious examples. The curves produced by a bent ruler or a string suspended at both ends provide simple practical examples where the ideas discussed above can be used to find an equation for a curve that fits.

Linking mathematics to items of local interest is often useful: as an example Figure 6.11 shows a picture of the Humber Bridge and a diagram showing approximate measurements. The origin is taken as the midpoint of a line joining the feet of the towers, which stand on two piers. The graph will have an equation of the form $y = ax^2 + c$. Since $y = 30$, when $x = 0$, it follows that $c = 30$. Since the distance between the two towers is 1410 metres and their height is 155 metres, $y = 155$ when $x = 705$ and solving the equation $155 = 705^2 a + 30$ gives an approximate value for a of 0.00025 or about $\frac{1}{4000}$. Further information and ideas related to the Humber Bridge will be found at **www.humberbridge.co.uk** and **www.mahumberside.eril.net**.

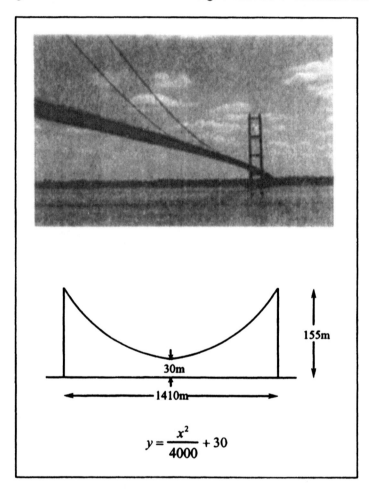

$$y = \frac{x^2}{4000} + 30$$

Figure 6.11 *An equation for the Humber Bridge (photo reproduced from www.humberbridge.co.uk)*

The effects of stretches in both directions are exemplified particularly clearly by the sine and cosine functions, and these have a very wide range of practical applications. Again, a dialogue serves to illustrate a very similar approach to that used in the case of translations. This time a graph of $y = \sin(x)$ is on display.

T: How can we stretch the graph of $y = \sin(x)$ so that the humps are three times taller? What form will the equation take?
A: *It's $y = 3\sin(x)$. [T displays this on the screen.]*
T: Fine. [T displays $y = \sin(x)$ on its own again.] Now, how can we stretch the curve so that the humps are twice as wide?
B: *It's $2\sin(x)$. No, that makes it taller. It must be $y = \sin(2x)$ [Without comment, T displays this on the screen with $y = \sin(x)$.] It's shrunk!*
T: So, what should it be?
B: *It must be $y = \sin(\frac{x}{2})$. [Retaining the previous graph, T displays the new graph on the screen, which now looks like Figure 6.12.] Yes, it's right now.*

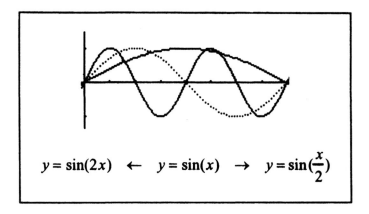

$$y = \sin(2x) \quad \leftarrow \quad y = \sin(x) \quad \rightarrow \quad y = \sin\left(\frac{x}{2}\right)$$

Figure 6.12 *Stretching a sine graph*

It is important to understand why the graph of $y = \sin(2x)$ corresponds to $y = \sin(x)$ stretched by a factor of $\frac{1}{2}$. Looking at one particular point helps to make it clear what is happening: the peak of the first wave is when the value of x is 45°, which corresponds to the peak of the original sine curve at 90°, the value $2x$. Each point on the curve moves towards the y axis with the distance stretched (or shrunk) by a factor of $\frac{1}{2}$. A similar argument explains how the graph of $y = \sin(\frac{x}{2})$ corresponds to $y = \sin(x)$ stretched by a factor of 2.

At some point, the appropriate language – period and amplitude – needs to be introduced, but the first priority is to establish the important effects of stretches in the two directions and to combine these in simple cases with translations. There are many examples of oscillating behaviour which can be modelled with sine or cosine graphs. The graph of Figure 6.13 shows the depth of the sea at some place as the tide rises and falls over a 12-hour period (a very rough approximation to reality, but it makes the numbers simple!). The units on the x axis are then 3 hours and with a maximum depth of 35 metres the units on the y axis are 5 metres. Since the minimum depth is 5 metres, the amplitude is 15 metres and the mean depth is 20 metres, so the curve has an equation of the form $y = 15 \sin(kx°) + 20$. The value of k is related to the stretch factor, but is found most easily by using the fact that $kx = 360$ when $x = 12$ which gives $k = 30$ and an equation for the graph of $y = 15 \sin(30x°) + 20$.

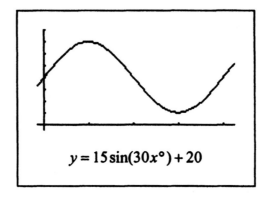

$$y = 15\sin(30x°) + 20$$

Figure 6.13 *Modelling the rise and fall of the tide with a sine graph*

Before leaving the subject of translations and stretches it is worth looking at the way that they may be applied to a circle with unit radius centred at the origin, whose graphical representation is achieved most simply by the pair of parametric equations $x = \cos(t)$ and $y = \sin(t)$. The effect of the two transformations is shown in Figure 6.14. In the first case, the circle has been translated by 3 units in the x direction and 2 units in the y direction, and in the second case 3 and 2 are taken as the scale factors for stretches in the two directions. The corresponding Cartesian equations can be derived readily from the parametric forms. The stretching also provides a simple way of thinking about the area of the ellipse. Since the area of the circle with unit radius is π, the area of an ellipse resulting from the two stretches with factors 3 and 2 is 6π. In general, for stretches with factors a and b in the x and y directions, the area is πab.

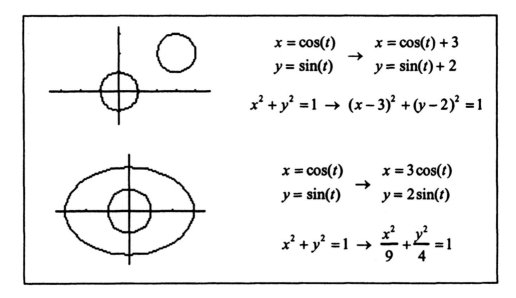

Figure 6.14 *Translating and stretching a circle*

Thinking about graphs in terms of transformations is particularly valuable because it focuses attention on the role of the parameters in an equation and the resulting families of curves that result from varying those parameters, which in turn highlights the properties of the curves that remain constant and those that change. The examples discussed in this section have referred specifically to quadratic functions and circular functions, but the ideas obviously apply to the graphs of all functions. The ideas can be summarized succinctly for a general function $y = f(x)$ as follows:

- Translation of p units in the x direction and q units in the y direction:

$$y = f(x) \rightarrow y = f(x - p) + q$$

- Stretch by factor a in the x direction and factor b in the y direction:

$$y = f(x) \rightarrow y = bf\left(\frac{x}{a}\right)$$

However, most students find it easier to understand and remember key ideas by references to specific examples rather than in a more general form, so that a summary like that of Figure 6.15 is usually more appropriate.

	Translating $y = x^2$	Stretching $y = \sin(x)$
2 in the x direction	$y = (x - 2)^2$	$y = \sin\left(\frac{x}{2}\right)$
3 in the y direction	$y = x^2 + 3$	$y = 3\sin(x)$
2 in the x direction and 3 in the y direction	$y = (x - 2)^2 + 3$	$y = 3\sin\left(\frac{x}{2}\right)$

Figure 6.15 *Summarizing the transformation of graphs*

CUBIC FUNCTIONS

Another aspect of sketching graphs is how the graph of a function created by adding or subtracting a pair of functions is related to the two parent graphs. Figure 6.16 shows the graphs of $y = x^3 - x$ and $y = x^3 - x^2$ with the graph of $y = x^3$ shown dotted in each case. One of these would provide a useful focus for class discussion and then students could be asked to think out the other one for themselves.

In the case of $y = x^3 - x$, it is clear that the curve must pass through the origin. When x is positive, a positive number is subtracted from x^3 at each point. It is as though the curve is pulled downwards, so that the graph lies below that of $y = x^3$. Since $x^3 - x = 0$ when $x = 1$, the curve crosses the x axis at that point and is negative when $x < 1$ and positive when $x > 1$. This fully determines the position of the part of the curve on the positive side. A similar analysis leads to the behaviour on the negative side, although it might also be observed that the graph has half-turn symmetry about the origin, since $x^3 - x$ is an odd function. Solving the equation $x^3 - x = 0$ by factorizing to give $x(x - 1)(x + 1) = 0$ serves as further confirmation of the three points of intersection with the x axis. When the ideas of the calculus are available later, the position of the maximum and minimum points can be determined precisely.

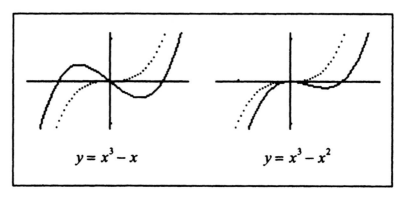

$$y = x^3 - x \qquad\qquad y = x^3 - x^2$$

Figure 6.16 *Graphs of some cubic functions*

Problems with volumes provide more practical examples that lead to cubic functions. For example, Figure 6.17 shows a square of card with 10cm edges where squares have been cut from each corner to give a net which folds up to make an open-topped rectangular box with a square base. If the edge of the base of the box is x cm, then the volume is given by the equation $V = \frac{1}{2}x^2 (10 - x)$, which can alternatively be written as $V = 5x^2 - \frac{1}{2}x^3$.

A graph will show how the volume varies as the size of the squares cut from the corners of the card varies. Producing a sketch of the graph again provides a useful exercise in algebraic thinking that can be aided by the practical situation. Students tend to focus their attention on the algebraic expression and need to be encouraged to relate their thinking to the situation it represents as well. It should be clear that the volume will be zero when $x = 0$, because the box would have no base, and $x = 10$, because the box is then all base and no height. Between these extremes, the volume must increase from zero and then decrease. Since the function is simple a single maximum would be expected. Outside this range the problem is not meaningful, but the form of the graph is useful in indicating the overall shape: it is helpful to see that the value of the function is positive when $x < 0$ and negative when $x > 10$.

Another useful way of looking at the function is to sketch the graph of $y = 5x^2$ first and then consider the effect of subtracting the term $\frac{1}{2}x^3$. This means that the graph of the volume function is above $y = 5x^2$ when $x < 0$ and below when $x > 0$, as shown by Figure 6.18.

The analysis in the various examples of this section uses algebraic thinking in a variety of ways and helps to develop further the vital skills of producing a quick sketch of the graph of a function and the reverse process of identifying a function whose graph is given.

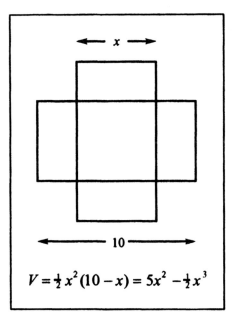

$$V = \tfrac{1}{2}x^2(10-x) = 5x^2 - \tfrac{1}{2}x^3$$

Figure 6.17 *The volume of an open-topped rectangular box*

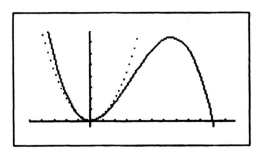

Figure 6.18 *Graph of $V = 5x^2 - \frac{1}{2}x^3$*

ALGEBRAIC FRACTIONS AND RATIONAL FUNCTIONS

The graph of $y = \frac{1}{x}$, like that of $y = x^2$, should be encountered at an early stage with the domain restricted to positive numbers. At the simplest level, as a graph with discrete points, it can be used to discuss the behaviour of the sequence of unit fractions: $1, \frac{1}{2}, \frac{1}{3}, \frac{1}{4}, \frac{1}{5}$ and so on. As the fractions get closer to zero there is a glimpse of limits and infinity and the idea of an asymptote. When the graph is extended to positive real numbers, the behaviour as x approaches zero offers similar insights, together with a link to the idea of reciprocal and its self-inverse properties. At a later stage, the implications of the equivalent form $xy = 1$ can be explored with its links to inverse proportion, discussed in Chapter 8.

The form $y = \frac{1}{x-p} + q$ for a translation of $y = \frac{1}{x}$ through p units in the x direction and q units in the y direction is no different to that for other functions, but its effect in moving the vertical asymptote to $x = p$ and the horizontal asymptote is $y = q$ is an important consideration. As with $y = x^2$, it is, for most purposes, better to consider stretches in the y direction only when interpreting the family of curves given by $y = \frac{c}{x}$, as displayed in Figure 6.19. Students tend to see the stretch as being in the direction indicated by the line $y = x$, but this is not so convenient as a stretch in either the x or y direction where the scale factor is simply c.

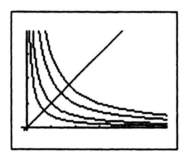

Figure 6.19 *The family of curves $y = \frac{c}{x}$ for $x > 0$*

Investigating the graph of the rational function $y = \frac{x-a}{x-b}$ by looking at the effect of varying the values of the constants a and b provides students a valuable opportunity to develop skills with algebraic fractions and graphical interpretation.

Figure 6.20 shows two functions of the form $y = \frac{x-a}{x-b}$, both with 2 as the value of b. If students are asked what they notice about these and other curves generated by the same function, they will comment on the intersections with the axes and the asymptotes. In Chapter 2 I referred to the notion of a 'procept', put forward by Gray and Tall (1993), to bring together the ideas of process and product. This relates well to $\frac{x-a}{x-b}$, which students initially see as representing a 'process' in the sense that it enables numbers to be calculated to determine points on a graph and can therefore serve as a label for a graph. However, the expression $\frac{x-a}{x-b}$ holds a lot of information and the teacher's task is to help students understand it as a 'product' which can be unpacked and repackaged to reveal what it has to say about the properties of the graph.

Using a graph plotter to plot particular families of graphs enables the student to focus on particular properties. Challenging students to draw some curves of the form $y = \frac{x-a}{x-b}$ which all intersect the x axis at $x = 1$ will focus attention on the role of the number 1 in the numerator. A similar challenge to find curves that intersect the y axis at a common point will focus on how the values of a and b relate to that property. The two graphs in Figure 6.20 clearly have the asymptote $x = 2$ in common, explained readily by the 2 in the denominator. However, the most striking property of the two graphs, and all others generated by $y = \frac{x-a}{x-b}$ apart from the special situation where $a = b$, is that $y = 1$ is always a horizontal asymptote, so why is this so?

There are a number of ways of explaining this property, but in the context of this chapter it is appropriate to think about it in terms of translations. The key is to look at equivalent forms for the expressions. Figure 6.21 shows what happens when the two expressions used above are expanded on a TI-89 calculator.

It is immediately clear why $y = 1$ is the horizontal asymptote because the other term tends to zero for large values of x. These equivalent forms can be used to explain how the two graphs

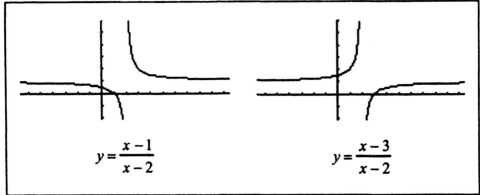

Figure 6.20 *Graphs of rational functions*

■ expand$\left(\dfrac{x-1}{x-2}\right)$	$\dfrac{1}{x-2}+1$
■ expand$\left(\dfrac{x-3}{x-2}\right)$	$1-\dfrac{1}{x-2}$

Figure 6.21 *Equivalent forms for algebraic fractions*

of Figure 6.20 are obtained by translating the graphs of $y = \frac{1}{x}$ and $y = -\frac{1}{x}$. The two examples have been carefully chosen so that the numerator is one in the fractional part. That is clearly not always the case, so there is certainly more to think about here. Furthermore, the effect of varying the position of the horizontal asymptote on the form of the expression merits careful consideration. Students can be asked to compare the effect of stretching and translating as a way of moving the asymptote. For example, $y = \frac{2(x-1)}{x-2}$ and $y = \frac{x-1}{x-2} + 1$ both have an asymptote at $y = 2$, but they are not equivalent functions and therefore do not have identical graphs.

It is not sufficient to accept uncritically the output of a calculator, because students should become fluent in the manipulations required to move between the two forms of the expression. However, the graphs and the calculator output do provide a useful motivation for understanding more fully how algebraic fractions behave. The two processes involved here have direct analogies with changing back and forth between improper and proper fractions. Thus $\frac{x-1}{x-2} = 1 + \frac{1}{x-2}$ becomes $\frac{5}{4} = 1 + \frac{1}{4} = 1\frac{1}{4}$ when $x = 5$, but clearly there are differences because $\frac{x-3}{x-2} = 1 - \frac{1}{x-2}$ does not behave in quite the same way. The algebraic key lies in being able to provide the linking step between the two forms, shown below using two contrasting examples whose graphs have an asymptote at $y = 2$:

$$\frac{2(x-1)}{x-2} = \frac{2(x-2)+2}{x-2} = 2 + \frac{2}{x-2} \quad \text{and} \quad \frac{x-1}{x-2} + 1 = \frac{x-1+x-2}{x-2} = \frac{2x-3}{x-2}$$

Students commonly have considerable difficulty with manipulations involving algebraic fractions, primarily because they lack fluency with the corresponding operations using numerical fractions, which underpin the algebraic skills. However, motivation is also a factor and the manipulations can become more meaningful, relevant and interesting by building on the link between algebraic fractions and graphs.

CONCLUSION

The visual appeal of graphs gives them an immediate intrinsic interest, but they also have a wide range of applications within and beyond mathematics that make them seem more immediately relevant to the student than symbolic algebra. Graphs have a very important role as a way of picturing functions so that drawing attention to their properties can give greater meaning to symbolic forms. In essence, algebraic expressions are succinct symbolic summaries of numerical patterns. Maintaining and extending the links between symbols, numbers and pictures is a vital part of students' algebraic development and discussions and tasks focused on graphs provide an abundance of opportunities for viewing ideas from these different perspectives.

Graph plotters are a particularly powerful tool because they enable both teacher and student to look at a far wider range of graphs than would be possible if they all had to be plotted by hand. By varying the parameters of a function the resulting family of curves highlights common properties and prompts questions which can be answered by manipulating and interpreting the algebraic expressions. However, a graph plotter cannot do all the thinking. There are two key types of task which embrace the essential ideas that students need to understand for all the various types of function that they encounter in a school mathematics course:

- sketching simple graphs by hand, given their equations, to identify the main features without using a graph plotter;
- suggesting an appropriate equation for a given graph, sometimes using a graph plotter as a way of exploring possibilities and checking.

In both cases, the problem for the teacher is how to help the student to acquire the necessary skills and understanding. Discussion is important as a means of developing understanding, but it must be accompanied by frequent opportunities to maintain familiarity with important facts and skills. Once a new idea has been introduced, this is best achieved in two ways:

- by rehearsing skills frequently using mental algebra – short questions given orally with written responses, which in the case of graphs will focus on the two key tasks above;
- by applying algebra to problems, explanations and proofs of all kinds in a variety of appropriate contexts, so that skills are rehearsed as students learn to make sense of algebraic arguments and generate their own chains of reasoning, with graphs used frequently as the focus of a problem and also to add an extra dimension or further insight.

Chapter 7

Puzzles and Problems: Creating and Solving Equations

But yesterday you said *x* equals 2!

(Cartoon by Rex F. May reproduced with permission)

CREATING AND SOLVING LINEAR EQUATIONS

T: Think of a number. Double it and add 5. What is your answer?
A: *11*
T: Can you work out A's number?
B: *3.*
T: Is that right A?
A: *Yes*
T: How did you do it?
B: *I took 5 from 11 to get 6 and then halved it.*

Simple linear equations are often introduced with a dialogue like this. Students usually have little difficulty in solving problems in this way, provided that the numbers are simple and the operations and their inverses are familiar. The procedure they usually use is to 'undo' the two operations. However, as soon as equations are represented symbolically and formal methods of solution are introduced many students begin to experience a variety of difficulties that are well known to teachers:

- difficulty in translating a 'word problem' into an algebraic form;
- reliance on informal methods which work well in simple situations, but are less suited to equations whose solution necessitates a more formal procedure;
- lack of fluency when operating with negative numbers and fractions;
- choosing the wrong inverse operation;
- difficulty in deciding the order in which to carry out operations;
- confusion over what is seen as a complicated written procedure.

The most difficult part of solving any problem is often translating it into an appropriate symbolic form. It is easy to neglect this aspect of solving problems and concentrate students' energies solely on learning techniques for solution. This has two bad effects: the first is that students fail to develop an ability to carry out this vital initial stage in solving problems and the second is that motivation is weakened because the reason for learning to solve equations is lost. Techniques should be developed alongside the problems that they are designed to solve so that students can see a purpose in what they are doing. This purpose does not need to be very sophisticated – the attraction of solving puzzles can be a strong source of motivation. A variety of starting points for algebra were discussed in Chapter 3 and each of these presented algebra in meaningful ways where a concrete situation was translated into algebraic terms. This requires an awareness of symbolic meanings and conventions and an ability to move freely between a statement in words like 'double a number and add 5' and its symbolic form $2x + 5$.

Booth (1984, p. 93) discusses how equations like $x + 5 = 8$ are often used by teachers to introduce students to formal equation-solving procedures, but notes that 'children typically proceed to the solution of such equations by inspection, 'guess and test', or the application of known number bonds'. They do not need to think in terms of subtracting 3 because the missing number denoted by x is either immediately obvious to them or because they think 'I know that $3 + 5 = 8$'. Introducing formal procedures to do something that students can do quite well without does not seem a very sensible tactic, because many students, quite justifiably, ignore difficult ways of doing simple things. It is only when a route to the answer is not immediately obvious, and informal methods are clearly inadequate, that such students will recognize that a formal procedure might be useful. In the context of 'think of a number', solving $24x + 53 = 137$ is less trivial than $2x + 5 = 11$, although the simpler problem may be useful in suggesting ways of approaching the harder one.

Many difficulties with algebra arise, as I have observed in earlier chapters, because students do not have sufficient understanding of essential numerical ideas or fluency in using them, and this obviously applies equally to equation solving. It would seem appropriate therefore, as far as possible in the early stages, to establish principles and procedures, using only those types of numbers which the student can use with fluency. Problems involving fractions and negative numbers should be delayed until confidence has been established with using these more demanding types of number and with the algebraic procedures through using simpler numbers. On the other hand, large whole numbers and decimals may be manageable when a calculator is used to help the solution process.

A common error in solving an equation like $3x - 2 = 7$ arises when students decide to subtract 2 from both sides 'to get rid of the 2 on the left' and arrive wrongly at $3x = 5$. This arises because text books and teachers refer to 'removing' or 'getting rid of' a particular number in order to isolate the unknown element. This suggests to the student that something has to be 'taken away' rather than that an operation has to be 'undone'. Clarity about the operation to use is helped by thinking what steps have been taken to set up the expression on the left hand side of the equation. Verbalizing the steps represented by an expression like $3x - 2$ and possibly writing them out as a flow diagram, as shown in Figure 7.1, makes it easier to see what has to be done to find the value of x. The flow diagram makes clear that, since 2 has been subtracted as the last step, it has to be added back on to 7 first when you are seeking the unknown starting number.

The flow diagram builds on students' intuitive ideas about how to solve 'think of a number' problems and serves both as a useful preliminary to representing and solving problems in an algebraic form and as a pointer to ways of overcoming some of the difficulties that students have with formal methods of solving linear equations.

Thinking about how the equation has been built up helps to overcome difficulties with the order in which to carry out operations leading to a solution. The idea that what has been done last has to be undone first is not immediately obvious if the student looks at the written form

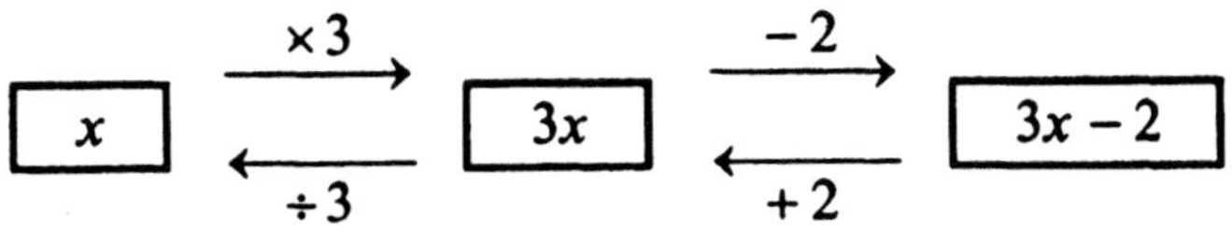

Figure 7.1 *Undoing with a flow diagram*

$3x - 2 = 7$. When you read the expression, '3 times something' comes to your attention first and that may dispose the unthinking student to try dividing by 3 as a first step. Although such an error may not be made in simple cases like this, it commonly arises when literal equations are involved. For example, in making a the subject of the literal formula $v = u + at$, it is not uncommon for students to give $a = \frac{v}{t} - u$ as a solution.

Insistence on a complicated written form of solution, like that shown on the left in Figure 7.2, where all the thinking steps are written down, makes a simple process look complicated and can create confusion rather than help understanding. The form shown on the right should be sufficient as a written solution, but there should be accompanying discussion to highlight the process of deciding on the two undoing steps – add 2 and divide by 3. A flow diagram is a valuable way of aiding that thinking and recording informally the steps that are involved.

Figure 7.2 *Complicating a simple procedure*

The use of flow diagrams helps to establish the important principle of carrying out the same operation to both sides of an equation to maintain the equality and to make explicit the order in which to carry out those operations. However, a flow diagram is not immediately applicable when the unknown appears in more than one place in an equation, because the unknown must appear in one place only in the equation. The additional steps required to achieve that are not difficult, once students have become fluent in solving a variety of linear equations where there is a single appearance of the unknown.

Equations should not always appear in a disembodied form in exercises which just practise solution techniques: formulating equations is as important as solving them. Here is a puzzle problem about ages followed by a dialogue with the focus on formulating the equation that has to be solved:

Jill is 27 years older than her son Jack and in 5 years time her age will be 4 times that of Jack. What are their ages now?

T: What are we trying to find here?
A: *Jack's age and Jill's age.*
T: What do we know about them?
B: *Jill is 27 years older than Jack.*
T: If we let Jack's age be *x* years at present, how can we write down Jill's age?
C: *Jill's age is x + 27 years.*
T: So, Jack is *x* years old and Jill is *x* + 27 years at the moment. What will their ages be in 5 years time?
D: *x + 5 for Jack and x + 32 for Jill.*
T: What do we do next?
A: *You know that Jill's age will be 4 times Jack's age in 5 years time.*
B: So, we can write 4(x + 5) = x + 32.

Students can then contribute the steps to take at each stage to arrive at a solution:

$$4(x + 5) = x + 32$$
$$4x + 20 = x + 32$$
$$3x + 20 = 32$$
$$3x = 12$$
$$x = 4$$

The final stage of solving a problem is to present the solution in the form required and to check that it is correct. In this case, Jack is 4 years old and Jill is 31 and in 5 years time their ages will be 9 and 36, which satisfy the stated requirements. It is easier to encourage students to check their solutions when they are solving an equation which arises from a problem, rather than as a disembodied example in an exercise, because the problem provides a clear context, even though it may be somewhat contrived.

Equations can be solved with an advanced calculator using the solve command as shown in Figure 7.3. This is clearly useful when a complicated equation arises in the course of mathematical work. However, students do need to understand the principles of solving a range of standard types of equations by hand and to develop considerable fluency with simple examples. The use of the solve facility on a calculator needs to be used judiciously so as not to subvert this essential requirement.

■ solve(5·x − 7 = 2·x + 5, x)   x = 4

Figure 7.3 *Solving an equation with an advanced calculator*

An advanced calculator can be used to help students understand how to solve equations quickly 'by hand' by focusing their attention on the choice of operations and by enabling them to see the effects of wrong choices. The screen from a TI-92 calculator shown in Figure 7.4 shows a sequence of operations applied to both sides of an equation so that *x* remains on the left and the solution appears on the right. The three operations are subtract 2*x*, add 7 and divide by 3. At each stage the equation is entered enclosed by brackets and the chosen operation is entered after the brackets. The result is then displayed as an equation on the right. This can be transferred to the entry line at each stage by highlighting with the cursor and entering.

The secret of success is to choose a suitable sequence of operations. With the calculator the student can concentrate attention on learning that important skill, because it becomes clear

```
▪ 5·x − 7 = 2·x + 5          5·x − 7 = 2·x + 5
▪ (5·x − 7 = 2·x + 5) − 2·x        3·x − 7 = 5
▪ (3·x − 7 = 5) + 7          3·x = 12
   3·x = 12
▪ ─────────                     x = 4
     3
⟨3*x=12⟩/3
```

Figure 7.4 *Displaying the steps in solving an equation*

immediately when an operation does not do what was expected. For example, Figure 7.5 shows what happens if 7 is subtracted rather than added as the second operation in the example from Figure 7.4. It does not make the equation any simpler so the student has to delete that line and think again!

```
▪ (3·x − 7 = 5) − 7               3·x − 14 = -2
```

Figure 7.5 *Choosing the wrong operation!*

Using advanced calculators as a way of developing students' understanding and skills in carrying out tasks independently of the machine is a relatively unexplored area, which needs handling with some caution because the student may take the view that the calculator appears to be able to do all work so that there is no need to understand what is going on. However, the ability to use equations intelligently and to create algebraic arguments is very dependent on familiarity and fluency with the rules and procedures of written algebra. A calculator does not solve all the problems!

Solving a literal equation, changing the subject of a formula and finding the inverse of a function are all equation solving tasks, where the difficulty of choosing the correct operations at each stage is an even greater challenge for students because the presence of additional variables complicates the situation. When values are given for all the other variables it is invariably simpler to substitute the values first and then solve the equation. For example, to find the value of a from the formula $v = u + at$ when $v = 25$, $u = 10$, and $t = 3$, it is much simpler to substitute and solve the equation $25 = 10 + 3t$, than to derive the formula $a = \frac{v-u}{t}$ and then substitute.

When it is necessary to retain the literal form of an equation, flow diagrams are again a useful tool for thinking about the steps to take. This is illustrated by the example of Figure 7.6 showing how to make l the subject of the formula $T = 2\pi\sqrt{\frac{l}{g}}$. For some students, flow diagrams may be a reliable procedure for continuing use, but for most they should only be an aid to thinking on the path towards fluency in choosing the correct operations in the correct order for a more conventional procedure, such as the following:

$$2\pi\sqrt{\frac{l}{g}} = T$$

$$\sqrt{\frac{l}{g}} = \frac{T}{2\pi}$$

$$\frac{l}{g} = \frac{T^2}{4\pi^2}$$

$$l = \frac{gT^2}{4\pi^2}$$

The expressions on each side of the equation at each step appear in corresponding boxes in the flow diagrams of Figure 7.6, a useful connection to make and one that could be further emphasized by setting out the two flow diagrams vertically.

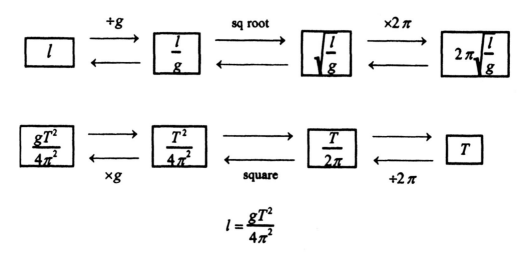

$$l = \frac{gT^2}{4\pi^2}$$

Figure 7.6 *Using a flow diagram to transform the formula* $T = 2\pi\sqrt{\frac{l}{g}}$

SIMULTANEOUS EQUATIONS

Sawyer (1964, p. 40) suggested that algebra could be introduced with problems which lead to simultaneous equations, because these may seem less trivial than simple linear equations and provide a greater motivation for an algebraic approach that gives meaning to symbols and develops important procedures. Sawyer's initial example is in the form of a puzzle question, neatly illustrated by the picture in Figure 7.7, which makes the solution to the problem immediately obvious and leads readily to an algebraic representation.

With m as the height of a man and s as the height of each son it is easy to see that the situation can be represented by the pair of simultaneous equations:

$$m + 2s = 14$$
$$m + s = 10$$

The diagram makes it clear how subtracting the two equations leads immediately to the solutions $s = 4$ and $m = 6$. The idea can then be applied readily to a variety of other pairs of

'A man has 2 sons. The sons are twins: they are the same height. If we add the man's height to the height of 1 son, we get 10 feet. The total height of the man and the 2 sons is 14 feet. what are the heights of the man and his sons?'

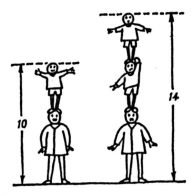

Figure 7.7 *A problem with a man and his sons (Taken from Sawyer, (1964), p. 41: reproduced with permission from Penguin Books.)*

equations involving different numbers of men and sons, and women and daughters, but perhaps not all four at once! A simple equation with subtraction arises by including an equation giving the difference between the heights of man and son:

$$m + s = 8$$
$$m - s = 2$$

A picture will suggest that $2s = 6$, the result of subtracting the equations, from which it follows that $s = 3$. Alternatively, such a pair of equations can be used to introduce the idea that adding equations is often a useful tactic, in this case giving $2m = 10$ and hence $m = 5$.

Another way of introducing simultaneous equations is to use two dice, one red and one yellow, and ask a student to roll them and note the scores.

T: What is the total score on the two dice?
A: 8
T: How can we record that?
B: r + y = 8
T: What is r?
C: The red dice.
T: Think carefully what it means.
B: The number on the red dice.
T: Yes, the letter stands for a number. And *y* is the number on the yellow dice. Now, what is the sum of the number on the red dice and 3 times the number on the yellow dice?
A: 14
T: How can we write that down?
B: r + 3y = 14
T: And how can we now find the two numbers *r* and *y*?

Again we have a puzzle situation with a pair of equations where students can be challenged to suggest a way to find the solutions:

$$r + 3y = 14$$
$$r + y = 8$$

Students readily see, as with the man and sons example, that subtracting the equations leads to a solution. In both examples the meaning of the equations is clear and the letters clearly refer to numbers. It is not difficult to add further refinements which require addition and subtraction of different multiples of two equations. The puzzles are designed to attract the interest of the students – solving them provides a simple purpose for the algebra. Moreover the students can themselves suggest solution procedures which can be refined, practised, extended and applied to a wide variety of examples.

QUADRATIC EQUATIONS

Simple quadratic equations without a linear term can be solved as soon as students are familiar with square roots. By extending the methods used for linear equations, students can easily solve equations such as:

$$x^2 + 3 = 12, \quad (x - 5)^2 = 81 \text{ and } 3x^2 - 8 = 40$$

A more challenging problem before formal procedures are introduced would be to find a number which is 1 less than its square by finding a solution (or solutions) to the equation $x^2 - x = 1$. It is clear from the spreadsheet shown in Figure 7.8 that a solution lies between 1.61 and 1.62. Evaluating the function for 1.615 then shows that the solution lies between 1.615 and 1.62 and that 1.62 is therefore the solution correct to 2 decimal places. Further evaluation gives 1.618 as the solution to 3 decimal places.

x	x^2-x
1.6	0.96
1.62	1.0044
1.61	0.9821
1.615	0.993225
1.618	0.999924
1.619	1.002161
1.6185	1.00104225

Figure 7.8 *Trial and improvement to solve* $x^2 - x = 1$

Trial and improvement is valuable in giving students a feel for a solution as a number that satisfies an equation, because it is a direct search for a number that is tested at each stage by trying it out. It also has a value in developing an understanding of the decimal form of numbers and the question of finding solutions to a suitable degree of accuracy. Trial and improvement has the virtue of providing a method that works for all equations, but it is not adequate as the sole method for solving equations, because multiple solutions are not identified readily and it does not give the exact form of a solution where that is possible, as in the important case of quadratic equations.

Graphical methods give valuable insights into equation solving both through highlighting the number of solutions and by providing solutions to a suitable degree of accuracy by zooming in on points of intersection. A hand-drawn sketch graph may be sufficient to identify the number of solutions, but as with trial and improvement zooming in on a solution will only give an approximate answer. However, graphical approaches to equation solving have a value in developing general understanding of graphs, particularly when alternative ways of solving the same equation are considered. Finding the intersection of the lines $y = x^2 - x$ and $y = 1$ is one way of solving $x^2 - x = 1$ graphically. Other possibilities include the intersection of the curve $y = x^2 - x - 1$ with the x axis and the intersection of the curve $y = x^2$ with the straight line $y = x + 1$. These three alternatives are illustrated in Figure 7.9 by calculator screens from a TI-89.

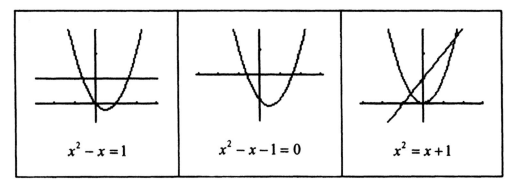

$$x^2 - x = 1 \qquad x^2 - x - 1 = 0 \qquad x^2 = x + 1$$

Figure 7.9 *Three graphical methods for solving the equation* $x^2 - x = 1$

In Chapter 5, quadratic functions were considered in the context of expanding and finding factors. Plotting the graph of a quadratic function such as $y = x^2 - 4x + 3$, shown in Figure 7.10, immediately prompts the question as to where it crosses the x axis. This in turn gives a purpose to expressing the function as a product of its factors $(x - 1)(x - 3)$.

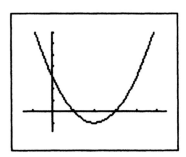

Figure 7.10 *The graph of* $y = x^2 - 4x + 3$

Solving equations by expressing them as a product of factors is an important idea with a wide range of applications. The essential idea is that one or more of the factors must be zero if the product is zero: $ab = 0 \Rightarrow a = 0$ or $b = 0$. This leads to the standard way of solving a quadratic equation:

$$x^2 - 4x + 3 = 0$$
$$(x - 1)(x - 3) = 0$$
$$x - 1 = 0 \text{ or } x - 3 = 0$$
$$x = 1 \text{ or } x = 3$$

Four difficulties commonly arise for students in relation to this procedure for solving quadratic equations:

- An equation like $x^2 - 4x = 0$ is often written as $x^2 = 4x$ and the common factor x is cancelled inadvisedly giving $x = 4$ and losing the other solution $x = 0$. It is important to alert students to the dangers of inappropriate cancelling and to encourage them to express equations like this in the form $x(x - 4) = 0$ so that solutions are not lost.
- An equation like $x^2 - 3x - 4 = 0$ is often written as $x^2 - 3x = 4$, factorized to give $x(x - 3) = 4$ and then solved by saying that $x = 4$ or $x - 3 = 4$, mistakenly using the zero product principle. Errors like this need to be discussed, firstly to make clear that both the solutions suggested must satisfy the equation and secondly to help students see that the principle does not work in this form for numbers other than zero. It may indeed be worth pointing out that 4 can be expressed as a product of integer factors in four ways as 1×4, $^-1 \times ^-4$, 2×2 and $^-2 \times ^-2$, and that only the first two of these lead to solutions.
- It is not always possible to solve an equation by finding factors. Students do not readily distinguish between situations where there are no real solutions and those where the solutions cannot be found readily because they are not rational. Examples like this need to be discussed as ideas about quadratic equations are developed: graphical interpretation and the role of the discriminant $b^2 - 4ac$ are particularly important.
- Once the general formula for solving a quadratic equation has been introduced, students have a strong tendency to use it regardless of whether an equation can be solved with a less complicated procedure, such as simple factorization. The attraction of the formula is that it 'always works' and so when it has become familiar students feel sure that they can get right answers. However, they should be helped to develop sufficient fluency in factorizing simple quadratic expressions so that becomes their obvious first approach, rather than the formula, when faced with a simple example.

Familiarity with the general method of solving quadratic equations is important because it is useful as a practical method of arriving at both exact and approximate solutions and as a way of discriminating between situations where there are 0, 1 or 2 solutions. The idea of completing the square, mentioned in conjunction with translating the graph of $y = x^2$ in Chapter 6, is valuable because it provides both a way of arriving at the quadratic equation formula and a simple way of sketching the graph of any quadratic function.

The equation $x^2 - 4x + 1 = 0$ is solved by completing the square as follows:

$$x^2 - 4x + 1 = 0$$
$$x^2 - 4x + 4 = 3$$

$$(x - 2)^2 = 3$$
$$x - 2 = \pm\sqrt{3}$$
$$x = 2 \pm \sqrt{3}$$
$$x \approx \text{ to } 3.73 \text{ or } 0.27$$

Students often have difficulty with the first step because it requires a ready familiarity with forms like $(x - 2)^2 = x^2 - 4x + 4$. It is helpful initially to look at examples where the coefficient of x^2 is 1 and the coefficient of x is even, so that the principle behind the procedure is understood before the complications caused by fractions are introduced. The procedure has greater relevance when it is linked to the graph of the quadratic function, because the completed square form provides a simple way of sketching graphs and determining the turning point, as well as showing the significance of the solutions of the corresponding quadratic equation.

Unnecessary complication can again be avoided in proving the formula for solving a general quadratic equation. As before the situation is simplified if the coefficient of x^2 is restricted to 1 initially, so that the equation considered is $x^2 + bx + c = 0$. The usual approach based on completing the square, shown in Figure 7.11, should be presented alongside a numerical example like the one above, stressing the role of the identity $(x + \frac{b}{2})^2 = x^2 + bx + \frac{b^2}{4}$. The general case $ax^2 + bx + c = 0$ can then be dealt with by replacing b and c with $\frac{b}{a}$ and $\frac{c}{a}$ to give the familiar formula:

$$x = \frac{-b \pm \sqrt{b^2 - 4ac}}{2a}$$

$$x^2 + bx + c = 0$$

$$x^2 + bx + \frac{b^2}{4} = \frac{b^2}{4} - c$$

$$(x + \frac{b}{2})^2 = \frac{b^2}{4} - c$$

$$= \frac{b^2 - 4c}{4}$$

$$x + \frac{b}{2} = \frac{\pm\sqrt{b^2 - 4c}}{2}$$

$$x = \frac{-b \pm \sqrt{b^2 - 4c}}{2}$$

Figure 7.11 *Proving the quadratic equation formula*

As with all other equations, added meaning and purpose are given to learning solution procedures when they are applied to interesting problems. Figure 7.12 shows why 3, 4 and 5 is the only Pythagorean triple with consecutive numbers, whilst Figure 7.13 presents a problem involving speeds where algebraic fractions are involved in the solution.

Applying Pythagoras' theorem to a right-angled triangle with sides of lengths x, $x+1$ and $x+2$:

$$(x+2)^2 = (x+1)^2 + x^2$$
$$x^2 + 4x + 4 = x^2 + 2x + 1 + x^2$$
$$x^2 - 2x - 3 = 0$$
$$(x+1)(x-3) = 0$$
$$x = -1 \text{ or } x = 3$$

$x = -1$ is clearly not a valid solution, so $x = 3$ is the only solution which leads to a Pythagorean triple. The only consecutive set of numbers that can form the sides of a right-angled triangle is 3, 4 and 5.

Figure 7.12 *3, 4, 5 is the only consecutive Pythagorean triple*

The current in a river is flowing at 3km/h. Find the maximum speed of a boat in still water if the minimum time for a journey of 1km up the river and back is 1 hour.

If the maximum speed of the boat in still water is x km/h the time in hours taken to go 1km up the river and back is given by the expression:

$$\frac{1}{x+3} + \frac{1}{x-3}$$

If the journey takes 1 hour, the resulting equation is solved to find x:

$$\frac{1}{x+3} + \frac{1}{x-3} = 1 \implies x-3+x+3 = (x+3)(x-3) \implies x^2 - 2x - 9 = 0$$

The two solutions are $x \approx 4.16$ or $x \approx -2.16$, and only the first of these is valid, because the negative solution would require part of the journey to be done in negative time!

Figure 7.13 *A Problem with Speeds*

These two problems illustrate well the two roles of algebra. In the first case the purpose is to explain or prove something, namely that only one Pythagorean triple is possible, whilst in the second a problem requiring a numerical solution is posed and solved. In both cases there are the usual three stages to solving the problems:

- expressing the situation in an algebraic form;
- manipulating the algebraic expressions, which includes deciding what to do next at each stage of the solution process;
- interpreting the results.

Mastering the first and last of these needs just as much emphasis as learning the all important manipulative skills, which have little purpose if they cannot be used to solve meaningful problems.

ITERATIVE PROCESSES

The iterative process known as Heron's method for finding square roots was known to the Babylonians over 3500 years ago. The process generates a sequence where each successive term is closer to the value of the square root required. It can be explained by referring to the problem of finding the sides of a square with an area of 5. If 2 is one side of a rectangle of area 5, as shown in Figure 7.14, the other side is obtained by dividing 5 by 2 to give 2.5. The mean of 2 and 2.5, namely 2.25, will be closer to the square root of 5, so the process is repeated with that as an approximation. If the process is then repeated with successive approximations, the terms of the sequence converge towards the square root. In algebraic terms, if x is taken as one side of the rectangle of area 5, then the other side is $\frac{5}{x}$. The mean of these two values is $\frac{1}{2}(x + \frac{5}{x})$.

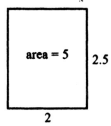

Figure 7.14 *Finding the square root of 5*

A spreadsheet can be set up to generate the sequence by entering $=(A1 + 5/A1)/2$ and filling down the column. It is then easy to use further columns to display simultaneously the results of varying the initial input as shown in Figure 7.15. The ANS facility on a graphical calculator is a convenient alternative means of generating such sequences, although a small screen cannot display several sequences at the same time.

The sequence converges very rapidly to the square root whatever the initial value and it is also easy to modify the procedure to find the square root of other numbers. The limiting value of the sequence is the solution to the equation $x = \frac{1}{2}(x + \frac{5}{x})$, whose equivalence to $x^2 = 5$ can be shown as follows:

$$x = \tfrac{1}{2}(x + \tfrac{5}{x}) = \tfrac{x}{2} + \tfrac{5}{2x} \;\Rightarrow\; \tfrac{x}{2} = \tfrac{5}{2x} \;\Rightarrow\; x^2 = 5$$

2.000000	3.000000	10.000000
2.250000	2.333333	5.250000
2.236111	2.238095	3.101190
2.236068	2.236069	2.356737
2.236068	2.236068	2.239157
2.236068	2.236068	2.236070
2.236068	2.236068	2.236068

Figure 7.15 *A sequence converging to* $\sqrt{5}$: $x_{n+1} = \frac{1}{2}\left(x_n + \frac{5}{x_n}\right)$

Cube roots provide another interesting application of iterative processes. One way of deriving a simple iterative formula for the cube root of 5 is as follows:

$$x^3 = 5 \implies x^4 = 5x \implies x = \sqrt{\sqrt{5x}}$$

This iteration, using the formula $x_{n+1} = \sqrt{\sqrt{5x_n}}$, can be carried out on a simple calculator by entering 1, or some other value, as a first approximation and then repeating the sequence of operations below to produce subsequent approximations:

Multiply by 5 $\rightarrow$ Square root $\rightarrow$ Square root

Alternatively, the sequence can be evaluated with a graphical calculator or a spreadsheet as in the square root example. A graphical representation of the process, shown in Figure 7.16, with a staircase diagram and corresponding table, provides a further source of insight into the convergence of the sequence.

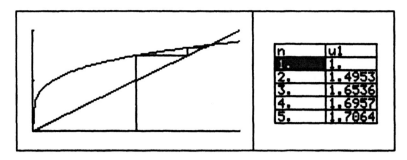

Figure 7.16 *Cube roots by iteration*

Different iterative methods for finding the cube root of 5 can be derived from the underlying equation $x^3 = 5$, but there is no guarantee that they will converge. For example, the sequence given by $x_{n+1} = \sqrt{\frac{5}{x_n}}$ converges, whereas $x_{n+1} = \frac{5}{x_n^2}$ diverges. The formula, $x_{n+1} = \frac{1}{3}\left(2x_n + \frac{5}{x_n^2}\right)$, gives a sequence which converges very rapidly. It can be derived in a similar way to Heron's method for square roots by letting two sides of a cuboid with volume 5 be x and then finding the mean of the 3 sides. Interestingly, both this result and Heron's method are the iterative formulae given by applying the Newton–Raphson formula, $x_{n+1} = x_n + \frac{f(x_n)}{f'(x_n)}$, to solve $f(x) = 0$ with $f(x) = x^3 - 5$ and $f(x) = x^2 - 5$, respectively. When sequences converge, the rates of convergence vary widely and the sequence may increase or decrease or it may oscillate on either side of the limiting value as it converges. Graphs provide an excellent way of examining this behaviour and the whole topic provides a wealth of material for students to investigate.

APPROXIMATE AND EXACT SOLUTIONS

Practical problems usually require an approximate answer accurate to an appropriate number of decimal places, but long strings of digits after the decimal point often hide fascinating underlying patterns and decimal forms may hinder an appreciation of the exact arguments that are the essence of mathematical thinking.

The solutions of the quadratic equation $x^2 - x - 1 = 0$ provide an interesting example. In decimal form to 3 decimal places, the solutions are 1.618 and −0.618, whereas in exact form they are $\frac{1+\sqrt{5}}{2}$ and $\frac{1-\sqrt{5}}{2}$. In both forms the sum of the roots is clearly 1, but multiplying the two decimal values gives a value of −0.999924, whereas applying the difference of two squares to the exact forms shows convincingly that the product of the roots is in fact exactly −1.

The positive root is known as the golden ratio and Figure 7.17 compares its successive powers in approximate and exact form. The decimals, apart from 2.618, do not look particularly interesting and indeed do not agree with the exact forms calculated to 3 decimal places after the fourth power because 1.618 has been rounded and the rounding errors grow. However, the numbers that appear in exact form have some very interesting properties – the coefficients of $\sqrt{5}$ are the Fibonacci sequence and the other whole numbers are the Lucas sequence, which has similar properties.

n	1.618^n	$(\frac{1}{2}(1+\sqrt{5}))^n$
1	1.618	$\frac{1}{2}(1+\sqrt{5})$
2	2.618	$\frac{1}{2}(3+\sqrt{5})$
3	4.236	$\frac{1}{2}(4+2\sqrt{5})$
4	6.854	$\frac{1}{2}(7+3\sqrt{5})$
5	11.089	$\frac{1}{2}(11+5\sqrt{5})$
6	17.942	$\frac{1}{2}(18+8\sqrt{5})$

Figure 7.17 *Powers of the golden ratio*

As a final pointer from the same source of the importance of exact values, the quadratic equation $x^2 - x - 1 = 0$ is solved using the iterative formula $x_{n+1} = 1 + \frac{1}{x_n}$. Starting with 1 and using rational numbers, each term is the ratio of successive terms from the Fibonacci sequence:

$$1, \quad 1 + \tfrac{1}{1} = \tfrac{2}{1}, \quad 1 + \tfrac{1}{2} = \tfrac{3}{2}, \quad 1 + \tfrac{1}{3/2} = \tfrac{5}{3}, \quad 1 + \tfrac{1}{5/3} = \tfrac{8}{5}, \quad 1 + \tfrac{1}{8/5} = \tfrac{13}{8}$$

Fascinating results like this are not revealed if the results are calculated in approximate form. Equations do not always have exact solutions and for many practical applications of algebra an approximate solution is all that is needed, but exact solutions have a great importance in revealing the underlying patterns and precision of mathematics.

CONCLUSION

The ability to formulate and solve equations has been an essential component of mathematics throughout its long historical development. Algebra had its origins in solving puzzles of the kind found in the writings of the ancient Egyptians. They found solutions to equations like $x + \frac{1}{7}x = 19$, which is Problem 24 from the Ahmes Papyrus referred to by Boyer and Merzbach (1991, p. 15). Problems were not expressed in a symbolic form and the Egyptians' methods of solution were very different from those used today, but none the less their fascination with solving number puzzles is very evident.

The intrinsic interest of solving problems is at least as strong a motivation for learning algebra as more mundane applications to real-world problems. In the early stages of learning algebra, puzzle problems are likely to have a greater appeal to students because they have an immediacy that is often lacking in attempts to relate algebra to practical situations. Puzzles may relate to a concrete situation, like the boat going up and down a river discussed earlier in this chapter, but essentially the problem of finding the speed is a puzzle rather than a real practical problem and is best presented as such.

The skills involved in solving equations clearly depend on understanding and fluency with substitution, simplification, expanding and factorizing as well as an appreciation of the role of graphs. As I have noted earlier, there are good reasons for not putting too much emphasis on solving equations in the early stages of learning because this tends to reinforce the notion of letters representing specific unknowns rather than variables. On the other hand, equations do have the big attraction that solutions can be checked: a determined student should always be able to persist until a correct solution has been achieved.

This chapter has concentrated on linear equations, simultaneous linear equations and quadratic equations, which form the major components of the part of an algebra course devoted to equation solving. Other types of equations such as cubic equations or trigonometrical equations involve the same principles, so the new ideas involved when it comes to mastering them are not extensive.

A variety of methods of solution have been discussed, particularly in relation to quadratic equations. Students need to acquire an initial feel for what is involved in solving equations. Trial and improvement methods offer this, but students need to recognize their limitations when exact methods are available. Graphical methods also give approximate solutions, but they also contribute in other ways in helping students to understand equations and the behaviour of a variety of functions. Exact methods are important partly because they provide simple, rapid ways of achieving solutions, but also because the form of the solutions they produce is often interesting in itself and in the extensions it suggests. Whilst trial and improvement has its limitations, more sophisticated numerical methods involving iterative processes offer a very different and powerful approach to solving equations which has a strong intrinsic interest.

It is essential to practise the skills of equation solving to achieve fluency, but this should be done alongside learning to apply those skills in solving problems, with due emphasis given to formulating problems algebraically and checking and interpreting solutions. It is the challenge of solving interesting problems that gives meaning and purpose to learning algebraic skills.

Chapter 8

Proportionality, Growth and Decay

The ability to handle all ratios necessitates the use of *multiplication* by a fraction
(Hart, 1981, p. 101)

PROPORTIONALITY: THE MULTIPLICATIVE PRINCIPLE

Proportionality is a fundamental idea underlying a wide range of situations involving a relationship between two sets of numbers. It arises in problems with quantities and costs, value for
money, conversion between units, currency conversion, percentages, speeds and other rates of
change, scales for diagrams and maps, lengths in similar figures and trigonometry. The
essential idea is that the ratio between corresponding pairs of number is constant, so that there
is a multiplicative relationship between the two sets of numbers. Students' ability to deal with
proportion problems is linked closely to their understanding of multiplication and division
with their inverse relationship and links to fractions. The general algebraic statement above
summarizes the two key ideas: that the ratio between two numbers determines the scale factor
relating them and that division is the inverse operation which 'undoes' multiplication. Figure
8.1 illustrates this with two numerical examples.

Figure 8.1 *Inverse operations*

Speed (mph)	Speed (kph)
50	80
30	
0	

Speed (mph)	Speed (kph)
50	80
30	**60**
0	**30**

Figure 8.2 *A student's errors in converting speeds*

Figure 8.2 shows a typical example of the errors students make in tackling problems involving proportionality. A thirteen-year-old student had been asked to complete the table on the left by converting the speeds in miles per hour to kilometres per hour. The table on the right shows the student's responses.

The 60 has been found either by subtracting 20 from 80, because 30 is 20 less than 50, or by adding 30 to 30, because 80 is 30 more than 50. In each case, the student is seeing an additive relationship either within the columns or across the rows. The final 30 in the right hand column has been determined in a similar way using an addition strategy. Stating that 30 kph is equivalent to 0 mph is clearly absurd and does draw attention to the way in which students so often fail to recognize that what they are writing down makes no sense at all. The essential misconception here though is a failure to recognize that there is a multiplicative relationship between the two sets of numbers.

Hart (1981, p. 95) gives another example, illustrated in Figure 8.3, of the way in which a large number of students adopt an addition strategy when asked to enlarge a rectangle with a base of 5 cm and height 3 cm to give a new rectangle with base 12 cm. The common response was to say that the height will be 10 cm obtained either by subtracting 2 from 12 or by adding 7 to 3 for the height. Scale diagrams immediately show that the dimensions of the enlarged rectangle cannot be correct, but it is a much harder step for many students to see that the rectangle has been enlarged by a scale factor of $\frac{12}{5}$ or 2.4, giving the correct height as 7.2 cm.

Base (cm)	Height (cm)
5	3
12	**10**

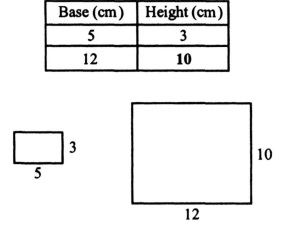

Figure 8.3 *Error in enlarging a rectangle*

The erroneous use of addition strategies for proportion problems is very widespread. Hart (1981) noted this with a variety of examples from a large sample of students who commonly used this strategy, except in cases where the familiar operations of doubling or halving were involved. She also observed that only a very small minority of students tested in 1976 (twenty out of 2257) attempted to solve proportion problems by writing down and solving an equation of the form $\frac{a}{b} = \frac{c}{d}$, based on the idea of equal ratios, where one of the elements is unknown.

Textbooks commonly approach proportion problems in one or more of three different ways, sometimes quite reasonably varying the strategy according to the type of problem and the numbers involved. Figure 8.4 shows an example involving costs that compares the three approaches.

The unitary method involves finding the cost of one unit as an intermediate step and is obviously the simplest method for this example. The approach is simple because the meaning

---

3 kg of potatoes cost £1.35. What is the cost of 5 kg of potatoes?

1. Unitary method:

3kg of potatoes cost £1.35.

1kg of potatoes cost $\dfrac{£1.35}{3} = 45\text{p}$.

5kg of potatoes cost $5 \times 45\text{p} = £2.25$.

2. Scale factor method:

$$3\text{kg} \xrightarrow{\times \frac{5}{3}} 5\text{kg}$$
$$£1.35 \xrightarrow{\times \frac{5}{3}} \quad ?$$

5 kg of potatoes cost $\dfrac{5}{3} \times £1.35 = £2.25$

3. Equal ratios method:

Let x be the cost in pence of 5 kg of potatoes.

Either $\dfrac{x}{135} = \dfrac{5}{3} \implies x = \dfrac{5}{3} \times 135$ or $\dfrac{x}{5} = \dfrac{135}{3} \implies x = 5 \times \dfrac{135}{3}$

Figure 8.4 *Three ways of solving a proportion problem*

of the intermediate step as the unit price is clear and moreover it can be used to calculate the cost for any quantity. The method is also adaptable because the 'unit' does not necessarily need to be taken as one: for example, to determine the cost of 250g given the cost of 150g of an item it would be sensible to find the cost of 50g, rather than 1g, as the intermediate step. An approach based on scale factors involves recognizing that the mass is increased by a factor of $\frac{5}{3}$ and that the cost has to be increased by the same factor. The numbers involved in the problem may conveniently be set out in a diagrammatic form with arrows to help the student see how the numbers are related to the scale factor. This approach is particularly appropriate in geometrical problems, including those involving the scales of plans and maps, where the idea of enlargement can be invoked.

The two alternatives using equal ratios reflect the other two methods, with the ratio corresponding either to the unit cost or to the scale factor. An algebraic approach involving an equation is more abstract because the interpretation of the ratio is not necessarily obvious to the student and the formality of setting up and solving an equation may add an additional barrier in solving a problem that is essentially numerical. However, there are problems where an algebraic approach is necessary. Familiarity and fluency with the first two approaches, which require understanding of the multiplicative principle and the use of fractions, are necessary requirements for solving more demanding problems. Figure 8.5 shows a geometrical

---

Find h, the height of the point P above the line AB.

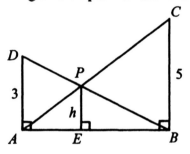

Using two pairs of similar triangles: $\dfrac{h}{3} = \dfrac{EB}{AB}$ and $\dfrac{h}{5} = \dfrac{AE}{AB}$.

Adding the two equations: $\dfrac{h}{3} + \dfrac{h}{5} = \dfrac{AE + EB}{AB} = 1 \ \Rightarrow\ h = \dfrac{15}{8}$.

Dividing the two original equations shows that E divides AB in the ratio 3:5.

In more general terms, if $a = AD$ and $b = BC$, then $\dfrac{1}{h} = \dfrac{1}{a} + \dfrac{1}{b}$ or $h = \dfrac{ab}{a+b}$

so, interestingly, the height h is independent of the length of AB.

Figure 8.5 *A geometrical problem using equal ratios*

example which requires explicit use of equal ratios and further situations which involve ratio are discussed in Chapters 9 and 10.

DIRECT PROPORTION

At the time of writing, the exchange rate between the US dollar and the pound is about $1.40 to the pound. The table in Figure 8.6 shows some corresponding pairs of values using p and d to stand for the number of pounds and dollars respectively.

Pounds (p)	Dollars (d)
1	1.40
2	2.80
3	4.20
4	5.60
5	7.00

$$p \xrightarrow{\times 1.40} d$$

Figure 8.6 *Direct proportion and the exchange rate*

The two sets of numbers are proportional – they are described as being in direct proportion. They are linked by the exchange rate, a scale factor which leads to the equation $d = 1.40p$ (not $p = 1.40d$, the error discussed in Chapter 2, which arises when students attempt to make a direct translation of the statement that £1 is equivalent to $1.40). The equation $d = 1.40p$ is an example of a simple linear relationship of the form $y = kx$, where k is a constant. Students encounter relationships of this form when they study straight-line graphs, so, in speaking of two sets of numbers that are in direct proportion, a different viewpoint and some new words are being introduced for what should be a familiar situation. The links need to be made explicit: changing the letters used to describe the variables immediately makes things seem different. Whilst $y = 3x$ may immediately be recognized as an equation whose graph is a straight line through the origin with a gradient of 3, the same connections will not be made so readily for $d = 1.40p$. Students have to be helped to see the common features and introduced to new ways of describing the situation. There are a number of key points to make about two sets of numbers that are in direct proportion:

- As one of the variables increases then so does the other. Equal increases in one variable correspond to equal, but different, increases in the other. In the exchange rate example, each increase of £1 is accompanied by an increase of $1.40. The increases may be described as proportional in the sense that when a value of one variable is doubled then so is the corresponding value of the other.
- When one variable is zero then so is the other: it is obvious that if you have no pounds then you will not get any dollars!
- Corresponding pairs of numbers are in the same ratio, which means that there is a single scale factor linking each pair.

- The scale factor, sometimes referred to as a constant of proportionality, has different interpretations as a rate of change – for example, exchange rate, cost per unit, speed – according to what quantities the numbers represent.
- Plotting one variable against the other gives a straight-line graph through the origin whose gradient is equal to the scale factor.
- Direct proportion is described symbolically as $y \propto x$, which means that $y = kx$ where k is a constant.
- The language can be applied to other relationships of a similar form where $y \propto x^2$ means, for instance, that $y = kx^2$ where k is a constant, although it is not the gradient of the corresponding graph.
- Inverse proportion arises when one variable decreases as the other increases, and $y \propto \frac{1}{x}$, which means that $y = \frac{k}{x}$ or $xy = k$, where k is a constant. Here the product of the variables is constant rather than their ratio and the graphical link is to $y = \frac{1}{x}$ with its very particular and peculiar properties, which were discussed in Chapter 6.
- Another important case is when $y \propto \frac{1}{x^2}$, referred to as the inverse square law. It arises frequently in scientific applications such as the laws governing gravitational and magnetic forces where, in both cases, the strength of the force between two bodies is inversely proportional to the square of the distance between them.

The crucial idea for students to appreciate with proportionality is that it is a multiplicative relationship, linked to the idea of a scale factor and equal ratios, which involve division, the inverse operation to multiplication. This is neatly encapsulated in the two equivalent forms that the defining equation can take:

$$\text{Variables linked by a constant scale factor: } y = kx$$
$$\text{Constant ratio between variables: } k = \frac{y}{x}$$

PERCENTAGE CHANGES

To increase an amount by 8 per cent students usually learn initially to calculate 8 per cent of the amount and add it on. Decreases are handled in a similar manner. This is a perfectly reasonable and practical procedure for many purposes. However, to deal with successive increases and decreases it is much more convenient to use a scale factor, multiplying the original amount by 1.08 for an 8 per cent increase and 0.92 for an 8 per cent decrease. This step is not an easy one for many students to take, but is made clearer by using money as an example and by pointing out that every £1 becomes £1.08 or £0.92.

1	1
2	1.08
3	1.1664
4	1.259712
5	1.36048896
6	1.469328076

Figure 8.7 *Increasing an amount by 8 per cent*

A sequence generated on a graphical calculator or spreadsheet, as shown in Figure 8.7, can provide a valuable focus for discussion. The sequence has been generated by successive multiplication by 1.08 and the terms of the sequence are powers of 1.08, so that the nth term is given by 1.08^n. Varying the rate per cent (r) and the initial value (a) leads to $a(1 + 0.01r)^n$ as a more general form for the nth term.

A key idea is that division by 1.08 moves you back through the sequence, an operation that students can perform readily with a calculator. It is very satisfying to keep multiplying by the same factor to obtain successively more impressive looking numbers, and then to undo what has been done by a succession of divisions to return to your starting point.

There is a common misconception that when an amount has been increased by a particular percentage, a reduction by the same percentage returns you to the original amount. It seems 'obvious' that an increase of 10 per cent followed by a decrease of 10 per cent should return you to your starting point, but this is not so, as the second 10 per cent is larger than the first because it is 10 per cent of a larger amount. Scale factors provide a more sophisticated explanation: multiplying successively by the two scale factors of 1.1 and 0.9 is equivalent to multiplying by the single scale factor of 0.99, which represents a 1 per cent decrease. It also follows from this that decreasing first and then increasing has the same effect. Another example which seems counter-intuitive is whether you should apply a discount to a bill before or after adding on VAT (Value Added Tax). In fact it makes no difference because the same result is obtained regardless of the order in which the amount is multiplied by the two corresponding scale factors. Similar arguments with scale factors serve to refute other related misconceptions like thinking, for example, that an increase of 10 per cent followed by one of 20 per cent is the same as a single increase of 30 per cent. Since $1.1 \times 1.2 = 1.32$, the increase is in fact 32 per cent.

The correct procedure for undoing the effect of a percentage change is to divide by the appropriate scale factor. As suggested above this idea can be reinforced by letting students explore how to move backwards and forwards through appropriate sequences. Using arrows to show the effect of operations is a useful way of helping students to think about the steps to take in solving problems involving percentage increases and decreases. Figure 8.8 shows a typical problem approached in this way.

After a 5% price increase the new price of a book is £12.50.
What was the price before the increase?

$$\xrightarrow{\times 1.05}$$

OLD PRICE   NEW PRICE

$$\xleftarrow{\div 1.05}$$

Old price = £12.50 ÷ 1.05 = £11.90 (to the nearest penny)

Figure 8.8 *Finding the old price*

Although this section has focused on numerical calculations there are important underlying algebraic ideas concerned with the order of operations and the inverse nature of multiplication and division, which go beyond the immediate examples of percentage changes and financial applications.

POWERS AND THE LAWS OF INDICES

Powers are a good example of the way in which an idea is initially defined in a simple concrete way in the context of positive whole numbers and then extended to give a meaning for a wider set of numbers. Moving beyond the simple idea that 2^3 is a shorthand notation for $2 \times 2 \times 2$ to the more abstract ideas involved in giving meaning to 2^0 or 2^{-3} involves a considerable conceptual leap for students. It is thus important to make clear the meaning and purpose of the new ideas and to stress that they are an extension of the original definition, besides expecting students to remember definitions in a suitable form and to acquire appropriate skills.

The sequence of powers of 2 is generated by starting at 1 and doubling successively. Moving back down through the sequence by dividing by 2 gives obvious meanings to powers where the index is zero or a negative integer. Furthermore, these meanings are compatible with the multiplication and division laws and indeed could be derived from them as an alternative way of formulating the definitions. Figure 8.9 displays particular examples with powers of 2 as a way of summarizing the key general ideas. Students often find it easier to appreciate and remember the general results and definitions through the more familiar form of special cases.

$$
\begin{array}{ll}
2^4 = 16 & \\
2^3 = 8 & \text{Multiplication Law: } 2^p \times 2^q = 2^{p+q} \\
2^2 = 4 & \quad 2^0 \times 2^3 = 2^3 \quad \Rightarrow \quad 2^0 = 1 \\
2^1 = 2 & \quad 2^{-3} \times 2^3 = 2^0 \quad \Rightarrow \quad 2^{-3} = \dfrac{1}{2^3} \\
2^0 = 1 & \\
2^{-1} = \dfrac{1}{2} & \text{Division Law: } 2^p \div 2^q = 2^{p-q} \\
2^{-2} = \dfrac{1}{4} & \quad 2^3 \div 2^3 = 2^0 \quad \Rightarrow \quad 2^0 = 1 \\
& \quad 2^0 \div 2^3 = 2^{-3} \quad \Rightarrow \quad 2^{-3} = \dfrac{1}{2^3} \\
2^{-3} = \dfrac{1}{8} &
\end{array}
$$

Figure 8.9 *Extending definitions with powers of 2*

Extending the definition to fractional powers raises further interesting issues. If the powers of 2 are represented graphically they are seen to lie on a smooth curve. The numbers could indicate the number of bacteria doubling at daily intervals and counted in thousands. If the initial value (on day zero) is taken as 1 thousand, the negative powers indicate the number in thousands on previous days. A meaning can now be given to intermediate points such as $2^{\frac{1}{2}}$ and $2^{\frac{3}{2}}$ using the argument displayed in Figure 8.10. Their numerical values will be seen to fit with the intermediate positions on the curve and a growth rate of $\sqrt{2}$ per half day corresponds precisely with doubling every day. These ideas can be extended to other rational values of x in a similar way with the graph suggesting then that a meaning can be given for all real values.

Understanding the notation and properties of powers with an accompanying fluency in applying them to simple situations is an essential aspect of elementary algebra. Constant

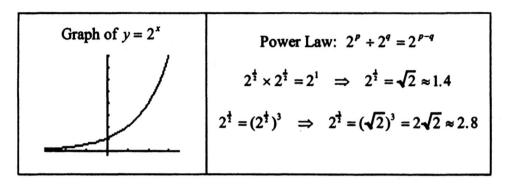

Figure 8.10 *Fractional powers of 2*

reference to simple examples, particularly the familiar powers of 2, together with reminders about how definitions have been extended so that the laws of indices always hold, provides students with a foundation for making sense of more complex applications.

GROWTH AND DECAY FUNCTIONS

Growth and decay in many different contexts are obvious features of the world around us and offer plenty of scope to apply mathematical ideas both at an elementary level, using functions like $y = 2^x$ and $y = 2^{-x}$, and at a more sophisticated level when the exponential function $y = e^x$, considered briefly in Chapter 12, has been introduced. Financial applications and population growth have already been referred to in this chapter; other examples include radioactive decay, the falling pressure in a tyre with a slow puncture, the temperature of a hot body as it cools down and the velocity of a parachutist as he or she tends to a terminal velocity.

Familiarity with the graphs of exponential functions is best developed by starting with the graph of a simple function like $y = 2^x$ and obtaining other graphs from it by applying simple transformations. Figure 8.11 shows a number of graphs illustrating the effects of reflection, translation and stretches. Replacing x with $-x$ causes a reflection in the y axis with $y = 2^{-x}$ as the simplest example of a decay function. It is worth noting the fact that this is equivalent to $y = (\frac{1}{2})^x$. Replacing x with $2x$ causes a stretch in the x direction with a factor of $\frac{1}{2}$ and here it is useful to note that $2^{2x} = 4^x$. Translation in the y direction is straightforward and the graph of $y = 3 + 2^{-x}$ has the form that would be taken by a graph of the temperature of a cooling body. Finally, the graph of $y = 3 \times 2^x$ is obtained by stretching $y = 2^x$ by a factor of 3 in the y direction and models a situation where a population with an initial value of 3 doubles in each unit of time.

Figure 8.12 shows the use of a simple exponential function to model the growth of population in England and Wales in the latter half of the nineteenth century. The two tables provide a comparison between the actual figures and the figures given by the function $y = 15.9 \times 1.127^x$, where $x = \frac{t - 1841}{10}$, when t is the year. The growth factor is calculated by noting that the population increased by a factor of $\frac{32.5}{15.9} \approx 2.044$ over the 60-year period. Therefore, over a 10-year period the growth factor is given by $\sqrt[6]{2.044}$, which is approximately 1.127 – about 12.7 per cent every 10 years. As an additional point of interest, calculating $\sqrt[10]{1.127} \approx 1.012$, tells us that the annual growth rate was about 1.2 per cent per annum.

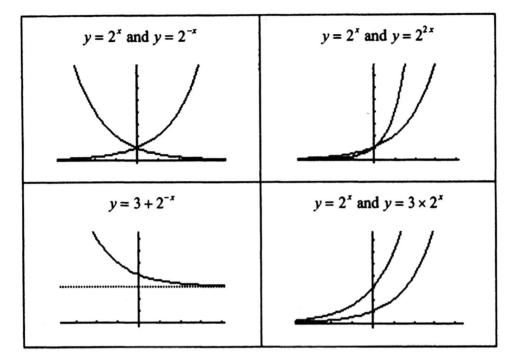

Figure 8.11 *Graphs of growth and decay functions*

The figures given by the function are a remarkably close fit, but not one that continues into the twentieth century. An example of this kind, besides providing opportunity for extending mathematical knowledge and understanding, does also provide a chance to discuss wider social and historical issues underlying the statistical data, something which surely ought to have an occasional place in the mathematics classroom.

CONCLUSION

Proportionality, growth and decay are ubiquitous features of a wide range of phenomena in the real world and they are important ideas within mathematics. However, there is plenty of evidence that students have difficulty in coming to understand these ideas whose essential characteristic is that they involve multiplicative relationships. Apart from simple problems involving doubling and halving the common error is that students think of increases and decreases solely in terms of addition and subtraction in situations where multiplication and division are the appropriate operations to consider. Understanding the nature of multi-plication, with its links to division and fractions and the situations to which it applies, lies at the heart of making sense of problems involving proportionality, growth and decay.

Two key ideas, summarized in Figure 8.13, are the crucial elements:

- the ratio of two numbers, whether expressed as a common fraction or as a decimal fraction, gives the scale factor which links the pair.
- multiplication and division are inverse operations: one operation undoes the other.

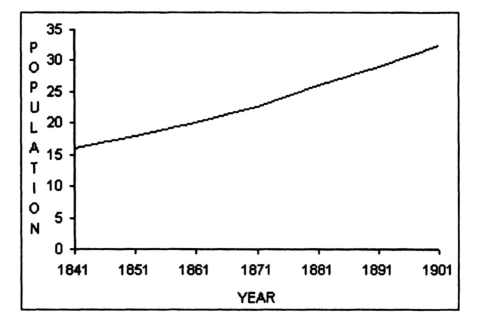

YEAR	POPULATION
1841	15.9
1851	17.9
1861	20.1
1871	22.7
1881	26.0
1891	29.0
1901	32.5

x	15.9*1.127^x
0	15.9
1	17.9
2	20.2
3	22.8
4	25.7
5	28.9
6	32.6

Figure 8.12 *Population of England and Wales: 1841 to 1901 (to the nearest 0.1 million)*

Problems involving proportionality can be solved in two different, although equivalent, ways: by using scale factors or by using equal ratios. Scale factors provide a simpler initial approach to proportionality problems, which extends readily to other situations involving growth and decay. Using equal ratios is more abstract and requires the student to set up and solve an

$$\xrightarrow{\times \frac{b}{a}}$$

$$a \qquad\qquad b$$

$$\xleftarrow{+\frac{b}{a} \ (\text{or} \times \frac{a}{b})}$$

Figure 8.13 *Growth and decay*

equation, an unnecessary complication in simple numerical problems, but an essential requirement in more complex situations. Students should learn simple ways of solving simple problems; more abstract, algebraic ways of thinking should be introduced through problems which are difficult to solve using simpler tools. The purpose and power of the more advanced tool is then much more likely to become clear.

Percentages are another related, ubiquitous feature of our world which are widely regarded by students as difficult and are a frequent source of misconceptions particularly when two or more percentage changes are involved. The misconceptions again arise at root through a failure to see changes in terms of multiplication, but the situation is complicated because a percentage increase certainly does involve adding something on! Scale factors are a powerful tool in handling many percentage problems and the availability of calculators prevents the relative complexity of the numerical calculations acting as an additional hurdle to under-standing the ideas.

Extending the definition of powers to indices other than natural numbers is another good example of the way in which ideas in mathematics become increasingly abstract. Students need to appreciate the meaning and purpose of new ideas and teachers need to appreciate that these need to be reinforced continually alongside practising the associated skills and applying them to problems.

Finally, exponential functions are an important class of functions that can be used both to model a wide range of growth and decay phenomena as well as to provide intrinsic interest and mathematical applications. Looking at them graphically provides another way of reinforcing the way in which graphs can be transformed whilst providing the familiarity needed to use them for modelling, but it also provides the familiarity and understanding needed for the later introduction of e and the important exponential function with all its intriguing properties.

Chapter 9

Links to Geometry

A picture is worth a thousand words. (Anon)

LINKING ALGEBRA AND GEOMETRY

The links between algebra and geometry are close, since geometry is concerned with relationships between variables like angle, length, area and volume and contributes to the language of algebra through words like square and cube. Geometrical diagrams are a rich source of insight for algebraic ideas, whilst algebraic methods are a powerful tool for solving geometrical problems and for presenting geometrical proofs. Graphs, considered at length in Chapter 6, are particularly significant as an idea which provides a remarkable bridge between geometry and algebra, both by succinctly summarizing the properties of functions in a pictorial form and by enabling geometrical properties to be represented symbolically.

Pictorial representations are immediately appealing and attractive to students and are therefore potentially valuable as a way of giving greater meaning to algebraic ideas by providing a variety of striking representations, many examples of which have appeared in earlier chapters. The idea of a variable is enhanced by linking it to angle and length which can vary continuously, as a counter to an often dominant emphasis in the early stages of learning algebra on variables which only take discrete whole number values. Many key algebraic relationships, like the difference of two squares, have geometric origins and are neatly summarized in a memorable way by a picture. Geometrical problems and proofs are an important application of algebraic ideas and as such add greater purpose to learning algebra.

Geometrical arguments and problems involving angles offer an early way of using letters in a context where the link with number is clear. For example, Figure 9.1 shows a simple argument linking the angles associated with parallel lines. The equality of the alternate angles is deduced from the pairs of corresponding and vertically opposite angles. Besides providing a rudimentary use of algebraic notation this provides a good example of the sort of simple deductive argument that students should constantly encounter in algebraic and geometrical contexts to develop their powers of reasoning.

Following on from this, the idea of alternate angles contributes to the simple way of proving

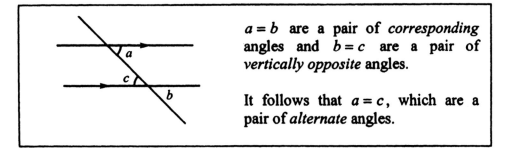

$a = b$ are a pair of *corresponding* angles and $b = c$ are a pair of *vertically opposite* angles.

It follows that $a = c$, which are a pair of *alternate* angles.

Figure 9.1 *Angles with parallel lines*

that the sum of the angles of a triangle is 180° shown in Figure 9.2. Although students will initially meet this key fact about a triangle in an experimental way through measuring, it is important to establish that it can be deduced from simpler properties. Presenting the argument in an algebraic form helps to reinforce the idea of letters representing variables.

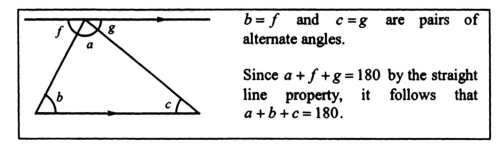

$b = f$ and $c = g$ are pairs of alternate angles.

Since $a + f + g = 180$ by the straight line property, it follows that $a + b + c = 180$.

Figure 9.2 *The angle sum of a triangle*

As various geometrical properties about angles are established they are used in 'angle chasing' problems where given angle facts in a figure are used to establish further facts. Such problems may sometimes lead to simple equations as in Figure 9.3, an interesting example because there are two possible solutions.

Two general points about the use of symbols in a geometrical context are worth making. The first, illustrated by the example of Figure 9.3, concerns the question of units. It is customary in mathematics to use letters to represent numbers rather than quantities, which are numbers with a unit attached. It is convenient both in labelling diagrams and in setting out an algebraic argument to omit any reference to the units, either assuming that the numbers refer to some consistent general system of units or by making reference to units only in the initial and closing comments. Confusion can be caused when units are combined with algebraic symbols because, to a student, the distinction between the two roles being assumed by letters is not necessarily clear. For instance, only the context makes clear the distinction between *mg*, meaning mass multiplied by acceleration due to gravity, and *mg*, meaning a mass of *m* measured in grams, or *a* m, meaning a length *a* measured in metres, and am, *ante meridiem*, meaning before midday. Examples like these may seem obscure, or even facetious, but to a student at an early stage in learning algebra the conventions are not necessarily obvious or

What are the angles of an isosceles triangle if one angle is twice one of the other angles?

Let the angles be x and $2x$ degrees and use the fact that the sum of the angles in a triangle is $180°$.

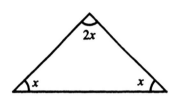

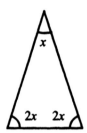

$$2x + x + x = 180 \qquad\qquad x + 2x + 2x = 180$$

$4x = 180$ and so the three angles are $45°$, $45°$ and $90°$.

$5x = 180$ and so the three angles are $36°$, $72°$ and $72°$.

Figure 9.3 *Finding unknown angles in an isosceles triangle*

even consistent, and the scope for confusion is considerable, until ideas and their applications are securely understood.

The other notational difficulty arises through the use of upper case letters to represent points and lower case letters to represent most algebraic variables. Again context should make clear what the letters represent, but to the novice ab^2 and AB^2 look similar and are not distinguished in the spoken form. Substituting values into ab^2 often causes problems, as noted in Chapter 4, because the correct order of operations differs from the order in which the terms in the expression are written. It is important therefore to frequently make explicit to students what an expression means and to draw to their attention at appropriate times how very similar forms can mean completely different things in different contexts.

ISOSCELES TRIANGLES

Geometric problems involving relationships between angles provide many useful examples to reinforce algebraic ideas. In a situation where one of the angles in a diagram can vary it can be instructive to look at how the other angles change. Figure 9.4 shows the side view of a typical arrangement for an 'up and over' garage door which is represented by the line BE. The point D on the door moves up and down the vertical door post and the point C is attached by a rod to a pivot at the top of the door post at A. The three lengths AC, BC and DC are equal, creating two isosceles triangles, ACD and ACB. Dynamic geometry software or a model made with plastic or card strips are very useful as way of showing how the garage door moves and to clarify the essential properties of the configuration.

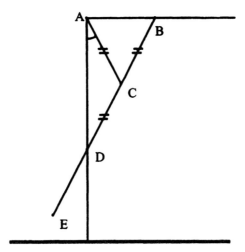

Figure 9.4 *An 'up and over' garage door*

Using the angle properties of the isosceles triangles students can calculate some of the other angles as the angle between the rod and the door post, *CAD*, varies when the door is opened and closed. Results can be presented in a table like that shown in Figure 9.5 where values of angle *CAD* are taken at intervals of 10°. Working numerically in this way makes a subsequent algebraic analysis of the situation more accessible as a way of proving that the top edge of the door represented by the point *B* moves horizontally.

∠CAD	∠ACD	∠ACB	∠CAB
10°	160°	20°	80°
20°	140°	40°	70°
30°	120°	60°	60°
40°	100°	80°	50°
50°	80°	100°	40°
60°	60°	120°	30°

Figure 9.5 *Angles in the garage door problem*

As students work on this they will see obvious patterns emerging in the sequences of values for each angle that should enable them to predict other values. They can also be encouraged to look for links between the sequences. There are obvious instances of doubling and halving, but perhaps the most striking feature is that the sum of angle *CAD* and angle *CAB* appears always to be a right angle. This interesting fact explains why the garage door moves horizontally as the door is opened, but to be more than a conjecture based on a few numerical observations it does need to be proved algebraically.

The four sequences are linear and can be expressed in algebraic terms as follows:

$$\angle CAD = x°$$
$$\angle ACD = 180° - 2x°$$
$$\angle ACB = 2x°$$
$$\angle CAB = 90° - x°$$

The relationships in the table of values between numbers in different columns are shown to be true generally by looking at the links between the algebraic forms for each angle. The power of algebra as a language in which to express relationships and present mathematical arguments becomes clear in an example like this, where so much is determined succinctly by simplifying expressions or expressing them in an equivalent form:

$$180 + (180 - 2x) = 2x \qquad 90 - x = \tfrac{1}{2}(180 - 2x) \qquad x + (90 - x) = 90$$

Another configuration of a similar type involving isosceles triangles, taken from Andrews and Sinkinson (2000), is shown in Figure 9.6. Again, the relationships between the angles can be investigated both numerically and with dynamic geometry before being cast in an algebraic form. The interesting feature is the angle that is three times the initial angle between the two intersecting lines upon which the figure is based, and the fact that this exercises a constraint on the initial angle because $3x \leq 90$, so the initial angle cannot exceed 30°.

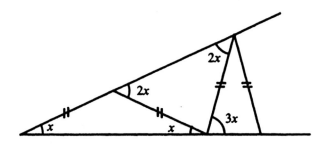

Figure 9.6 *Another isosceles triangle problem*

Isosceles triangles are a frequent feature of geometrical configurations, particularly those which feature circles. As a final example in this section, Figure 9.7 shows a diagram which leads to a proof of the theorem that states that the angle at the centre of a circle is equal to twice the angle at the circumference standing on the same arc. Using the angle properties of the two isosceles triangles in the diagram, the two angles at the centre of the circle are $2x$ and $2y$ given that the angles at the circumference are x and y. The total angle at the centre is $2x + 2y$, which is twice $x + y$, the total angle at the circumference. For a complete proof, it is necessary to consider the special cases obtained by moving the point determining the angle at the circumference so that the angle is $x - y$ or $y - x$. Other angle properties of circles can be proved in a similar way or as a direct deduction from this result.

Students meet isosceles triangles at an early stage in their study of geometry so that the

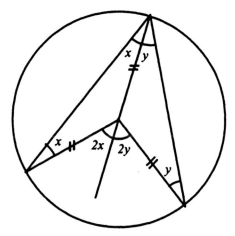

Figure 9.7 *The angle at the centre theorem*

relationship between their angles rapidly becomes very familiar. This makes configurations involving isosceles triangles particularly useful as an algebraic application, whether the problem is to calculate an angle by solving an equation or to prove a simple theorem. Geometrical configurations using such familiar angle properties offer a good source of examples for students to learn how to express a problem in an algebraic form from an early stage.

THE ANGLES OF POLYGONS

The sum of the angles of a polygon can be determined in more than one way. Typically students would be asked to look at a number of examples numerically before proceeding to generalize. Two ways of subdividing a polygon, in this case a hexagon, into triangles are shown in Figure 9.8.

In the first case, diagonals are drawn from a single vertex to give four triangles, so that the angle sum is $4 \times 180° = 720°$. In the general case with n sides, the number of triangles is $n - 2$, two less than the number of sides, giving an angle sum of $180(n - 2)$ degrees. In the second case, lines are drawn from an interior point to each vertex to give six triangles. The angle sum of the triangles is $6 \times 180° = 1080°$, but this includes the six angles at the interior point so that the angle sum for the polygon is $1080° - 360° = 720°$. In the general case with n sides, the angle sum is given by $180n - 360$ degrees. From an algebraic point of view, the equivalence of two expressions for the angle sum is reinforced by the geometrical arguments:

$$180(n - 2) = 180n - 360$$

The last diagram provides a different route to the second formula for the angle sum. The sum of the exterior angles of any polygon is 360°, a property that can be demonstrated easily by considering the angle turned through when you walk right round a polygon. At each vertex the sum of the exterior angle and the corresponding interior angle is 180°, giving again a total for the interior angles of $180n - 360$ degrees.

For regular polygons, all the interior angles are equal so that the size of one angle is obtained by dividing the expression for the angle sum by n:

$$\frac{180n - 360}{n} = 180 - \frac{360}{n}$$

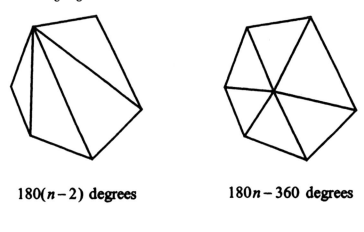

180(*n* − 2) degrees   180*n* − 360 degrees

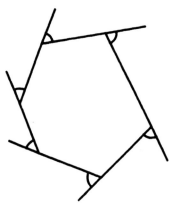

180*n* − 360 degrees

Figure 9.8 *Angle sum of a polygon*

Alternatively, a more direct approach is to say that one of the exterior angles is given by $\frac{360}{n}$, so that the corresponding interior angle is $180 - \frac{360}{n}$. Displaying the interior and exterior angles on a graph, as shown in Figure 9.9, provides a useful task for students, whether done by hand or using a spreadsheet or graph-plotting software.

The graphs provide a number of significant points for discussion with students which link the algebraic expressions and the features of the graphs to the angle properties of regular polygons:

- the graphs are not continuous, so that intermediate points have no meaning – it is not possible to have a polygon with $4\frac{1}{2}$ sides!
- the graphs are not defined for values of *n* less than 3 – reference to the impossibility of one- and two-sided polygons makes this clear;
- the graphs intersect at the point where *n* = 4, corresponding to a square where the interior and exterior angles are equal;

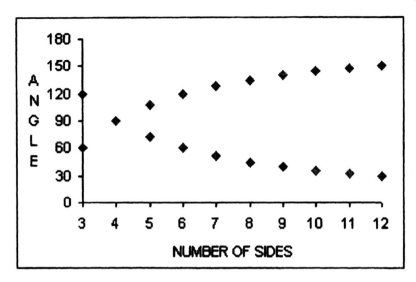

Figure 9.9 *Graphs of the interior and exterior angles of a regular polygon*

● the graphs are symmetrical about the 90° line, because the sum of the interior and exterior angles is 180°.
● As the number of sides increases the exterior angle tends to 0° and the interior angle tends to 180°, whilst the polygon is approximating ever more closely to a circle.

While students will calculate the angles numerically in the initial stages of learning about polygons, this section has shown that there are many ways in which the relationships involved can be represented algebraically. Besides adding to students' geometrical understanding, this serves also to reinforce algebraic understanding and skills.

PERIMETER AND AREA

Like angles, lengths are a simple, concrete examples of a variable which can be used in expressions for perimeters, a useful idea that has already been discussed in Chapter 4. In the two very similar looking examples of Figure 9.10, a square with edges of length x has been removed from a rectangle of length l and width w. The problem is to find the perimeter of the resulting shape.

In the first case, a rather long-winded initial approach would be to add the lengths of each of the straight sections only to find, perhaps to the surprise of some students, that no x is left when the expression is simplified:

$$l + w + (w - x) + x + x + (l - x) + w = 2l + 2w$$

Upon reflection it is clear that this happens because the two lower horizontal lines are equivalent to the length of the rectangle and the same is true for the two vertical lines on the right being equivalent to its width. At first sight, the second example appears to lack information because the position of the removed square along the lower edge has not been specified.

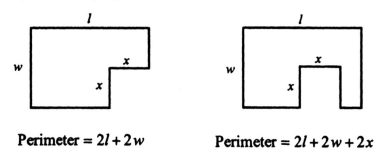

$$\text{Perimeter} = 2l + 2w \qquad\qquad \text{Perimeter} = 2l + 2w + 2x$$

Figure 9.10 *Two Perimeter Problems*

However, the first case provides a clue when it is realized that the three lower horizontal lines have a total length of *l*, so that only two edges of length *x* are required in the expression for the perimeter: $2l + 2w + 2x$. Examples like this are valuable both for the exercise of simplification skills and for the geometric insight involved.

It is natural to move from perimeter to area, but the formula $lw - x^2$, which applies to both cases in Figure 9.10, does not offer anything of significance. Other shapes present much greater possibilities. The formula for the area of a trapezium is $\frac{1}{2}(a + b)h$, where *a* and *b* are the parallel sides and *h* is the height. This result can be derived from formulae for the areas of a parallelogram and a triangle in many different ways, some of which are shown in Figure 9.11. The first two cases involve simplifying the sum of two expressions representing the areas of the two parts. In the third case the formula for the area can be written down directly. The interest resides in the fact that the length of the line midway between the two parallel sides is the mean of the two lengths: $\frac{1}{2}(a + b)$. Since the length of the base of the shaded triangle is $\frac{1}{2}(b - a)$, the segment designated as the mean length is either $a + \frac{1}{2}(b - a)$ or $b - \frac{1}{2}(b - a)$, both of which simplify to give $\frac{1}{2}(a + b)$.

The trapezium is only one among many shapes where the derivation of the area formula can be a source of algebraic insight. Volume formulae obviously offer the same possibilities. Such formulae make much better sense to students if they appreciate how they have been obtained by seeing some alternative approaches.

SIMILAR TRIANGLES

Similar triangles were discussed as an example of proportionality in Chapter 8, where approaches to solving problems using scale factors and equal ratios were compared. Similarity is an important geometrical idea which arises in a diverse range of problems whose solutions frequently require an algebraic approach.

Figure 9.12 shows three of the five diagonals of the regular pentagon *ABCDE* and these create two similar isosceles triangles, *DFC* and *EFB*. The presence of two pairs of alternate angles proves the similarity. In the diagram the pentagon has sides of unit length and the diagonals are of length *d*. Calculating angles will show that triangle *BFC* is isosceles, so that the *BF* is of unit length and *FC* is of length $d - 1$. Returning to the original pair of similar triangles, it is clear from the lengths of the parallel sides that triangle *DFC* is enlarged by a scale factor of *d* to give triangle *EFB*. Applying this scale factor to the sides *BF* and *FC* results in the equation $d(d - 1) = 1$, whose solution is as follows:

$$d(d - 1) = 1 \;\Rightarrow\; d^2 - d - 1 = 0 \;\Rightarrow\; d = \frac{1 \pm \sqrt{5}}{2}$$

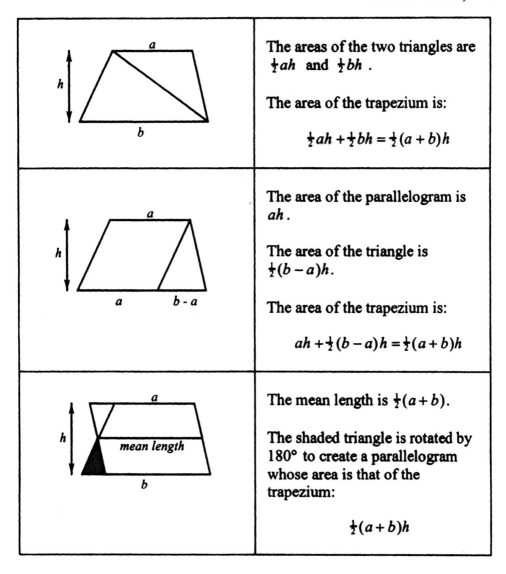

	The areas of the two triangles are $\frac{1}{2}ah$ and $\frac{1}{2}bh$. The area of the trapezium is: $$\frac{1}{2}ah + \frac{1}{2}bh = \frac{1}{2}(a+b)h$$
	The area of the parallelogram is ah . The area of the triangle is $\frac{1}{2}(b-a)h$. The area of the trapezium is: $$ah + \frac{1}{2}(b-a)h = \frac{1}{2}(a+b)h$$
	The mean length is $\frac{1}{2}(a+b)$. The shaded triangle is rotated by 180° to create a parallelogram whose area is that of the trapezium: $$\frac{1}{2}(a+b)h$$

Figure 9.11 *Three ways to determine the area of a trapezium*

Only the positive value, which approximates to 1.618, is appropriate for the length of a diagonal. This value of d is known as the golden ratio and some of its remarkable properties have been referred to in Chapter 7.

If a pot in the form of a truncated cone – like a flower pot or a yoghurt pot – is rolled without slipping on its curved surface the top edge (and the bottom edge) traces out a circle. Calculating the radius is an obvious problem both for a particular numerical instance and to find a general formula – which is what we do here. In Figure 9.13, which shows a side view, the diameters of the top and bottom of the pot are denoted by a and b, and the slant edge by l. The

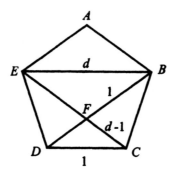

Figure 9.12 *Diagonals of a regular pentagon*

apex of the cone formed by producing the curved surface is the centre of the circle whose radius r we are trying to find.

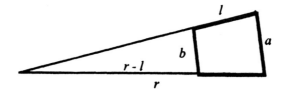

Figure 9.13 *Radius of a circle formed by a rolling pot*

There are two similar isosceles triangles in the diagram with the sides a and b corresponding to the sides r and $r - l$. Using equal ratios we obtain an equation that can be solved as follows to produce a formula for the radius:

$$\frac{r-l}{r} = \frac{b}{a} \implies rb = ra - la \quad \rightarrow \quad r(a - b) = la \implies r = \frac{la}{a - b}$$

A similar argument would produce the formula $\frac{da}{a-b}$ for the height of the larger cone when the depth of the pot is taken as d. The height of the smaller cone is then $\frac{db}{a-b}$. The volume of a cone of radius r and height h is $\frac{1}{3}\pi r^2 h$, which becomes $\frac{1}{12}\pi a^2 h$ for a diameter a. From this, a formula for the volume of the pot can be calculated as the difference in the volume of two cones:

$$\frac{\pi}{12}\frac{da}{a-b}a^2 - \frac{\pi}{12}\frac{db}{a-b}b^2 = \frac{\pi d(a^3-b^3)}{12(a-b)} = \frac{\pi d(a^2+ab+b^2)}{12}$$

The identity for the difference of two cubes, $a^3 - b^3 = (a - b)(a^2 + ab + b^2)$, is used in the final step.

THE THEOREM OF PYTHAGORAS

The theorem of Pythagoras has the distinction of being one of the most famous theorems in mathematics. The theorem is usually named after Pythagoras, although it was known to the Chinese and the Babylonians a long time before he lived. The relationship between areas states that in a right-angled triangle the square on the hypotenuse is equal to the sum of the squares

on the other two sides, summarized pictorially and symbolically by Figure 9.14. It is both
surprising and highly useful that the sides of a right-angled triangle should be related in this
simple way.

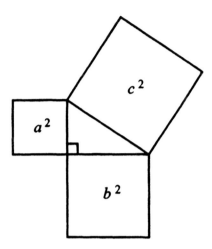

Figure 9.14 *The theorem of Pythagoras:* $a^2 + b^2 = c^2$

There is a rich variety of different proofs of the theorem, many of which involve algebraic
arguments as well as requiring geometric insight. Proofs using the two diagrams of Figure 9.15
are based on the expansions of $(a + b)^2$ and $(a - b)^2$. In both cases, four right-angled triangles
are arranged around a square to leave a smaller square shown shaded in each case. Students
should be asked to verify that the sides are equal and the angles are right angles to be certain
that the shapes are squares. Each of the triangles has an area of $\frac{1}{2}ab$ so that the total area of the
four triangles is $4 \times \frac{1}{2}ab = 2ab$. In each case, equating an expression for the area of the large
square to expressions for the areas of the smaller square and the four triangles leads to the
theorem in the form $a^2 + b^2 = c^2$.

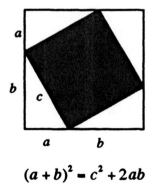

$$(a+b)^2 = c^2 + 2ab$$

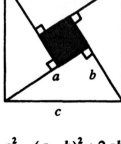

$$c^2 = (a-b)^2 + 2ab$$

Figure 9.15 *Two proofs of the theorem of Pythagoras*

Two further proofs use similar triangles. The first of these, based on the similar triangles in the left-hand diagram of Figure 9.16, equates the areas of the squares on the two shorter sides to two rectangles which form the square on the hypotenuse. The two rectangles are shown in the right hand diagram with one pair of equal areas shaded. The proof is an algebraic version of the proof given in Euclid's *Elements* (Euclid, 1967), which shows that the corresponding areas are equal using an argument involving congruent triangles.

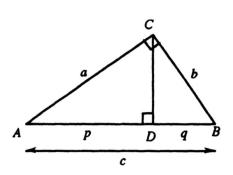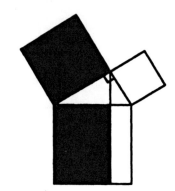

Figure 9.16 *A proof with similar triangles*

In the right angled triangle ABC, D is the foot of the perpendicular from C to the side AB. The argument uses equal ratios derived from the fact that the three right-angled triangles ABC, ACD and CBD are similar. The first two lines show that the two smaller squares are equal in area to the two rectangles and the third line shows that the sum of these two areas is indeed equal to the area of the square on the hypotenuse.

Using triangles ACD and ABC: $\dfrac{p}{a} = \dfrac{a}{c} \Rightarrow a^2 = cp$

Similarly, with triangles CBD and ABC: $\dfrac{q}{b} = \dfrac{b}{c} \Rightarrow b^2 = cq$

It then follows that $a^2 + b^2 = cp + cq = c(p + q) = c^2$

Although the argument is a purely algebraic one concerning lengths, interpreting it in terms of areas aids understanding of the argument, which helps students to appreciate links between algebra and geometry and adds interest to what otherwise may appear to be just an exercise in manipulating symbols.

A second related proof of the theorem of Pythagoras uses similar triangles in conjunction with the right-angled triangle ABC in the semi-circle with centre O shown in Figure 9.17. D is the foot of the perpendicular from C to the diameter AB with CD forming one side of the right-angled triangle ODC whose sides are denoted by a, b and c. The two angles denoted by x are equal. The semi-circle is not strictly necessary, but it does make it easy to construct the right angle. If this is done with a dynamic geometry package the point C can be moved to vary the whole configuration, whilst maintaining its essential characteristics.

Using the two similar right-angled triangles ADC and CDB each of which contain the angle x:

$$\frac{b}{c+a} = \frac{c-a}{b} \text{ (note that these ratios are equal to } \tan x)$$

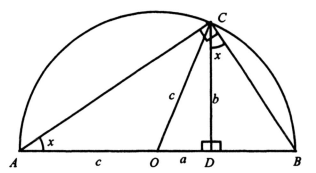

Figure 9.17 *A second proof using similar triangles*

It then follows that $b^2 = (c + a)(c - a)$, which implies that $a^2 + b^2 = c^2$.

Here the difference of two squares, whose importance was emphasized in chapter five, has appeared alongside an equation involving equal ratios, effectively demonstrating the need for students to acquire familiarity and fluency with a range of diverse ideas in order to create and to follow algebraic arguments.

This section ends with two very different problems, which again illustrate the application of algebra in a geometric context. The first, shown in Figure 9.18, involves paper folding.

Fold a paper square in half to give a 2 by 1 rectangle. Fold the rectangle so that one pair of opposite vertices coincide. Investigate the dimensions of the right-angled triangle that is formed.

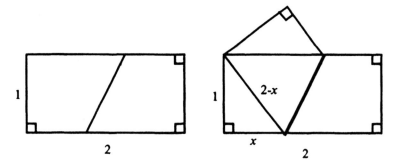

Figure 9.18 *A paper-folding problem*

With the length x as one side of the right-angled triangle, the other side is of length $2 - x$. Applying Pythagoras' theorem to the triangle gives an equation for x, which can be solved as follows:

$$(2 - x)^2 = x^2 + 1 \implies 4 - 4x = 1 \implies 4x = 3 \implies x = \tfrac{3}{4}$$

The sides of the triangle are $\tfrac{3}{4}$, 1 and $\tfrac{5}{4}$, proportional to the sides of a 3, 4, 5 triangle. This is certainly rather an unexpected and surprising result, but becomes immediately obvious if the initial rectangle is taken as 8 units by 4 units. The problem can be extended readily by asking students to investigate a 3 by 1 rectangle, or more generally an *m* by *n* rectangle.

The second problem involves finding a simple formula that gives the approximate distance to the horizon from a point whose height above sea level is known. The formula takes a particularly simple form if distances are measured in miles and heights in feet: finding a metric version is left as an exercise for the reader!

The problem then is to find an approximate formula for *d*, the distance of the horizon in miles, from a point which is *h* feet above sea level. In Figure 9.19, *R* denotes the radius of the earth in miles and *H* is the height above sea level in miles, noting the need to work with a consistent system of units to produce a formula relating lengths.

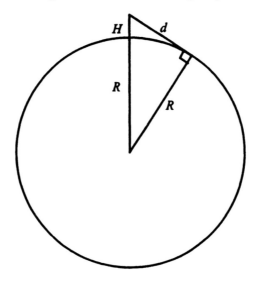

Figure 9.19 *How far is the horizon?*

Since there are 5280 feet in a mile and the radius of the earth is approximately 3960 miles it follows that $R = 3960$ and $H = \frac{h}{5280}$. Applying Pythagoras' theorem to the right-angled triangle in Figure 9.19 leads to the following:

$$d^2 = (R + H)^2 - R^2 = 2RH + H^2 \approx 2RH, \text{ since } H \text{ is small}$$

Substituting for *R* and *H* results in a drastic simplification because by chance the particular numbers have a large common factor:

$$d^2 \approx 2RH = \frac{2 \times 3960 \times h}{5280} = \frac{3h}{2}$$

The approximate formula is $d = \sqrt{\frac{3h}{2}}$, which is easy to remember and use, so do encourage your students to try it out when they are high up in the world! For example, for a height of 300 feet above sea level, the approximate distance to the horizon is about 21 miles and from the top of Mount Everest, at about 29000 feet, the distance is over 200 miles. In theory, you can see one mile from a point $\frac{2}{3}$ of a foot (8 inches or about 20 centimetres) above sea level. This may be a little difficult to observe in practice, but it does have an interesting implication. If three posts are placed at one mile intervals in a straight line across a stretch of still water so that each protrudes the same distance above water level, the top of the middle post will be about 8 inches above the horizontal line joining the tops of the other two posts.

The various proofs and problems in this section show how algebra can be applied to geometrical situations involving the theorem of Pythagoras, a result which offers a very rich range of possibilities of wide interest and extensive opportunities to practise and extend algebraic skills. There are many websites that offer useful material on various aspects of the theorem: two examples can be found at **www.ies.co.jp/math/java** and **www.cut-the-knot.com/ pythagoras**.

CONCLUSION

Geometry is a rich source of problems to solve and propositions to prove providing abundant applications to motivate algebraic thinking at all levels. Length and angle are excellent examples of variables because they relate directly both to numbers and to pictures and they are involved in the related concepts of perimeter, area and volume as well as the wealth of ideas linked to the properties of different configurations. They therefore give a particularly appropriate way of giving both meaning and purpose to algebraic expressions. Algebraic arguments, whether used to solve an equation or to prove a theorem, have a clear purpose in a geometrical context. In this chapter I have sought to convey this richness by examining a few geometrical ideas in detail to show some of the possibilities they present for using and understanding algebra.

Isosceles triangles are a common feature of many configurations and the simple relationship between their angles provides a valuable exercise in elementary algebra. If x denotes the number of degrees in each of the two equal angles then the third angle is given by $180 - 2x$, whereas if y denotes the other angle, the two equal angles are given by $\frac{1}{2}(180 - y)$ or $90 - \frac{1}{2}y$. Fluency in representing relationships like this is aided by the corresponding fluency developed with numbers. The angle properties of polygons offer another simple situation where results can be first generated numerically and then expressed in an algebraic form. Finding a general expression for the angle sum in more than one way helps students appreciate the equivalence of two expressions like $180(n - 2)$ and $180n - 360$, and finding an expression for an angle of a regular polygon as $180 - \frac{360}{n}$ gives greater sense to the operation of dividing by a variable n. Graphing the angles of regular polygons is a good example of a task that is worth considering in depth because it brings together a lot of important ideas. Graphs have already been considered in detail in Chapter 6 because they are an important tool that bring algebra and geometry together in a very special way.

Deriving formulae for perimeter, area and volume, and using similar triangles in a variety of ways, makes use of lengths as the underlying variable, and results can be reinforced by looking at numerical cases. Seeing alternative strategies for arriving at a result, and then showing that different expressions are equivalent, reinforces algebraic understanding as well as making standard formulae more familiar and memorable. The idea of proportionality, considered at length in Chapter 8, is reinforced by the frequent occurrence of similar triangles in geometrical situations where strategies using scale factors and equal ratios are needed that require the use of algebraic fractions.

The final section of this chapter looked at the applications of algebra to proofs of the important theorem of Pythagoras and problems that depend upon it. These particularly draw on the identities involving squares – the square of a sum and the difference of two squares –

that were considered at length in Chapter 5, besides providing another application of similar triangles. The two final problems provide a fine contrast between the two attractions of mathematics – the intrinsic interest of a paper-folding exercise which generates a 3, 4, 5 triangle and the extrinsic interest of a formula that enables you to calculate how far you can see from the top of a hill. The theorem of Pythagoras provides the relationship between the lengths of the sides of right-angled triangles, but we also need to establish relationships linking the lengths to the angles. This is the subject of Chapter 10, which discusses how students can be helped to make sense of trigonometry and to appreciate the fascinating properties and wealth of applications of the sine, cosine and tangent functions.

Chapter 10

Trigonometry and Circular Functions

In every right triangle, if we describe a circle with a centre a vertex of an acute angle and radius the length of the longest side, then the side subtending this acute angle is the right sine of the arc adjacent to that side and opposite the given angle; the third side is equal to the sine of the complement of the arc. (Regiomontanus (1436–1476) in Fauvel and Gray, 1987, p. 245)

INTRODUCING SINE AND COSINE

The geometrical task of finding lengths and angles in triangles requires familiarity with the circular functions – sine, cosine and tangent – whose role in mathematics is extensive and important, going way beyond the solution of triangles that originally inspired their development. Understanding the properties of these functions and their application to a variety of problems requires an interplay between geometric and algebraic ideas. Unfortunately, students often come to regard the subject as difficult, seeing it as a matter of remembering a lot of apparently unrelated formulae and procedures. It is essential to develop an understanding of how the three functions relate to right-angled triangles and then, as they are developed further, to appreciate the link to circles, the behaviour and properties of their graphs and the connections between identities as a web of interrelated ideas rather than as a set of disparate facts.

Many school textbooks, working with right-angled triangles, define sine, cosine and tangent initially as ratios, which, as has been pointed out in Chapter 8, is an idea that students often find difficult. A ratio provides a comparison between two numbers and is not necessarily itself seen as a number that can be interpreted, in particular, as a length. In fact, a length is a ratio because there is an implicit comparison with whatever is being taken as the unit of measurement. However, students think of lengths as something simple and concrete that can be represented by numbers. This simple understanding of length, together with the ideas of enlargement and scale factor, has many advantages over definitions involving ratios in the early stages of learning trigonometry, although some explicit use of ratios is inevitably involved in solving trigonometrical problems. Sine and cosine as length is not a new idea – it reflects the historical development of the subject in the fifteenth century by Regiomontanus (see the quotation that heads this chapter), and was advocated by Nunn (1919) and in the early text books of the *School Mathematics Project*, SMP (1966). Maor (1998) advocates 'a shift in emphasis from the abstract to the practical' by linking trigonometry closely to circles with definitions based on projections, the directed lengths or displacements needed to extend the ideas to general angles.

The availability of calculators and a variety of computer software can also influence the way in which the subject is presented as well as providing the means to carry out calculations. The links between the various functions, the behaviour of their graphs and their representation as directed line segments in diagrams can be enhanced in a variety of ways by the wise use of technology. So, let us begin with a calculator.

A thirteen-year-old student once asked me what the SIN key was for on a calculator, no doubt thinking that something exciting might be in store! Investigating the numbers that are generated by the sine and cosine keys on a calculator (taking care to ensure that the calculator is set to operate in degrees) is a very good way to begin the study of trigonometry. A starting point is provided by Figure 10.1, which appears in the *Key Stage 3 National Strategy Framework for Teaching Mathematics* (DfEE), 2001). It shows a table of values of cosθ and sinθ rounded to two decimal places for values of θ taken from 0 to 90 degrees. Drawing the graph of cosθ against sinθ gives a quadrant of a circle with unit radius centred at the origin, a result that often intrigues students when they encounter it for the first time.

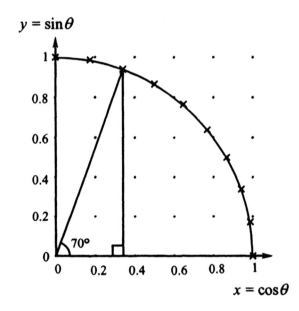

θ	cos θ	sin θ
0	1	0
10	0.98	0.17
20	0.94	0.34
30	0.87	0.50
40	0.77	0.64
50	0.64	0.77
60	0.50	0.87
70	0.34	0.94
80	0.17	0.98
90	0	1

Figure 10.1 *Co-ordinates of points on a circle*

It is a small step to extend the range of values of θ beyond 90 to give a full circle, but the quarter circle alone offers plenty of scope for discussing the table and the graph with students. With some prompting from the teacher, a number of significant observations, whose interconnections can be explored, should arise:

● the points are equally spaced round the circumference of the quarter circle;
● the values of θ correspond to the angle measured in degrees anti-clockwise from the *x* axis;

- the co-ordinates (cosθ, sinθ) give the point on the circle corresponding to any angle of θ degrees;
- the values in the table for cosθ and sinθ are the same, but they appear in reverse order. As cosθ decreases, sinθ increases;
- the values do not decrease, or increase, by the same amount at each stage. cosθ decreases by small steps at first, but the steps get bigger;
- when the same value arises, the sum of the two angles is 90 degrees. At a later stage this is summarized as cosθ = sin (90 − θ), reminding us that cosine was originally defined as the sine of the complementary angle;
- cosθ and sinθ take the same value for θ = 45;
- the quadrant is symmetrical about the line corresponding to θ = 45.

There is a lot to say about this simple graph: it is a rich source of ideas about the basic properties of the two circular functions, sine and cosine. Drawing the graphs of cosθ and sinθ against θ, referred to elsewhere, can provide further food for thought.

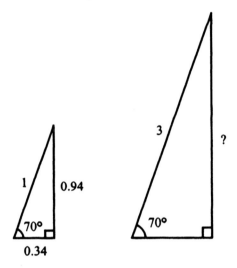

Figure 10.2 *Calculating the height of a ladder up a wall*

The link with right-angled triangles is made by a triangle superimposed on the circle graph, like that with an angle of 70° shown in Figure 10.1. If the graph is displayed on an overhead projector, this can be done very effectively by placing a separate acetate sheet on the display on which the triangle is drawn, with the angle and the lengths of the three sides labelled. The triangle can then be displayed independently of the graph, as shown on the left in Figure 10.2, and used as a starting point to extend the ideas to solving right-angled triangles in general. As always, a problem provides a good starting point that is developed here through an idealized dialogue between teacher and students:

T: How can we find how high up a wall a 3 metre ladder reaches if it makes an angle of 70° with the ground?
A: *Draw a diagram* [the right-hand triangle in Figure 10.2].
T: What are you assuming here?

B: The ground is horizontal and the wall is vertical, so there is a right angle.
T: What can you say about the two triangles?
C: They are similar.
D: One is an enlargement of the other.
T: What is the scale factor of the enlargement?
A: It's 3, because the hypotenuse is 3.
T: So, how can you find the height?
B: It's 3 × 0.94, which is 2.82.
T: Is that a sensible answer?
C: Well, you would expect it to be a bit less than 3.
D: It would be better to round it to 2.8 – 2.8 metres – because 2.82 looks a bit too accurate for measuring a height up a wall.
T: What is the distance along the ground from the foot of the ladder to the wall?
A: That's 3 × 0.34, which is 1.02 – just over a metre.
T: How would we work out the height if the ladder was 5 metres long?
B: It would be 5 × 0.94.
T: And what if the angle was 75° instead of 70°?
C: You would have to change the 0.94.
T: Where did 0.94 come from?
D: The calculator – it was sin 70°. We need sin 75°. We must work out 5 × sin 75°.
T: And how do we find the distance along the ground in this case?
A: It is 5 × cos 75°.

The enlargement displayed in the two diagrams in Figure 10.2 readily suggests to students how to solve the problem of calculating the lengths of the two shorter sides of the right-angled triangle. With judicious use of questions, the teacher can then lead students to see how to solve the problem in a general case, a skill that can then be practised and applied to a variety of problems presented in words and diagrams.

This approach has defined the sine and cosine of an angle as a length, initially as co-ordinates of points on a circle and then as the two shorter sides of a right-angled triangle with unit hypotenuse. Enlargement provides the key to solving problems in a general right-angled triangle. Figure 10.3 summarizes these ideas, using the variables x and y to refer to the two sides in the general case.

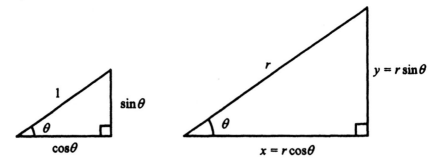

Figure 10.3 *Defining sine and cosine using an enlargement with scale factor r*

The two statements, $x = r\cos\theta$ and $y = r\sin\theta$, for the lengths of the shorter sides could in themselves be taken as the defining relationships for cosine and sine and they are equivalent to the traditional ratio definitions:

$$\cos\theta = \tfrac{x}{r} = \frac{\text{ADJACENT SIDE}}{\text{HYPOTENUSE}} \text{ and } \sin\theta = \tfrac{y}{r} = \frac{\text{OPPOSITE SIDE}}{\text{HYPOTENUSE}}$$

Length is a simpler concept than ratio, and calculation of lengths comes more naturally before the calculation of angles, for which the ratio form is necessary. Furthermore, students find it much simpler to work algebraically and numerically from a statement involving a product rather than a quotient. It is simpler for a student whose algebraic skills are still being developed to begin with $a = bc$ and derive $b = \tfrac{a}{c}$ or $c = \tfrac{a}{b}$, than it is to work the other way round, particularly when a move between the two quotient forms is required.

There is a parallel here with other common formulae that have similar forms. Students have little difficulty using the formula for the area of a rectangle as $A = lw$, and from this they can see that length is given by $l = \tfrac{A}{w}$ and width by $w = \tfrac{A}{l}$. On the other hand, when velocity, v, is defined in terms of distance, d, and time, t, by $v = \tfrac{d}{t}$, they find it much more difficult to derive the equivalent forms $d = vt$ and $t = \tfrac{d}{v}$ – particularly the latter. Indeed, some textbooks seem to imply that students should remember all three formulae in this case, rather than remember one and understand how to derive the others from it.

	$y = 5\sin 34^\circ$	$\sin 34^\circ = \dfrac{y}{5}$
(triangle: hypotenuse 5, opposite y, angle 34°)		$y = 5\sin 34^\circ$
(triangle: hypotenuse 6, adjacent 5, angle θ)	$6\cos\theta = 5$ $\cos\theta = \dfrac{5}{6}$ $\theta = \cos^{-1}\dfrac{5}{6}$	$\cos\theta = \dfrac{5}{6}$ $\theta = \cos^{-1}\dfrac{5}{6}$
(triangle: hypotenuse r, opposite 3, angle 27°)	$r\sin 27^\circ = 3$ $r = \dfrac{3}{\sin 27^\circ}$	$\sin 27^\circ = \dfrac{3}{r}$ $r = \dfrac{3}{\sin 27^\circ}$

Figure 10.4 *Comparing length and ratio definitions of sine and cosine*

Figure 10.4 contrasts the use of length- and ratio-based definitions of cosine or sine by comparing the algebraic steps required to find each of three possible unknowns in a right-angled triangle – shorter side, angle and hypotenuse. Once an initial statement of the appropriate definition in terms of the given values is written down, all that remains is to solve an equation. When calculating a length using the length definition, the initial statement is the solution, but in all other cases an algebraic step or two is needed to solve the equation.

The major new idea in this respect will be that of solving an equation like $\cos\theta = \tfrac{5}{6}$. Rather than tell students straight away about the inverse cosine, they can be challenged to try and find an angle with a cosine of the correct value using just the cosine key on the calculator. This may seem an arduous task, but it does emphasize the nature of what they are trying to find and makes the introduction of the inverse cosine much more meaningful, not least because they can see it as a valuable labour-saving device. Without this preamble there is the danger that it becomes yet another calculator key to press and another rule to remember. Square roots, although much simpler to understand, provide a good parallel where some initial calculations using successive approximation are useful to make sense of an idea, as a prelude to frequent calculator use.

TANGENTS AND GRADIENTS

The tangent may be introduced before sine and cosine, or it may follow at later stage, but there is little to choose between the arguments about which should come first. Introducing all three together certainly has little to recommend it because the scope for confusion is great and is likely to detract from a secure understanding of the ideas. Sine and cosine have much in common so there are clear advantages in introducing them together. Moreover, they have a wide variety of interesting properties and applications, including the link with circles and the wave form of their graphs, that can be pursued at an elementary level. However, simple practical problems like finding the height of a tree using the angle of elevation and finding the angle of a slope from its gradient provide good introductory examples for tangent. Familiarity with a definition of tangent and fluency with procedures for calculating lengths and angles can be developed with the one idea, before the potentially confusing task of choosing between two or three functions arises.

The early stages of learning about tangents have much in common with ways of introducing sines and cosines, with similar issues concerning definition and equation solving, so these are not rehearsed in detail again here, except to note that the link with gradient, discussed below, does make tangent as ratio at least as important as tangent as length. None the less, lengths are a simpler starting point.

Figure 10.5 shows distances stepped off along a tangent to a circle of unit radius by line segments drawn from the centre of the circle with the angles at the centre in intervals of 10°. The length along the tangent from the point of contact is the tangent of the corresponding angle. The values of these lengths can be measured and then verified using the tangent function on a calculator. Alternatively, in the style of the earlier sines and cosines exercise, the calculator values can be used to plot the points on the tangent so that students observe the angle property for themselves.

The triangle on the right in Figure 10.5 is the right-angled triangle with an angle of 60° extracted from the circle diagram. Enlargements of this triangle and others with different angles enable lengths to be calculated in appropriate situations and, when the two shorter sides are given, the angle determined.

The right-angled triangle of Figure 10.6 shows the general case with x and y used to denote the two shorter sides, so that $y = x \tan\theta$, which is equivalent to the usual ratio, or gradient, definition of the tangent:

$$y = x\tan\theta \quad \Leftrightarrow \quad \tan\theta = \frac{y}{x} = \frac{\text{OPPOSITE SIDE}}{\text{ADJACENT SIDE}} = \text{GRADIENT}$$

Gradient is an important mathematical idea that the tangent function links directly to the angle in a right-angled triangle. Calculating the angle of slope of a hill, the angle that a straight

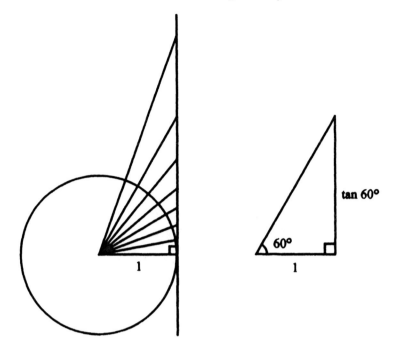

Figure 10.5 *Length along a tangent*

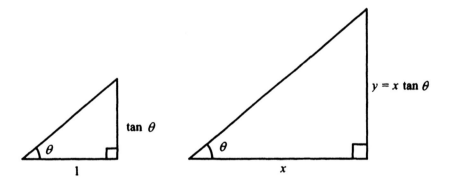

Figure 10.6 *Defining tangent as a length using an enlargement with scale factor x*

line like $y = 2x$ makes with the x axis, the direction of a vector from its components and the argument of a complex number all require a simple calculation involving gradient and tangent. The relationship between gradient and angle provided by the tangent function is not one of direct proportion, but it is a common misconception that doubling the angle will double the gradient. Reference to the circle diagram of Figure 10.5 or a simple counter example like 45°, with a gradient of 1, and 90°, where the gradient is clearly not 2, makes the error obvious, but like many misconceptions it is very persistent.

SOLVING TRIGONOMETRICAL PROBLEMS

In solving right-angled triangles when one of the angles is involved, the students' first source of difficulty and error lies in choosing between sine, cosine and tangent in order to make a correct initial statement. The difficulty lies in remembering definitions and identifying correctly the sides of a triangle to which they refer. The second source of difficulty is the algebraic one of solving an equation, which was referred to earlier with the three examples in Figure 10.04. There are then various smaller technical difficulties associated with notation, using a calculator correctly and rounding answers appropriately. Overcoming the difficulties that students encounter is clearly not a simple matter, but the way in which ideas are introduced should aim to give them definitions that make sense in their own terms and procedures that build on an established fluency with equation solving.

Frequent practice in using new ideas is necessary, but this requires more than repetitive routine exercises. Chapter 4 uses the phrase 'mental algebra' as a way of referring to frequent practice through orally given questions with immediate feedback, whereby misconceptions can be addressed and understanding developed. In a trigonometrical context, these will relate to labelled triangles displayed for students to see and will focus on asking students to make correct initial statements rather than on doing calculations. For example, given one side and an angle in a right-angled triangle, they can be asked to write down an expression for one of the other sides, or, given two sides, they can be asked to make a statement involving one of the angles. Alongside this, students can practise skills by applying them to solve a wide variety of problems to provide the meaning and purpose that is so often lacking in many traditional textbook exercises.

Many problems involve interpreting a written description, identifying an appropriate right-angled triangle, and using sine, cosine or tangent in a routine way to find a solution. More demanding problems require some additional algebraic manipulation for their solution – possibly involving other ideas like Pythagoras' theorem. A good example is provided by Figure 10.7, where h, the height of a tree has to be found in terms of the angles of elevation α, and β, and the distance d, between two points in a straight line from the foot of the tree. The distance from the nearer point to the foot of the tree is taken as w.

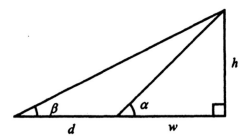

Figure 10.7 *A problem with heights*

The two right-angled triangles give two equations:

$$h = w \tan\alpha \text{ and } h = (w + d) \tan\beta.$$

Since w is not required in the solution, one possible strategy is to make w the subject of each equation, equate the results and solve the resulting equation:

$$\frac{h}{\tan\alpha} = \frac{h}{\tan\beta} - d \;\Rightarrow\; h = \frac{d\tan\alpha\,\tan\beta}{\tan\alpha - \tan\beta}$$

Finding a result in a general form like this requires considerable algebraic understanding and fluency. A first step towards this is taken by posing the same problem with carefully chosen numbers. If the angles are taken as 11.3° and 26.6°, the corresponding tangents to one decimal place are 0.2 and 0.5. Then, with a distance of 60 metres between the two points, the initial pair of equations become:

$$h = 0.5w \text{ and } h = 0.2(w + 60)$$

These two equations are much simpler to solve than the previous general equations and give a solution of 20 metres for the height. Attempting to solve the problem with less convenient numbers will show the advantages of having a general formula, even when a calculator can be used for the calculations. However, it is none the less a good teaching strategy to use a simple numerical example that can act as an indicator of the algebraic steps that need to be taken.

A new result like the cosine formula can be introduced as a problem, such as finding the third side in a triangle when two sides and an angle are given. Students should be challenged to solve a problem like the following for themselves:

Find the length of the third side of a triangle with sides of 5 centimetres and 8 centimetres and an angle between them of 39°.

A procedure to solve the particular problem can then be used as a basis for generalization to arrive at the cosine formula in its conventional form. A typical approach would be to apply the theorem of Pythagoras to the two right-angled triangles in Figure 10.8, to give two equations

$$a^2 = (c - x)^2 + h^2 \text{ and } b^2 = x^2 + h^2$$

The equations are then manipulated to find an expression for a^2 in terms of b and c and the angle θ.

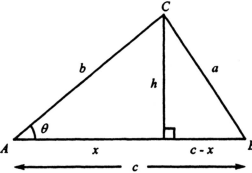

Figure 10.8 *Proving the cosine formula*

If the two equations are subtracted, h^2, is eliminated giving a relationship between the three sides and the additional length x.

$$a^2 - b^2 = (c - x)^2 - x^2 = c^2 - 2cx$$

Substituting $x = b\cos\theta$ and rearranging gives the cosine formula:

$$a^2 = b^2 + c^2 - 2bc\cos\theta$$

A common error arises when values are substituted into the cosine formula. Using the numbers from the problem referred to above, the formula gives $a^2 = 89 - 80\cos34°$, which students are commonly tempted to simplify to give $a^2 = 9\cos 34°$. This is an understandable error that they should be able to detect for themselves because it gives a value of less than 3 for a. Since that is the difference between 8 and 5, the lengths of the other two sides, it cannot be the correct length for the third side. It is important to acknowledge that errors will be made and to encourage students to check that their answers are reasonable. Focusing on a particular error like this by following through its consequences and discussing the algebraic convention that has been flouted serves both to clarify the correct procedure for this particular problem and to emphasize more general mathematical strategies.

The cosine formula is likely to make much better sense if the sort of problem it is designed to solve is presented initially as a challenge so that there is some appreciation of where it comes from and how it can be derived. Furthermore, the formula should not be seen as an isolated fact, but rather as a powerful extension of Pythagoras' theorem, as illustrated by this short dialogue:

T: What happens when the angle θ is 90°?
A: *Cosine is zero, so it becomes* $a^2 = b^2 + c^2 - Pythagoras'\ theorem.$
T: So, what about a if the angle is less than 90°?
B: *It will be less than before.*
C: *You take off* $2bc\cos\theta$ *to make it less.*
T: And what if the angle is more than 90°?
A: *You would have to add something on.*
B: *You have to use the cosine of an obtuse angle.*
C: *And that is negative, so you are taking a negative number. You do add something on!*

The cosine formula is usually introduced alongside the sine formula, a result that is easy to prove and takes a very simple form, although it does make very explicit use of ratios:

$$\frac{a}{\sin A} = \frac{b}{\sin B} = \frac{c}{\sin C}$$

Difficulties in using the sine and cosine formulae to find sides and angles in general triangles have much in common with those encountered in solving right-angled triangles and related problems. The two essential ingredients are to produce correct expressions to be evaluated or equations to be solved and to apply appropriate algebraic skills to reach a solution. The first stage should not be neglected through a rightful concern to develop the second stage.

THE GRAPHS OF THE SINE AND COSINE FUNCTIONS

One advantage of making the link between sines and cosines and the circle at an early stage and expressing definitions in terms of variables x, y and r is that the extension to general angles outside the range from 0° and 90° becomes a natural and straightforward step. The graphs of sine and cosine have already been discussed in Chapter 6 in conjunction with transformations and applications to periodic phenomena. An interactive computer diagram is a good way of emphasising the link between variation in the co-ordinates of a point as it moves round a circle

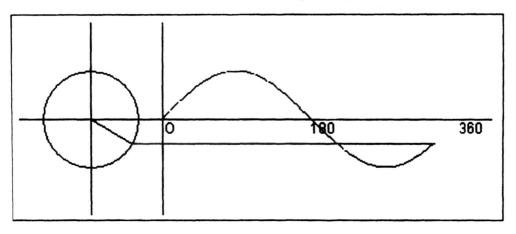

Figure 10.9 *A sine graph from a point moving round a circle*

and the periodic form of the graphs. Figure 10.9 shows an example taken from the website: **www.ies.co.jp/math/java**.

Graphs also provide a valuable reference point when considering properties of the sine and cosine functions. An advanced calculator like the TI-89 often responds in unexpected ways thereby providing examples which can provoke curiosity and demand explanation. Figure 10.10 shows the effect of entering three fairly innocuous expressions with the calculator set to operate in exact mode rather than approximate mode, which would give numerical values. Using symmetry the pair of bold vertical lines on each of the various graphs provides a simple graphical justification for the corresponding result, whose general form is stated as well. Graphs used like this not only provide students with a simple explanation, but they are an effective way of deriving such results.

Students do not find it difficult to remember the form of the graphs or to recognize their symmetry. Sketching a suitable graph or graphs makes it easy to determine whether a sine or cosine is positive or negative for a particular angle or to determine which angles have sines or cosines of the same or opposite sign. These are important skills when determining multiple solutions to trigonometrical equations.

TRIGONOMETRICAL IDENTITIES

Students commonly view trigonometry as a difficult subject because it is associated with remembering a large number of formulae whose purpose often appears obscure. There are certainly some results like the initial definitions of sine, cosine and tangent and a few key results that have to be remembered, but many others can be worked out readily once their meaning and the interconnections between them are understood. It is much easier to remember a formula that makes sense, because it is seen as something more than a symbolic form, through its links to graphs, diagrams and associated numerical examples.

The right-angled triangle with unit hypotenuse on the left in Figure 10.11 shows the lengths of the other two sides designated by sine and cosine. Two important identities follow as an immediate consequence of designating the sides in this way. The gradient of the hypotenuse tells us that $\tan \theta = \frac{\sin \theta}{\cos \theta}$ and Pythagoras' theorem gives $\cos^2\theta + \sin^2\theta = 1$. Extending ideas linked

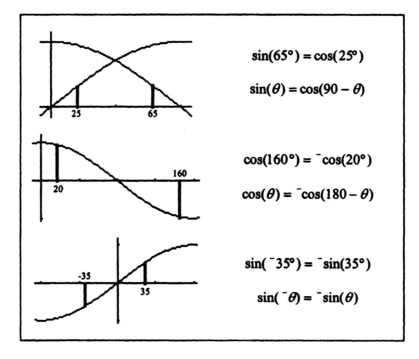

Figure 10.10 *Explaining with graphs*

to the circle diagrams used earlier in the chapter, these results can be seen to apply for all values of θ and not just the acute angles of a right-angled triangle. However, the diagrammatic representation for the acute-angled cases is a valuable peg for both understanding and memory. It is worth noting at this stage that knowing the value of one of the functions for a particular value of θ enables the values of the other two to be calculated either using the two identities directly in their symbolic forms or by relating the value given to lengths in a triangle. Exploring this idea is a useful source of small problems.

The other triangle of Figure 10.11 has been obtained by enlarging the first triangle by dividing each of its sides by $\cos\theta$. Dividing by a number which is less than one, like the value of $\cos\theta$ here, does indeed make the triangle larger, a fact that merits discussion because it may not be immediately obvious to all students! The function $\sec\theta$, which is the reciprocal of $\cos\theta$, arises naturally as the length of the hypotenuse of the enlarged triangle, and the identity $1 + \tan^2\theta = \sec^2\theta$ then follows immediately from the theorem of Pythagoras. It is perfectly possible to derive $1 + \tan^2\theta = \sec^2\theta$ symbolically from $\cos^2\theta + \sin^2\theta = 1$ by dividing both

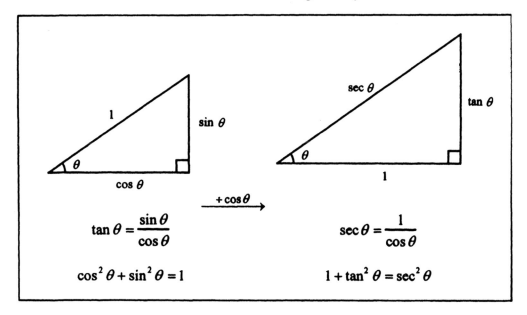

Figure 10.11 *Some important trigonometrical identities*

sides by $\cos^2\theta$, but the result is easier both to understand and to remember when it is linked directly to a picture. The function $\sec\theta$ is an unnecessary complication when solving triangles, but its importance becomes very clear when the surprising fact that $\sec^2\theta$ is the derivative of $\tan\theta$ arises in the study of the calculus.

The definitions of $\csc\theta$ and $\cot\theta$ leading to the identity $\cot^2\theta + 1 = \csc^2\theta$ can be introduced in a similar way by dividing each side in the first triangle by $\sin\theta$ instead of $\cos\theta$. It is also worth observing that the names cotangent and cosecant arise because they are respectively the tangent and secant of the complementary angle, so all that is required is to label the other acute angle as θ.

The other important set of trigonometrical identities are those related to the addition formulae for expanding $\sin(\theta + \phi)$ and $\cos(\theta + \phi)$. A common misconception is to suppose that $\sin(\theta + \phi) = \sin\theta + \sin\phi$. Although it is easy enough to use a counter example to show that this is incorrect – for instance, $\sin 45° + \sin 45°$ is certainly not equal to $\sin 90°$ – misconceptions like this are very persistent and will not necessarily be eradicated by one counter example on one occasion.

Figure 10.12 shows how the addition formula for sine can be derived by considering the position of the upper vertex as a basic triangle with unit hypotenuse and angle θ is rotated through an angle ϕ. The formula for cosine can be derived in a similar way as the difference of two horizontal lengths in the diagram. As with the previous identities the extension to general angles needs separate consideration, but the acute angled case provides a memorable diagrammatic derivation, particularly when it is illustrated with an interactive diagram on a computer screen.

Two other pairs of identities immediately follow from the first pair by making small changes, replacing ϕ with $^-\phi$ for one pair and by θ for the other pair:

$$\sin(\theta - \phi) = \sin\theta\cos\phi - \cos\theta\sin\phi \text{ and } \cos(\theta - \phi) = \cos\theta\cos\phi + \sin\theta\sin\phi$$

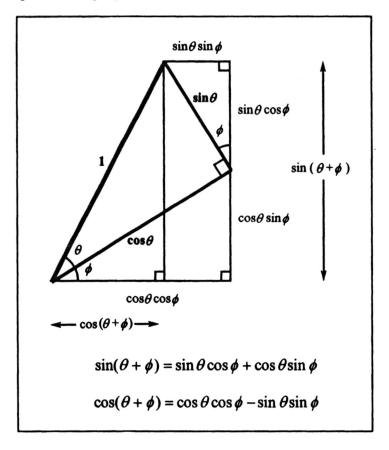

Figure 10.12 *Addition formulae for sine and cosine*

$$\sin 2\theta = 2\sin\theta\cos\theta \text{ and } \cos 2\theta = \cos^2\theta - \sin^2\theta$$

There are a variety of other results that can be derived in a similar fashion, including alternative forms for cos 2θ and identities involving tangent. Trigonometrical identities should be introduced judiciously because it is easy to overwhelm students if too much is encountered too rapidly. They need to become familiar with diagrammatic representations first to aid understanding and memory and to acquire an appreciation of the interconnections, which then enables a lot of results to be derived with relative ease from a small number of key identities.

SOME NOTATIONAL MATTERS

There are some inconsistencies that can cause confusion in the notation used for trigonometrical functions. The advent of calculators and computer software that can handle symbolic expressions particularly emphasizes these anomalies. The conventional notation used for a general function of θ is $f(\theta)$, yet with trigonometrical functions like sine it is usual to write sin θ

when it would be more consistent to write sin(θ), something which is a necessary requirement in using many calculators.

When sin θ is squared, the usual convention is to write $\sin^2\theta$, but with a calculator it has to be written as $(\sin(\theta))^2$. This again is consistent with general function notation because $f^2(\theta)$ means $f(f(\theta))$ – a double application of the function. Strictly speaking, therefore, $\sin^2\theta$ ought to mean sin (sinθ). The conventional notation with the trigonometrical functions is not even self-consistent, because $\sin^{-1}\theta$ is the inverse function, not $(\sin\theta)^{-1} = \frac{1}{\sin\theta}$, whereas $\sin^{-1}\theta$ does agree with the meaning we give to $f^{-1}(\theta)$.

Finally it has to be noted that there are two other forms for the inverse function: $\sin^{-1}\theta$ may be written as arcsin θ or possibly invsinθ following the practice of some calculator key definitions.

Whilst there is not a lot of evidence that these notational inconsistencies cause major difficulty, teachers do need to be aware of them as a possible occasional source of confusion. Sometimes, a small matter like this can cause a disproportionate amount of difficulty for a particular student.

CONCLUSION

Trigonometry brings together a wide range of mathematical ideas, including many that are algebraic, and it is an important problem-solving tool. It has the unfortunate reputation of being a difficult subject that students associate with having to remember a large number of formulae and difficulty in choosing which one to use for each problem they encounter. There are indeed many potential difficulties and misconceptions associated with learning trigonometry, so, as with learning any mathematical ideas, the early stages are crucial in establishing both meaning and purpose. This chapter has presented a variety of approaches to learning trigonometry based on a careful analysis of ways in which it can be made both more accessible and more interesting. Some of the key issues are highlighted below.

- The link between the trigonometrical functions and a circle with unit radius needs to be established at an early stage. Besides providing an interesting initial step towards defining cosine and sine, it extends naturally to general angles and the graphs of the functions.
- Initial definitions of cosine, sine and tangent as lengths of the sides of right-angled triangles are much simpler to understand and work with than ratio definitions. Later this can be extended by referring to displacements or directed line segments.
- Ratio is none the less a vital idea in trigonometry because the solution of right-angled triangles is dependent on the idea of enlargement applied to similar triangles.
- Many elementary trigonometrical problems involve the algebraic skills involved in moving fluently between the three equivalent forms illustrated here with $x = r\cos\theta$, $\cos\theta = \frac{x}{r}$ and $r = \frac{x}{\cos\theta}$. There are clear advantages in the early stages for students to start with a statement like the first, because it often allows them to calculate the length of a side directly. In other cases, it is easier to derive the other two forms from the first rather than to use the second as starting point or, worse still, to attempt to memorize all three forms for each of cosine, sine and tangent.
- The link between tangent and the idea of gradient is an important one.
- Calculating angles involves an understanding of the role of inverse functions for cosine, sine and tangent. The associated notation $\cos^{-1} x$ need not be introduced immediately, although

it is often used as a label for calculator keys. At a later stage, the form of the notation can create confusion with the reciprocal of cos x.

- Most early work with trigonometry is associated with solving right-angled triangles. Deciding which of the three functions cosine, sine or tangent to use as a first step in solving a right-angled triangle is a major hurdle for many students. Frequent practice is necessary to achieve familiarity and fluency, something which can often be done through orally given questions with immediate feedback to address misconceptions and reinforce understanding. The challenge of solving significant problems gives real purpose to learning trigonometrical ideas and enables them to be related to other important results, such as the theorem of Pythagoras.

- Graphs as a way of representing trigonometrical functions are valuable both to explore and explain their properties and to apply them in modelling a variety of periodic phenomena.

- Understanding and remembering trigonometrical identities are both greatly enhanced by relating them to explanatory diagrammatic representations and by emphasizing their interconnections. Knowledge of a few key results enables others to be derived rather than remembered.

In his fascinating and informative book, *Trigonometric Delights*, Maor (1998) comments that it 'grew out of my love affair with the subject, but also out of my frustration at the way it is being taught in our colleges'. His book demonstrates admirably the wealth of interesting properties and applications displayed by the trigonometrical functions, which have been reflected at an elementary level in this chapter. Overcoming the limited view of the subject presented by many school textbooks and helping students to make better sense of trigonometrical ideas is a major challenge that embraces both geometrical and algebraic understanding. Trigonometry is peculiarly rich in links to other areas of mathematics and in applications: as such it is important to give students the understanding and skills to gain access to the wide range of possibilities.

Chapter 11

Sequences and Series

$$\tfrac{1}{3} + \tfrac{1}{3^2} + \tfrac{1}{3^3} + \tfrac{1}{3^4} + \tfrac{1}{3^5} + \tfrac{1}{3^6} \ldots \rightarrow \tfrac{1}{2}$$

ARITHMETIC SEQUENCES AND SERIES

The sequence of odd numbers and other sequences discussed in Chapter 3 are examples of arithmetic sequences. The focus in that chapter was on determining an expression for a general term by comparing the sequence with the multiples of the common difference. In the simple case of the odd numbers, this leads to the simple idea that any odd number is one less than the corresponding even number, so that the nth term is given by the expression $2n - 1$. Giving meaning to linear expressions of this kind, with the variables taking positive whole number values, and learning to manipulate them and combine them in various ways plays an important part in the early stages of learning algebra. There is a natural progression to expressions where the variable refers to a wider set of numbers, including zero, and rational, negative and real numbers. This is typified by the wider meaning given to the variable x in an expression like $2x - 1$ compared to the use of n in $2n - 1$.

Much of school algebra is concerned with problems where the variables are real numbers, but sequences, which are functions of a positive whole number variable typically denoted by n, have a continuing importance. Finding an expression for the nth term of a simple arithmetic sequence becomes one of the first challenges in learning algebra. It is usually simpler, however, to define a sequence inductively because it is natural to see the link between one term and the next. Typically at a later stage it is looked at from this perspective as a prelude to looking at the sum of an arithmetic series. The dialogue which follows is a first step on this path.

T: Start with 5 and keep adding 7. What do you get?
A: 5, 12, 19, 26, 33, . . .
T: So tell us the 10th term.
B: 5, 12, 19, 26, 33, 40, 47, 54, 61, 68 [counted on fingers]. *It's 68.*
T: Can anybody find the 10th term without counting out all the numbers?
C: 10 times 7, and then 5 more. No, that's 75 – too much.
D: It should be 7 less – that's 68. Only 9 lots of 7.
T: Why only 9 lots of 7?

A: You start with 5 and then you have 9 gaps of 7 between the numbers, so it is 9 times 7.
T: What would the 20th term be then?
B: You need to work out 19 times 7. That is ... 133.
T: How did you do that?
B: Well it is 10 times 7 which is 70 and then 9 more, 63, which makes 133.
T: Did anybody do it a different way?
C: You could do 20 times 7, 140, and then 7 less.
T: So, the 20th term is 133?
D: No, we forgot to add on the 5. It's 138.

The purpose of a discussion like this, which in passing draws on and rehearses mental calculation skills, is to arrive at any term in the sequence by using the inductive property directly. Students find it easy to see that a number of 7s have to be added to the starting number of 5, but understandably their first thought is to add on one too many. An example of the same error is provided by asking for the distance between the first and last post in a fence which has 10 posts with the posts 2 metres apart. It is all too easy to jump to the wrong conclusion that the distance is 20 metres, by counting the number of posts, rather than 18 metres by counting the number of gaps between the posts. With a sequence it is the number of gaps that is crucial: discussion should reinforce this to explain why $n - 1$ appears in a general formula.

T: Can you give a general rule?
A: You do one less than the number of terms times 7 and then add on 5.
T: What would that be for the nth term?
B: $7(n - 1) + 5$
T: How can we simplify that?
C: $7n - 2$
T: What does that tell you about the numbers?
D: They are all 2 less than a multiple of 7.

This links the 'gaps' method to the more direct ways featured in Chapter 3 by which students will have approached finding an expression like $7n - 2$. However, generating the form $7(n - 1) + 5$ is a useful step in helping students to understand the form of the more general formula $a + (n - 1)d$ for the n th term of an arithmetic sequence with first term a and common difference d. Such a formula is easy to remember, or indeed to derive when needed, if its structure is understood through relating it readily to a simple numerical example.

The two words 'sequence' and 'series' are often confused in everyday language where statements like 'a sequence is a series of terms' are not at all uncommon. The word progression, as in 'arithmetic progression' and 'geometric progression', is another source of confusion because it is often not clear whether it refers to a sequence or a series. It is a word that is best avoided if possible because it is rarely used in conjunction with sequences of other types. The distinction in meaning between the two words sequence and series need to be emphasized so that they are used correctly. It is easier to do this by referring to their meaning in the context of their use rather than by attempting to give formal definitions.

Returning to the earlier sequence, the next problem is to find the sum of the corresponding series for a particular number of terms and then to find a general procedure. The usual approach, which was referred to in Chapter 3 to sum consecutive odd numbers and to find the triangle number formula, is illustrated here by finding the sum of the first ten terms. The series has been written out twice with the second series underneath in reverse order and then corresponding terms have been added.

$$5 + 12 + 19 + 26 + 33 + 40 + 47 + 54 + 61 + 68$$
$$68 + 61 + 54 + 47 + 40 + 33 + 26 + 19 + 12 + 5$$
$$\overline{73 + 73 + 73 + 73 + 73 + 73 + 73 + 73 + 73 + 73}$$

The sum is then half of 10×73 because each term of the series has been included twice in that total. By observing that 73 is the sum of the first and the last term, a general procedure follows that can be expressed in a brief verbal form as 'half the number of terms times the sum of the first plus the last', or symbolically as $\frac{1}{2}n(a + l)$, using l to denote the last, or nth, term. Another way of looking at the result is to think of $\frac{1}{2}n(a + l)$ as the mean (or average) term so that the sum is 'the mean term multiplied by the number of terms'.

Textbooks commonly give the formula $\frac{1}{2}n(2a + (n - 1)d)$ for the sum with l replaced by the formula for the nth term, $a + (n - 1)d$. This is a good example of the tendency of textbooks to over-complicate, because it is much simpler to understand, and therefore remember, that the sum is $\frac{1}{2}n(a + l)$ (or its verbal form), together with how to work out l, the nth term. Attempting to remember the complicated form without understanding its structure is much more difficult and is not necessary, even when it comes to solving a typical rather formal problem. For example, suppose that we are asked to find the last term in an arithmetic series whose sum is 222, with a first term of 2 and a common difference of 3. To do this we need to find and solve an equation to give the number of terms in the series which can be done as shown below:

- The last, or nth, term $= 2 + 3(n - 1) = 3n - 1$
- Mean term $= \frac{1}{2}(2 + 3n - 1) = \frac{1}{2}(3n + 1)$
- Sum of first n terms $= \frac{1}{2}n(3n + 1)$
- Equation for sum: $\frac{1}{2}n(3n + 1) = 222 \Rightarrow 3n^2 + n - 444 = 0$
- Solving the equation: $(n - 12)(3n + 37) = 0 \Rightarrow n = 12$ or $n = -\frac{37}{3}$
- The only sensible solution is $n = 12$, since the number of terms must be a positive whole number, and so, by substituting into $3n - 1$, the last term is 35.

Arithmetic sequences and series are essentially very simple to understand and use if the necessary formulae are presented in a simple, possibly verbal, form which can be related easily to numerical examples. The procedure above has been designed to make each step towards the solution meaningful in itself, and easy to check. A blind substitution of numbers into a complicated looking formula may lead straight to the equation of the fourth line, but greater insight is obtained by leading up to it in the way shown. When students are confident with ideas they can modify and abbreviate their approach to problems, but for many it is better to use a slightly lengthier argument whose components are understood than a shorter one that relies just on memorized results.

GEOMETRIC SEQUENCES AND SERIES

Starting a new topic with a problem and letting students arrive at key results for themselves is potentially more motivating and can make them more memorable. The pocket money problem is one way of introducing some of the ideas of geometric sequences and series. The plan is for students to propose to their parents a plausible sounding pocket money scheme that turns out to be very rewarding. The idea is to ask for 1p the first week, 2p the second week, 4p the following week, and so on, doubling the amount each week. The problem is to see what happens over a year by asking them how much they would receive on the 52nd week and what the cumulative total would be for the year. The next step is to generalize these results for *n* years and see what happens if the scheme is changed to trebling and multiplying by other factors.

A table of values, like that on the left of Figure 11.1, shows the effect of the doubling proposal for the first 7 weeks. It is not difficult for students to observe that the amount is a power of 2 and that the total is 1 less than the next amount, so that the amount in pence for the 52nd week is 2^{51} with a total for the year of $2^{52} - 1$ pence. It is, of course, revealing to calculate how much this is in pounds! The results generalize readily to give:

$$\text{Amount for } n\text{th week} = 2^{n-1}$$
$$\text{Total at } n\text{th week} = 2^n - 1$$

The way these two expressions are verbalized has great potential for confusion: '2 to the power *n* minus 1' needs a significant pause either before or after the *n* depending on the intended meaning. Indeed, the written form can cause confusion because the size and position of the symbols is crucial to the meaning. These are small, but significant, details which do need to be pointed out to students.

Week	Amount	Total
1	1	1
2	2	3
3	4	7
4	8	15
5	16	31
6	32	63
7	64	

Week	Amount	Total
1	1	1
2	3	4
3	9	13
4	27	40
5	81	121
6	243	364
7	729	

Figure 11.1 *The pocket money problem*

The results of trebling are shown in the right-hand table of Figure 11.1. It is easy to see that the amount is given by 3^{n-1}, but annoyingly $3^n - 1$ does not give the correct totals. However, it is not difficult to spot that halving it does produce the correct results so that the total is given by $\frac{1}{2}(3^n - 1)$. This suggests that the corresponding results for quadrupling will be 4^{n-1} and $\frac{1}{3}(4^n - 1)$, which can be checked. This all leads to a pair of general results where *r* denotes the common ratio:

$$\text{Amount for } n\text{th week} = r^{n-1}$$
$$\text{Total at } n\text{th week} = \frac{r^n - 1}{r - 1}$$

The usual formulae for geometric series have now emerged, apart from the need to allow for different initial values. Students will, however, see readily that starting with 50p just means that all the values have to be multiplied by a factor of 50. This helps them to see that for a geometric series with common ratio *r* and first term *a*, the two results become:

$$n\text{th term} = ar^{n-1}$$
$$\text{Sum of the first } n \text{ terms} = \frac{a(r^n - 1)}{r - 1}$$

Letting the two results emerge in this way makes them more meaningful to most students and provides a useful memory peg on which to hang the idea. The teacher can always say: 'geometric series – remember the pocket money problem'. Further reinforcement is given by applying the ideas to a wide variety of problems. For example, regular savings schemes provide an interesting application. Suppose that you save £10 a month for a year in a scheme that pays interest which works out at 0.5 per cent per month. The total amount immediately after the last payment can be expressed as a geometric series and summed as shown below:

$$10 + 10 \times 1.005 + 10 \times 1.005^2 + \ldots + 10 \times 1.005^{11} = \frac{10(1.005^{12} - 1)}{1.005 - 1} \approx 123.34$$

Using an example like the pocket money problem to arrive at results investigatively is very different from the common practice of proving results before using them. When students meet an elaborate argument at the start of a new topic they commonly find it much more difficult to follow than the subsequent application of the results that have been obtained. As a consequence, they often dismiss the proof as irrelevant and concentrate on remembering and using the results, without acquiring a deep understanding. If the ideas are explored in a more informal way first and used to solve some problems, this gives an understanding and familiarity that provides a much better foundation for making sense of the algebraic arguments subsequently used to prove the results.

Finding the nth term of a geometric sequence is directly comparable to the corresponding procedure with an arithmetic sequence and is explained in a similar way, but proving the general formula for the sum of the first n terms requires a more elaborate algebraic argument. A particular numerical case showing how to determine directly the cumulative total for the pocket money problem is a valuable way to show the form of the general argument. In the example that follows, S_7 is used to denote the sum of the first seven amounts. Doubling the terms of the expression for this sum and then subtracting the original expression leads immediately to the required total:

- Sum of first seven terms: $S_7 = 1 + 2 + 2^2 + 2^3 + 2^4 + 2^5 + 2^6$
- Doubling: $2S_7 = 2 + 2^2 + 2^3 + 2^4 + 2^5 + 2^6 + 2^7$
- Subtracting: $S_7 = 2^7 - 1 = 127$

This provides a pattern for a proof of the general case with S_n denoting the sum of the first n terms:

- Sum of first n terms: S_n: $S_n = a + ar + ar^2 + \ldots + ar^{n-2} + ar^{n-1}$
- Multiplying both sides by r : $rS_n = ar + ar^2 + ar^3 + \ldots + ar^{n-1} + ar^n$
- Subtracting: $(r - 1)S_n = a(r^n - 1) \Rightarrow S_n = \dfrac{a(r^n - 1)}{r - 1}$

The most interesting aspect of geometric series is when the value of r is numerically less than 1. Since r^n tends to zero as the number of terms increases, the sum tends to a limiting value of $\frac{a}{1-r}$, usually referred to as the sum to infinity and denoted by S_∞.

A simple example of an infinite geometric series, illustrated by figure 11.2, has $\frac{1}{2}$ as the first term and a common ratio of $\frac{1}{2}$. The square is halved and at each stage the remaining part is halved again leaving a smaller and smaller remaining piece in one corner. It is clear from the

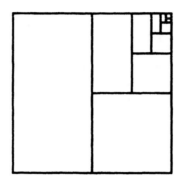

$$\tfrac{1}{2}+\tfrac{1}{2^2}+\tfrac{1}{2^3}+\tfrac{1}{2^4}+\tfrac{1}{2^5}+\tfrac{1}{2^6}+\ldots=\tfrac{1}{2}+\tfrac{1}{4}+\tfrac{1}{8}+\tfrac{1}{16}+\tfrac{1}{32}+\tfrac{1}{64}+\ldots=1$$

Figure 11.2 *Half and half again*

diagram that the sum of the series tends to one. Further reinforcement is provided by calculating the sequence of partial sums and observing how successive terms get closer to one:

$$\tfrac{1}{2},\ \tfrac{3}{4},\ \tfrac{7}{8},\ \tfrac{15}{16},\ \tfrac{31}{32},\ \tfrac{63}{64},\ldots$$

Finally, we can see that this limiting value of one is in agreement with the result obtained by
substituting $a = r = \tfrac{1}{2}$ into the formula $\frac{a}{1-r}$.

Figure 11.3, adapted from a diagram in Nelsen (1993, p. 120), provides a neat visual proof
of the formula for the sum of an infinite geometric series. The point E lies on the side BC of the
square $ABCD$, which has unit sides, and the length BE is denoted by r. A sequence of trapezia
similar to $ABED$ is constructed as shown and then the result follows by considering ratios of
corresponding sides (equivalent to $\tan\theta$ with θ as shown) in the two similar right-angled
triangles CDE and BFE. A diagram constructed using dynamic geometry software is useful
here as a way of demonstrating the effect of moving the point E along the side BC. The more
general formula is obtained by enlarging the diagram by a scale factor of a, which corresponds
to multiplying both sides of the equation by a.

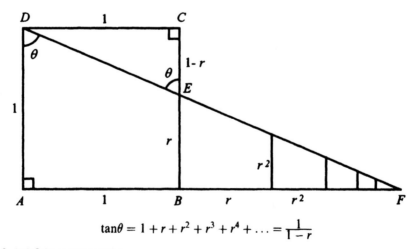

$$\tan\theta = 1 + r + r^2 + r^3 + r^4 + \ldots = \frac{1}{1-r}$$

Figure 11.3 *An infinite geometric series*

Recurring decimals provide an interesting application of geometric series. The formula for the sum to infinity can be used to convert the decimal form to the corresponding rational form. For the example of $0.\dot{3}\dot{6}$ shown below the common ratio, r, is 0.01 with 0.36 as the first term, a:

$$0.\dot{3}\dot{6} = 0.36 + 0.0036 + 0.000036 + \ldots = \frac{0.36}{1 - 0.01} = \frac{36}{99} = \frac{4}{11}$$

The idea of a sequence approaching a limit was discussed in Chapter 7 in conjunction with iterative procedures for solving equations. Infinite geometric series provide students with example of the important idea of the limit of a sequence because the sum to infinity is the limit of a sequence of partial sums. Infinite series of many different kinds are of general importance in mathematics. They provide many interesting insights into the curious and fascinating world of the infinite.

SIGMA NOTATION AND STATISTICAL FORMULAE

Arithmetic sequences provide a simple context for introducing the ideas of sigma notation with Σ used as a shorthand for the phrase 'the sum of the first n terms'. Extending the notation to include the limits above and below the Σ symbol only becomes necessary when there might be ambiguity about the number of terms involved in the sum. The sum of the natural numbers, introduced through the triangle numbers in Chapter 3, can be denoted by Σi, where i is a 'formula' for the general term:

$$1 + 2 + 3 + 4 + 5 + \ldots + n = \Sigma i = \tfrac{1}{2}n(n + 1)$$

This then gives an alternative way of arriving at the sum of an arithmetic sequence. In the first section of this chapter we considered an arithmetic sequence with 5 as the first term and a common difference of 7. The general term of the sequence was shown to be $7n - 2$, so that the sum to n terms could be denoted by $\Sigma(7i - 2)$, but the reason for changing the letter for the variable needs to be made clear, pointing out the need for an expression for a general term that is independent of n, the number of terms. The expression can be expanded as follows:

$$\Sigma(7i - 2) = 7\Sigma i - \Sigma 2 = 7\Sigma i - 2n$$

Some further explanation is clearly needed of the two facts: $\Sigma 7i = 7\Sigma i$ and $\Sigma 2 = 2n$, which can be done by looking at the structure of the first few terms of the sequence expressed in the same form as the general term $7i - 2$:

$$7 \times 1 - 2 = 5$$
$$7 \times 2 - 2 = 12$$
$$7 \times 3 - 2 = 19$$
$$7 \times 4 - 2 = 26$$
$$7 \times 5 - 2 = 33$$

It is then easy to see that the two columns of terms correspond respectively to $\Sigma 7i = 7\Sigma i$ and $\Sigma 2 = 2n$. Substituting the triangle number formula for Σi leads to a formula for the sum to n terms:

$$7\Sigma i - 2n = \tfrac{7}{2}n(n + 1) - 2n = \tfrac{1}{2}n(7n + 3)$$

Another nice example that uses the same principle is the fact that the sum of consecutive odd numbers is the square of the number of terms, referred to previously in Chapter 3. This is proved easily as follows:

$$\Sigma(2i - 1) = 2\Sigma i - \Sigma 1 = n(n + 1) - n = n^2$$

The sum of an arithmetic series can be found easily without using sigma notation, but the procedures involved are an important tool for handling most other types of sequence and are used very widely in statistics. Sigma notation is in fact most commonly first encountered in the context of statistical formulae, where Σx is used to stand for 'the sum of a set of data values which have been denoted by the variable x'. It is then incorporated into a formula for the mean of a data set as $\frac{\Sigma x}{n}$, where n is the number of values in the set. When frequencies are involved, with values denoted by f, the formula for the mean becomes elaborated to $\frac{\Sigma f x}{n}$. A corresponding simple formula for standard deviation, with $\bar{x}$ denoting the mean, takes either of the forms

$$\sqrt{\frac{\Sigma(x - \bar{x})^2}{n}} \quad \text{or} \quad \sqrt{\frac{\Sigma x^2}{n} - \bar{x}^2},$$

with similar results incorporating frequencies.

The idea of standard deviation and the two alternative formulae noted above make much better sense if they are introduced using sets of small numbers. The purpose of standard deviation is to compare the spread of different data sets, so let us compare the first five odd numbers 1, 3, 5, 7, and 9 and the five consecutive numbers 3, 4, 5, 6 and 7. Both sets have a mean of 5, but in the first case the squares of the deviations from the mean is $16 + 4 + 0 + 4 + 16 = 40$ and in the second case it is $4 + 1 + 0 + 1 + 4 = 10$. Dividing by 5 and taking the square root gives values of $2\sqrt{2}$ and $\sqrt{2}$, respectively, for the standard deviations. The first is double the second as might be expected by comparing the spreads of the two data sets.

Using the alternative formula has little advantage here because the numbers are simple, but it is instructive to see how the calculation proceeds and to be reassured by arriving at the same results as before. In the case of the odd numbers the sum of the squares is $1 + 9 + 25 + 49 + 81 = 165$. Dividing by 5 to get 33 and then subtracting 25, the square of the mean, gives 8 whose square root is indeed $2\sqrt{2}$. The other result, $\sqrt{2}$, follows in the same way.

Proving that the two formulae for standard deviation are equivalent is a useful exercise in algebraic manipulation involving sigma notation:

$$\frac{\Sigma(x-\bar{x})^2}{n} = \frac{\Sigma(x^2 - 2x\bar{x} + \bar{x}^2)}{n} = \frac{\Sigma x^2}{n} - 2\bar{x}^2 + \bar{x}^2 = \frac{\Sigma x^2}{n} - \bar{x}^2$$

The second step depends on the two simplifications shown below, which both depend on understanding the distributive property of sigma notation and realizing that the mean has to be treated as a constant:

$$2\bar{x}\frac{\Sigma x}{n} = 2\bar{x}^2 \quad \text{and} \quad \frac{\Sigma \bar{x}^2}{n} = \frac{n\bar{x}^2}{n} = \bar{x}^2$$

Success with simplification like this is much more likely if students have mastered the ideas of sigma notation in the context of the simpler examples like those linked to arithmetic sequences in the first part of this section. In the early stages of learning statistics, the over-complication in the use of sigma notation in statistical formulae that is sometimes a feature of textbook introductions is confusing to the student and quite unnecessary. Sigma notation is a valuable tool and confidence in its use should be developed over a period of time with extra refinements introduced only when there is a clear need for them.

SUMS OF SQUARES AND CUBES

The formulae for the sums of the squares and cubes of the natural numbers are both useful and interesting, but students often see them as yet more results to remember and acquire little sense of where they come from or what they mean. Both results can be demonstrated in a variety of different ways, which can add both interest and insight. The ideas that follow, taken from French (1990), are similar to some of those that appear in Nelsen (1993), a particularly rich source of pictorial proofs.

The formula for the sum of the cubes can be derived from a table of values as shown in Figure 11.4. The numbers in the last column are square numbers, which very conveniently turn out to be the squares of the triangle numbers. It is therefore a simple matter to obtain the formula by squaring $\frac{1}{2}n(n + 1)$, the formula for Σi. Although it is easy to derive the formula in this way, the method gives little insight into why it takes this form and it certainly does not constitute a proof. There are many ways of obtaining greater insight and, following our customary strategy, let us begin by posing a problem.

n	n^3	$\Sigma i^3 = (\Sigma i)^2$
1	1	$1 = 1^2$
2	8	$9 = 3^2$
3	27	$36 = 6^2$
4	64	$100 = 10^2$
5	125	$225 = 15^2$
6	216	$441 = 21^2$

$$\Sigma i^3 = 1^3 + 2^3 + 3^3 + 4^3 + 5^3 + \ldots = (\Sigma i)^2 = \tfrac{1}{4}n^2(n + 1)^2$$

Figure 11.4 *The sum of the cubes of the natural numbers*

It is an interesting challenge for students to calculate the sum of all the numbers in a multiplication table square. Figure 11.5 shows a six by six square with the rows in the left hand table highlighted by shading and the sum of the numbers in each row shown alongside. Each row total is a multiple of 21, which is the sum of the top row and the sixth triangle number. The total number of 21s is $1 + 2 + 3 + 4 + 5 + 6$, which is 21 again. So the overall total is 21^2, which is 441 as obtained previously in the table of values. This result generalizes readily: the sum of the numbers in a multiplication table square is given by the square of the corresponding triangle number or $(\Sigma i)^2$.

The right-hand table squares have been shaded to indicate squares in the form of a reversed letter L and the sum of the numbers in each is shown to the left. Rather strikingly, these are cubes, so that the total for the whole square is Σi^3, a result which again readily generalizes. The two different ways of summing the numbers in the square provides a very neat illustration of the identity $\Sigma i^3 = (\Sigma i)^2$, which gives the formula for the sum of the cubes, $\frac{1}{4}n^2(n + 1)^2$.

It is not immediately obvious why the sum of the numbers in the reversed Ls should be

1	2	3	4	5	6
2	4	6	8	10	12
3	6	9	12	15	18
4	8	12	16	20	24
5	10	15	20	25	30
6	12	18	24	30	36

21
42
63
84
105
126
‾‾‾
441

1
8
27
64
125
216
‾‾‾
441

1	2	3	4	5	6
2	4	6	8	10	12
3	6	9	12	15	18
4	8	12	16	20	24
5	10	15	20	25	30
6	12	18	24	30	36

Figure 11.5 *The sum of the numbers in a multiplication table square*

cubes. One way of seeing this surprising fact is to note that any one of the reversed Ls is the difference of the squares of two consecutive triangle numbers, because the sum of the numbers in the multiplication square is the square of a triangle number. If the nth triangle number is denoted by T_n and the one before by T_{n-1}, then two simple properties of triangle numbers, which are demonstrated pictorially in Figure 11.6 and may be proved using the two formulae $\frac{1}{2}n(n+1)$ and $\frac{1}{2}n(n-1)$, show directly that the difference of the squares is a cube:

$$T_n - T_{n-1} = n \text{ and } T_n + T_{n-1} = n^2 \;\Rightarrow\; T_n^2 - T_{n-1}^2 = n^3$$

Unlike the sum of the cubes, a table of values does not make it at all obvious what the formula for the sum of the squares of the natural numbers might be. Some textbooks suggest that the numbers in the last column of Figure 11.7 should be multiplied by six to make it easier to spot a pattern, but why should we choose to multiply by six apart from knowing in advance that it leads to the right answer?

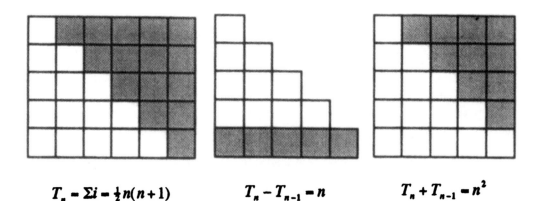

$$T_n = \Sigma i = \tfrac{1}{2}n(n+1) \qquad\qquad T_n - T_{n-1} = n \qquad\qquad T_n + T_{n-1} = n^2$$

Figure 11.6 *Some properties of triangle numbers*

n	n^2	Σi^2
1	1	1
2	4	5
3	9	14
4	16	30
5	25	55

$$\Sigma i^2 = 1^2 + 2^2 + 3^2 + 4^2 + 5^2 + \ldots = \tfrac{1}{6}n(n+1)(2n+1)$$

Figure 11.7 *The sum of the squares of the natural numbers*

A model using coloured cubes is a good way of representing the sum of the squares. The squares form the layers of a skewed pyramid, with the case of $n = 3$ shown on the left in Figure 11.8. Rather like the step diagram used in Figure 11.6 to show the formula for the triangle numbers, six of these pyramids fit together as shown on the right to make a cuboid with dimensions 3 by 4 by 7. This generalizes readily to give $n(n+1)(2n+1)$, where n is the height of the cuboid, $n + 1$ is its width and $2n + 1$ is the length with the central stepped portion contributing the 1 with a length of n on each side. This provides an ingenious pictorial proof, which both explains the mysterious six and the general structure of the otherwise rather obscure-looking formula:

$$\Sigma i^2 = \tfrac{1}{6}n(n+1)(2n+1).$$

There are many other related formulae which can be demonstrated using models and diagrams, but it is also important to develop algebraic skills to derive results. The three formulae

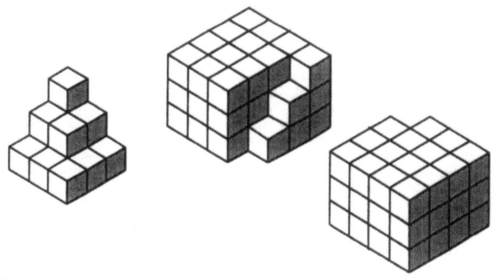

Figure 11.8 *Six pyramids to make a cuboid*

for Σi, Σi^2 and Σi^3 do not display any obvious common pattern that might help in predicting Σi^4 and subsequent results. However, there is an obvious pattern in the results for Σi, $\Sigma i(i + 1)$, $\Sigma i(i + 1)(i + 2)$ which does generalize:

$$\Sigma i = \tfrac{1}{2}n(n + 1)$$

$$\Sigma i(i + 1) = \tfrac{1}{3}n(n + 1)(n + 2)$$

$$\Sigma i(i + 1)(i + 2) = \tfrac{1}{4}n(n + 1)(n + 2)(n + 3)$$

Finding the formula for the second of these provides a good exercise in algebraic manipulation and brings out well the virtues of seeking common factors in the course of simplifying complicated expressions:

$$\Sigma i(i + 1) = \Sigma i^2 + \Sigma i$$

$$= \tfrac{1}{6}n(n + 1)(2n + 1) + \tfrac{1}{2}n(n + 1)$$

$$= \tfrac{1}{6}n(n + 1)(2n + 1 + 3)$$

$$= \tfrac{1}{6}n(n + 1)(2n + 4)$$

$$= \tfrac{1}{3}n(n + 1)(n + 2)$$

Additionally, $\Sigma i(i + 1)$ can be represented by a model. The two constituent elements are the skew pyramid for Σi^2 and the step model of a triangle number for Σi. Three pyramids fit together to make the solid in the middle diagram Figure 11.8. With the addition of three additional triangle numbers, like the steps on the right of the block, it is easy to create a cuboid to represent $n(n + 1)(n + 2)$.

This section has shown that the formulae for sums of squares and cubes are more than obscure symbolic forms. Different ways of representing them numerically and pictorially serve to make them much more interesting and meaningful, besides providing plenty of opportunity for exercising algebraic and other mathematical skills.

CONCLUSION

Sequences and series are mathematical ideas with a range of applications at different levels including links to the intriguing world of the infinite where numbers become very large or very small and lead to the important idea of limit. A number of significant issues in teaching and learning algebra have arisen which reinforce and build on ideas from earlier chapters about giving greater meaning and purpose to algebra by avoiding over-complication and using a variety of approaches that provide memorable concrete numerical and geometrical images.

Finding the nth term of a sequence and the sum of the first n terms of a series are the two key problems. In the case of arithmetic sequences and series the formulae should arise, and be frequently reinforced, by expressing them in a verbal form which refers back to their underlying meaning and structure. The expression $a + (n - 1)d$ is the first term plus $n - 1$ gaps, or jumps, to take you to the nth term, and the sum, $\tfrac{1}{2}n(a + l)$, is the mean, or average, term multiplied by the number of terms, a structure that can be demonstrated both numerically and by using variations on the step model of a triangle number.

With geometric sequences and series, the difficulty comes with the formula for the sum. Establishing this with an investigative approach linked to a problem, like the pocket-money problem, is more motivating than an initial formal derivation and provides a better foundation for making sense of a formal proof since some familiarity with the result has been developed. Examples using the sum to infinity can be illustrated geometrically in a variety of ways as a way of adding insight and interest.

Σ notation is a valuable tool in representing and manipulating series of all kinds, but it needs to be introduced and used judiciously so that procedures are understood and the meaning of expressions is not lost. From this perspective, statistical applications may not be the best medium for the first encounter with Σ!

The three formulae for Σi, Σi^2 and Σi^3 offer a particularly rich field for using numerical patterns and two- and three-dimensional diagrams to illustrate algebraic ideas and enhance understanding. Representations of this kind are an attractive and memorable way to exercise algebraic skills and maintain the link between algebra and both numbers and geometry.

The topic of sequences and series, besides bringing together a multiplicity of algebraic ideas, has also brought together a number of important principles of effective algebra teaching, which are summarized below.

- Start with a problem to give a sense of purpose, to develop thinking skills and to provide a memory peg, which can be referred back to.
- Make the meaning of expressions and the structure and steps of arguments clear through an awareness of common misconceptions and sources of difficulty.
- Avoid over-complication by introducing formulae and their refinements only when there is an obvious need for them.
- Use numerical patterns and examples both to demonstrate new ideas and to reinforce the structure of formulae.
- Enhance understanding, and memory, by illustrating algebraic results with diagrams and models.
- Provide challenging problems and proofs to make students think.

Chapter 12

The Calculus: Differentiation and Integration

There is no part of mathematics for which the methods of approach and development are more important than the calculus ... the early development must be gradual ... it will be found that pupils who have learnt to apply processes mechanically are mystified by the principles, and are therefore liable to serious error in any matter that is slightly outside the usual routine. (The Teaching of Calculus in Schools, Mathematical Association, 1951)

ALGEBRA AND CALCULUS

Since the calculus is far too big a subject to discuss in a single chapter in a book on algebra, I have chosen to use this final chapter to exemplify the ideas about teaching and learning algebra developed in this book by discussing some selected aspects of the calculus and its application to problems.

Derivatives and integrals are concerned with two very important ideas: the gradient of a curve, with its links to rate of change, and the area under a curve with its links to summation. It is customary to introduce derivatives before integrals, but practice varies with regard to the approach to integration. One approach is to define it as an anti-derivative and then to show that it can be used to determine the area under a curve. The idea of an anti-derivative is obviously relevant when it comes to differential equations, but it does not seem to be the obvious starting point for considering integrals because it lacks an immediate purpose. The other approach is to define integrals directly in terms of the area under a curve and then let it emerge that the process of finding an integral is the reverse of finding a derivative. This second approach has the considerable merit of letting the link between differentiation and integration, the fundamental theorem of the calculus, emerge as a surprise. It does seem rather unlikely that there should be a simple connection between the two very different concepts of the gradient of a curve and the area under a curve and this is brought out much more forcibly if the two ideas are developed independently.

As with algebra generally it is very easy for calculus to become a set of results and procedures which students practise through formal exercises and apply to standard types of problem. The quote from the Mathematical Association (1951) that heads this chapter highlights the importance of understanding where results come from and what they mean if they are to be applied successfully to new situations. Unfortunately, assessment items are usually concerned with skills and standard applications rather than deeper understanding and, as a consequence, these commonly become the sole focus for student and teacher. It is indeed much more difficult to assess students' conceptual understanding and some might argue that the important thing is to be able to use calculus effectively as a tool. The physicist and engineer, Sylvanus Thompson, in his classic book *Calculus Made Easy* (Thompson and Gardner, 1999), originally published in 1910, was outspoken in his criticism of what he saw as an over-rigorous approach to the calculus on the part of mathematicians. None the less, he went to considerable pains to present the ideas in ways that made it clear where they came from and what they meant, as well as how they could be used. Current school calculus textbooks invariably provide a careful introduction to the subject, but for many students this is either neglected, because it is considered difficult, or else there is no subsequent reinforcement of underlying principles after a suitable beginning. Practising and using results rapidly tend to become the sole tasks.

Success with calculus is very dependent on algebraic understanding and fluency, particularly in relation to graphs and the properties of different functions, and the key underlying concept of a limit. Informal work related to the significance of the gradient of a curve and the area under a curve is also important. The use of a motion-sensing device with younger students in conjunction with distance–time graphs has been described in Chapter 6 as a valuable way of giving a qualitative feel to the link between gradient and velocity. Interpreting the area under a simple velocity–time graph as distance travelled can similarly be considered well before the idea of integration is introduced.

Shuard and Neill (1977) provide a very thorough discussion for teachers of the ideas that should be encountered before the calculus is introduced, although the book obviously did not take account of the possibilities of more recent technology. In a subsequent book (Shuard and Neill, 1982), there is an extensive review of the school calculus curriculum with an emphasis on introductory approaches with a strong numerical basis using the calculators and computers that were available at that time. Innovative software packages produced by Tall (1986) linked numerical and graphical approaches and opened the way to the more powerful possibilities available using today's calculators and computers. However, technology does not solve all the problems and needs to be used judiciously to help students come to understand the underlying ideas and the use of algebra in representing and applying them.

GRADIENT FUNCTIONS

Students who have followed an elementary course in calculus are always very familiar with the fact that when $y = x^2$, the derivative $\frac{dy}{dx} = 2x$. They should know that it tells them the gradient of the curve, and that in general this enables them to find the turning points on a curve where it is zero and the rate of change in appropriate applications. They will be able to determine the derivatives of various functions with some degree of fluency, but they are invariably less confident, or even totally ignorant, about where the results come from. As I have suggested in the previous section, the underlying ideas which relate to a limiting process are important and should be emphasized in the introductory stages and subsequently reinforced.

Looking at the behaviour of the gradient as you move along a graph gives a feel for the meaning of a derivative as a gradient function. Using a straight edge as the tangent to a graph, students can be asked to observe and describe the way the gradient changes as the straight edge is moved along the curve. From this a graph of the gradient function can be sketched. This is

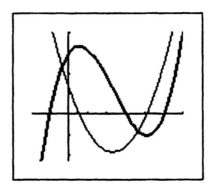

Figure 12.1 *Graphing the gradient function*

illustrated with the graph shown in bold in Figure 12.1, by noting the two points where the gradient of the bold curve is zero, and then considering how the gradient changes and where it is positive and negative. After discussion of an example, students can be asked to produce sketches for a selection of graphs for themselves without any mention of the equations of the curves at this stage. Some graph plotters have a facility to plot gradient functions, but to get a feel for what is happening it is much better to first arrive at a sketch by thinking about the behaviour and only then to pose the problem of finding an equation for the graph of the gradient function.

The next step is to determine the precise form of the gradient function for a given function, so we need some method of calculating the gradient at a point on a curve. Successive approximations tending to a limiting value provide a way of doing this. Let us consider the gradient at the point P with co-ordinates (3,9) on the curve $f(x) = x^2$, as shown in Figure 12.2. If Q is the point (4,16), then the gradient of PQ is $\frac{16-9}{4-3} = 7$. The gradient of PQ is greater than the gradient of the tangent to the curve at P, but the value of 7 gives a crude approximation to the gradient at P.

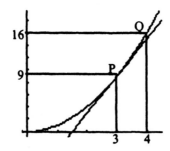

Figure 12.2 *Finding the gradient at a point on a curve*

We get a better approximation by taking a point Q which is closer to P. With an x coordinate of 3.1 the co-ordinates of Q are (3.1,9.61) and then the gradient of PQ is calculated as $\frac{9.61-9}{3.1-3} = 6.1$. It is arduous to do a lot of calculations like this, which means that it is sensible to mechanize the process, something that can be done in a variety of different ways using a calculator or a computer.

	A	B	C
1	x	h	Gradient
2	3	1	7.0000
3	3	0.1	6.1000
4	3	0.01	6.0100
5	3	0.001	6.0010
6	3	0.0001	6.0001

Figure 12.3 *Using a spreadsheet to find a gradient*

Figure 12.3 shows a spreadsheet that has been set up to find approximations to the gradient of $f(x) = x^2$ at a general point, using an interval of width h and seeing what happens as h gets closer to zero. To generate the numbers in the third column of the spreadsheet, the formula for the gradient of a line joining a pair of points on the graph is required:

$$\text{Gradient} = \frac{(x+h)^2 - x^2}{h}$$

It is unfortunate that spreadsheet notation is not quite the same as conventional algebraic notation, but students who are familiar with spreadsheets do not find it unduly difficult to translate this into ((A2 + B2)^2 − A2^2)/B2 to go into cell C2. Creating a spreadsheet provides a strong motivation for introducing a formula for the gradient which is a step away from the general result:

$$\text{Gradient} = \frac{f(x+h) - f(x)}{h}$$

Besides showing the gradient tending to the limit of 6, as in Figure 12.3, the great beauty of this spreadsheet is that it is a simple matter to change the value of both h in cell B2, as shown in Figure 12.4, and also x in cell A2, to see how the sequence changes to suggest a value for the gradient each time.

	A	B	C
1	x	h	Gradient
2	3	-1	5.0000
3	3	-0.1	5.9000
4	3	-0.01	5.9900
5	3	-0.001	5.9990
6	3	-0.0001	5.9999

Figure 12.4 *Negative values of the interval*

Following some investigation it is easy to see that the gradient appears to be given by $2x$. Why this should be so can be seen by simplifying the expression used for the gradient column:

$$\text{Gradient} = \frac{(x+h)^2 - x^2}{h} = \frac{2xh + h^2}{h} = 2x + h$$

The algebraic simplification involved here is not in any way difficult. The meaning of the formula is reinforced by the numerical approach and the simplified form corresponds neatly to the results that have been generated. There are serious problems here, concerned with what happens when the value of h is zero. We appear to be considering that possibility and yet at an earlier stage substituting $h = 0$ would lead to the worrying fraction $\frac{0}{0}$. To avoid dividing by zero we have divided by h first and then set it to be zero, something which seems somewhat questionable – although it seems to produce sensible answers! This matter took a long time and much controversy before it was resolved by mathematicians, but it should be pointed out to students as a fascinating dilemma for them to take up again later.

Having reached this stage, the way is open to generate all the standard results by looking graphically, numerically and algebraically at $f(x) = x^n$ for different values of n to show that the derivative of $f(x) = x^n$ is $f'(x) = nx^{n-1}$ and seeing how this extends to general polynomial functions.

The introduction here of the symbol $f'(x)$ to denote the derivative of the function $f(x)$ raises the question of notation. Students need to become familiar with both forms for the derivative – $f'(x)$ and $\frac{dy}{dx}$. Both are in common use and have their respective merits, but which should come first is open to debate. I would argue that it avoids additional complication at an introductory stage to use h to denote a small interval rather than the more difficult δx or dx. Whenever $\frac{dy}{dx}$ is seen for the first time it must be pointed out that it is not a fraction in the normal sense – the ds may not be cancelled as if they were a conventional variable!

AREA UNDER A CURVE

The approximate area under a graph can be found by dividing it into a number of strips and calculating the area of each by considering it as a rectangle. This can be done in several different ways: the two diagrams of Figure 12.5 show the area under $f(x) = x^2$ approximated by five upper and five lower rectangles, which give very poor estimates above and below the correct value, as follows:

$$\begin{aligned}
\text{Area of upper rectangles} &= 0.2(0.2^2 + 0.4^2 + 0.6^2 + 0.8^2 + 1^2) \\
&= 0.2^3(1^2 + 2^2 + 3^2 + 4^2 + 5^2) \\
&= 0.44 \\
\text{Area of lower rectangles} &= 0.2(0^2 + 0.2^2 + 0.4^2 + 0.6^2 + 0.8^2) \\
&= 0.2^3(0^2 + 1^2 + 2^2 + 3^2 + 4^2) \\
&= 0.24
\end{aligned}$$

A much better estimate of 0.34 is obtained by taking the mean of these two values. This is equivalent to using a trapezium to approximate the area of each strip, the method known as the trapezium rule. Alternatively, the accuracy can be improved by increasing the number of strips, but this requires lengthy calculations so that a calculator or computer is an appropriate tool. A spreadsheet or a program of some kind are two ways of doing this: I have chosen here to use some of the symbolic facilities of a TI-92 calculator.

The sum of the upper rectangles for the area under the graph of $f(x)$ between $x = 0$ and $x = a$ with strips of width h is given by the expression $\Sigma h f(x)$. The products $h f(x)$ give the area of each rectangle. If there are n strips, then $h = \frac{a}{n}$, and the values of x corresponding to each upper rectangle are given by hi, where i takes values from 1 to n. For the lower rectangles, the corresponding values of x are given by $h(i - 1)$.

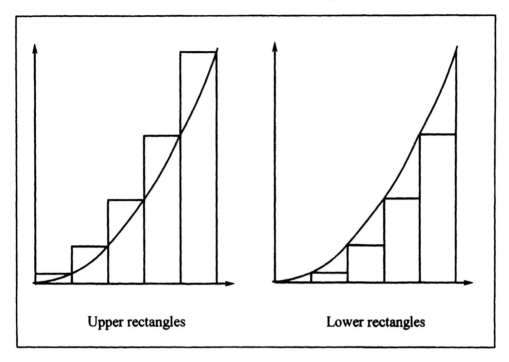

Figure 12.5 *Upper and lower rectangles to find an approximate area*

On the first screen in Figure 12.6, the function $f(x)$ has been defined as x^2 and an area function, area (a,n), has been defined to calculate the area of n upper rectangles with the upper limit set at a. Two values for the area between $x = 0$ and $x = 1$, using 10 and 100 strips, are displayed. On the second screen, the area function has been modified to give the corresponding results for lower rectangles. Note that in this case the screen is not wide enough to simultaneously dislay the whole of the definition. Again, the mean of corresponding results, equivalent to using the trapezium rule, gives better approximations.

At a later stage, the area functions can be changed to area(a,b,n) for a general pair of limits $x = a$ and $x = b$ by setting $h = \frac{b-a}{n}$ and $x = a + hi$ or $x = a + h(i - 1)$.

Figure 12.7 shows similar results using an alternative area function, the mid-ordinate rule, which gives a very good approximation to the area under a curve. The heights of the rectangular strips are taken at the mid-points of each interval. Determining the definition of the area function is an interesting algebraic task, which is aided by seeing that the x coordinates of the midpoints are given by $\frac{1}{2}h$, $\frac{3}{2}h$, $\frac{5}{2}h$, and so on.

Having established a suitable means of calculating approximate areas, students can be set a task like that shown in Figure 12.8, which asks them to investigate numerically the areas under the graphs of simple functions of the form $y = x^n$, where n is a natural number. The questions ask them to look at the effect of varying the number of strips and, importantly, to explain their results in graphical terms.

I have found that students using such a task readily establish the standard result that the area under the graph of $y = x^n$ between $x = 0$ and $x = a$ is given by $\frac{a^{n+1}}{n+1}$, whilst seeing a limiting process in action through increasing the number of strips. Questions 5 and 6 look at the effect on the area and the corresponding area formulae of translating and stretching the

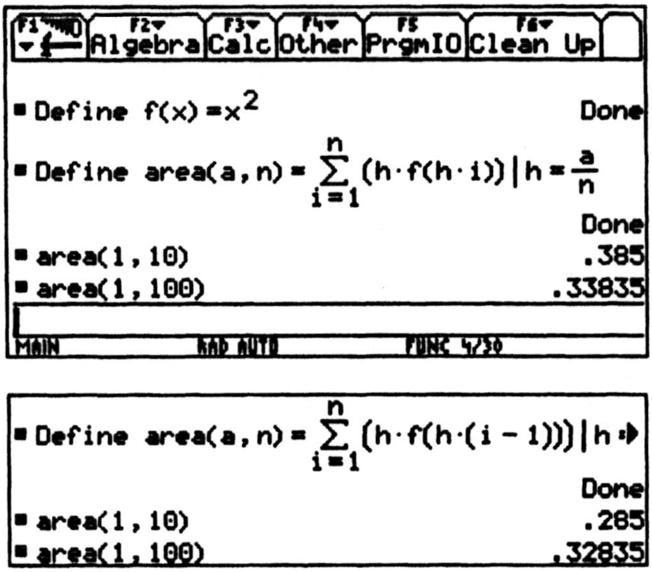

Figure 12.6 *Calculating area under a curve with a TI-92 calculator*

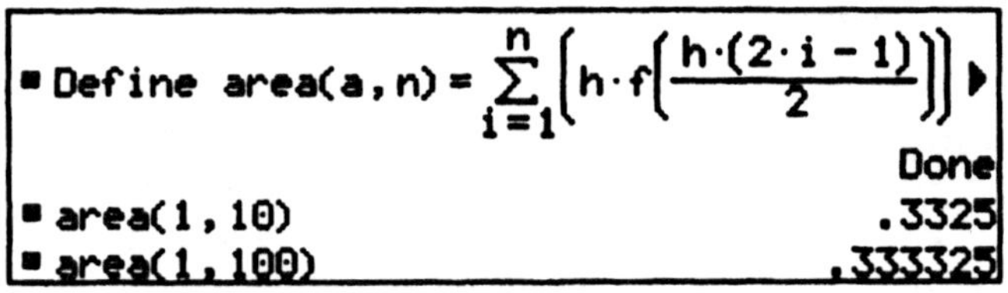

Figure 12.7 *Using the mid-ordinate rule to find approximate areas*

curves. As a leading example at this stage, students might be asked to sketch a graph and suggest a formula for the area under $y = 8x - x^2$ between $x = 0$ and $x = 8$, comparing the values given by their formula and by a numerical approximation. This leads on naturally to the application of the ideas to general polynomial functions and the introduction of standard notation for integration with areas between a general pair of limits, including negative values, and areas below the x axis. The ideas can then be applied to a wide variety of problems, extended to other functions, and the all-important link with derivatives established.

Approaching integration by using a numerical limiting process gives students a good initial sense of how integration formulae arise and what they mean. It also makes a strong link between the integral symbol, $\int$, from S for sum, and sigma, Σ, denoting summation. As with derivatives, the notation for integration can seem very strange and arbitrary. Furthermore, a good basis is established for students to make sense of an algebraic derivation of the results that have been determined numerically, something which is commonly regarded as difficult. A simple presentation, like the following for the integral of x^2, uses the formula for Σi^2, discussed in Chapter 11, and builds on the ideas of this section:

Finding Approximate Areas under Curves using Numerical Methods

Sketch graphs to illustrate your results for each question.

1. Find the area under the graph of $y = x^2$ between $x = 0$ and $x = 1$, by trying different values of n. What does the exact area appear to be?

2. Find the area under $y = x^2$ between $x = 0$ and $x = a$ for values of a from 0 to 5. Think carefully about appropriate values of n to use to maintain suitable accuracy as the number of strips increases. What simple fractions are approximately equal to your decimal answers? Suggest a formula for the area under the curve in terms of a.

3. Investigate some other simple functions such as x^3 and x^4 in the same way and try to find formulae.

4. Find formulae for the areas under $y = x$ and under $y = 1$ from $x = 0$ to $x = a$, without using a calculator.

5. Investigate areas under $y = x^2 + c$ for various values of c and compare these with the corresponding areas under $y = x^2$. Explain what happens with the aid of graphs.

6. Investigate areas under $y = kx^2$ in a similar way for various values of k.

Figure 12.8 *An introductory task on integration*

$$\text{Area of } \textit{upper} \text{ rectangles} = \frac{a}{n}\left[\left(\frac{a}{n}\right)^2 + \left(\frac{2a}{n}\right)^2 + \ldots + \left(\frac{na}{n}\right)^2\right]$$

$$= \frac{a^3}{n^3}\left[1^2 + 2^2 + \ldots + n^2\right]$$

$$= \frac{a^3}{n^3}\tfrac{1}{6}n(n+1)(2n+1) \text{ since } \sum_{i=1}^{n} i^2 = \tfrac{1}{6}n(n+1)(2n+1)$$

$$= \frac{a^3}{6}\left(1 + \tfrac{1}{n}\right)\left(2 + \tfrac{1}{n}\right)$$

$$\to \frac{a^3}{3} \text{ from } \textit{above} \text{ as } n \to \infty$$

If the same process is applied to the lower rectangles the last step becomes

$$\frac{b^3}{6}\left(1 - \tfrac{1}{n}\right)\left(2 - \tfrac{1}{n}\right) \to \frac{b^3}{3} \text{ from } \textit{below} \text{ as } n \to \infty$$

This neatly illustrates the way that the area is sandwiched between two values which converge to the same limit from above and below.

The introductory stages of learning about both derivatives and integrals are very important in establishing a sound basis for further developments. Calculus can so easily become a matter of remembering and applying a set of standard procedures and yet it is not difficult to use numerical and graphical approaches to give a feel for the underlying ideas, including an understanding of algebraic approaches to the limiting processes.

RADIANS AND CIRCULAR FUNCTIONS

Radians, as a measure for angle, seem like an unnecessary complication to students unless they appreciate that they are a vital simplifying idea in extending the calculus to circular functions. It is therefore important to emphasize the role of radians when the derivative of the sine function is introduced. By using a straight edge as a tangent to a sine curve, it is easy to see that the gradient function looks like a cosine curve, but it is necessary to establish that its value at $x = 0$ is 1 and that the curve is actually what it appears to be. The value at $x = 0$ is the gradient of the sine curve at the origin.

If radians have been introduced beforehand, an interesting approach is to plot the graph of the sine function, $f(x) = \sin x$, and then to superimpose the graph of an approximate gradient function, $g(x) = \frac{\sin(x+h)-\sin(x)}{h}$, using a small value such as 0.1 for h. As Figure 12.9 shows, this approximates very closely to the graph of $\cos(x)$, which is further reinforced by considering smaller values of h. Repeating this exercise with the graph plotter set in degrees demonstrates clearly that working in degrees is a much less convenient proposition!

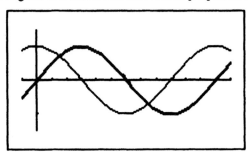

Figure 12.9 *Graphing the gradient function for sine*

The immediate advantage of using radians is that the gradient of the sine curve at the origin is 1. An approximation for this gradient at the origin is given by $\frac{\sin h}{h}$, when h is small, and it is instructive to evaluate it for increasingly small values of h comparing the effect of using both degrees and radians. The usual way of determining the precise limiting value is to use the sector of a circle with unit radius shown in the left-hand diagram of Figure 12.10. If the angle h is small and measured in degrees, the arc length, $AB = \frac{\pi h}{180}$, is approximately equal to the perpendicular, $AC = \sin h$. It then follows that $\frac{\sin h}{h} \approx \frac{\pi}{180}$. However, if h is measured in radians $AB = h$ and $\frac{\sin h}{h} \approx 1$. The right-hand diagram of Figure 12.10, showing the tangent to the sine curve at the origin, helps to make it clear why radians are defined by saying π radians are equivalent to 180°.

The limiting value of $\frac{\sin h}{h}$ also arises when we prove algebraically that the derivative of $\sin x$ is $\cos x$. For this purpose, it is simpler to use an alternative form for the gradient of a line joining two points on a curve, namely:

$$\text{Gradient} = \frac{f(x+h) - f(x-h)}{2h}$$

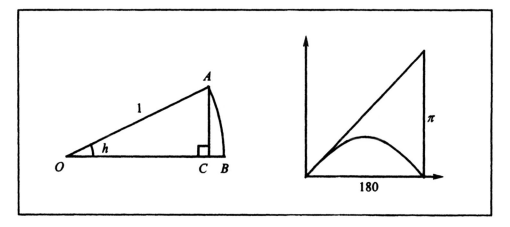

Figure 12.10 *The gradient of the sine curve at the origin*

This is applied to the sine function, as follows:

$$\text{Gradient} = \frac{\sin(x + h) - \sin(x - h)}{2h}$$

$$= \frac{(\sin x \cos h + \cos x \sin h) - (\sin x \cos h - \cos x \sin h)}{2h}$$

$$= \frac{\cos x \sin h}{h}$$

$$\rightarrow \cos x \text{ as } h \rightarrow 0, \text{ since } \frac{\sin h}{h} \rightarrow 1$$

This section only touches on a few aspects of calculus involving circular functions, but it does serve to illustrate ways in which students can be given a feel for the underlying ideas through the interplay between numerical, graphical and algebraic approaches. It also shows the way in which an algebraic argument like that shown above, although brief, is dependent at each step on a deep understanding of a whole range of ideas. If students are to make sense of such arguments it is essential to develop their understanding of these ideas before bringing them together, but also to further review what they mean as the argument is developed. However, in constructing and in making sense of any mathematical argument, the details must not detract from an understanding of the whole argument. It is always important to be able to see the wood as well as the trees.

EXPONENTIAL AND LOGARITHMIC FUNCTIONS

The derivative of the exponential function can be approached in a similar way to that of sine. Figure 12.11 shows the graphs of the two exponential or growth functions 2^x and 3^x. It is easy to see, by using the straight edge as tangent technique, that their gradient functions will also be growth functions with a similar form and that the gradient of the curves when $x = 0$ will be a significant parameter.

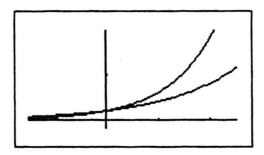

Figure 12.11 *The graph of* 2^x *and* 3^x

Using the formula $\frac{f(x+h)-f(x)}{h}$ to find the gradient function for $f(x) = 2^x$ gives:

$$\frac{2^{x+h} - 2^x}{h} = \frac{2^x(2^h - 1)}{h}$$

At $x = 0$, this takes the value $\frac{2^h-1}{h}$, which can be evaluated by substituting small values of h to determine the limiting value to a suitable number of decimal places. In the case of 2^x, the value is 0.69 to 2 decimal places and for 3^x it is 1.10 to the same degree of accuracy. That means that the corresponding derivatives for 2^x and 3^x are given approximately by 0.69 × 2^x and 1.10 × 3^x.

The key property of these exponential functions is that the rate of growth, given by the gradient function or derivative, is directly proportional to the value of the function at each point. Clearly, the presence of an awkward constant makes these derivatives somewhat clumsy and that leads us to ask if there is some value between 2 and 3 where the value of the constant is 1. There is, of course, such a value and we refer to it by the letter e. In the case of such a function e^x, we require the gradient at $x = 0$, given by the limiting value of $\frac{e^h-1}{h}$ as h tends to 0, to be 1. This gives us a way of determining a value for the constant e, as follows:

$$\frac{e^h - 1}{h} \approx 1 \;\Rightarrow\; e^h - 1 \approx h \;\Rightarrow\; e^h \approx 1 + h \;\Rightarrow\; e \approx (1 + h)^{\frac{1}{h}}$$

One might expect the expression $(1 + h)^{\frac{1}{h}}$ to approach a limiting value of 1 as h approaches 0, but the spreadsheet displayed in Figure 12.12 shows successive approximations to e as the limiting value of a sequence.

h	e
0.1	2.59374
0.01	2.70481
0.001	2.71692
0.0001	2.71815
0.00001	2.71827
0.000001	2.71828
0.0000001	2.71828

Figure 12.12 *Evaluating e*

Expanding $(1 + h)^{\frac{1}{h}}$ using the binomial theorem and taking the limit as h tends to 0 leads to the series expansion, which provides an alternative way of evaluating e:

$$e = 1 + 1 + \frac{1}{2!} + \frac{1}{3!} + \frac{1}{4!} + \frac{1}{5!} + \dots$$

The function e^x has the remarkable property that its derivative is the same function, which makes it very suitable for representing any situation involving continuous growth or decay. Again, the interplay between graphical, numerical and algebraic approaches is an important means of helping students come to understand the ideas that underpin subsequent development of the properties and applications of the exponential function.

Before the days of calculators, logarithms were introduced to students as a way of doing multiplication and division, the purpose that led to their original invention. That is not now an appropriate way of introducing logarithms, but it does mean that their properties are less familiar when they are eventually encountered in the context of algebra and calculus. On the other hand, a calculator keyboard does serve to emphasize that the natural logarithm function is the inverse of the exponential function and that is an important link to establish. As with many algebraic ideas, a simple numerical example is useful to focus attention on the key property:

$$2 \approx e^{0.693} \iff 0.693 \approx \ln 2$$

$$y = e^x \iff x = \ln y$$

The laws of logarithms can then be seen as a logical consequence of the laws of indices, which were discussed in Chapter 8 and should have been established at an earlier stage. The derivation of the addition law for logarithms from the corresponding law for indices is shown in Figure 12.13. The laws for $\ln\frac{a}{b}$ and $\ln a^n$ can be derived in a similar way.

$$a = e^p \iff p = \ln a$$
$$b = e^q \iff q = \ln b$$
$$ab = e^{p+q} \iff p + q = \ln ab$$
$$e^p \times e^q = e^{p+q} \iff \ln ab = \ln a + \ln b$$

Figure 12.13 *The addition law for indices and logarithms*

The importance of the natural logarithm is that it provides a means of integrating the reciprocal function. The formula $\frac{x^{n+1}}{n+1}$ for the indefinite integral of x^n does not work in the case of the reciprocal function, $\frac{1}{x}$, where $n = {}^-1$. This has to remain a mystery to students until the natural logarithm is introduced. The mystery can be resolved directly by investigating the area under $y = \frac{1}{x}$, in ways similar to those considered in the earlier section on integration, to show that the natural logarithm is involved.

The result can also emerge algebraically by considering the derivative of the natural logarithm, which is linked to the derivative of the exponential function. The argument is as follows:

$$y = \ln x \implies x = e^y \implies \frac{dx}{dy} = e^y = x \implies \frac{dy}{dx} = \frac{1}{x}$$

Alternatively, this argument can be reversed by starting with a differential equation to solve:

$$\frac{dy}{dx} = \frac{1}{x} \implies \frac{dx}{dy} = x = e^y \implies x = e^y \implies y = \ln x$$

Either way we arrive, very surprisingly, at the important fact:

$$\int \frac{1}{x} \, dx = \ln x + \text{constant}$$

This section has provided a brief review of a number of ways of approaching the introduction to the exponential function and the natural logarithm function. These are two very important functions, both of which involve many conceptual difficulties for students, so that the initial stages are crucial in providing a secure foundation from which fluency with skills and applications can be developed.

PROBLEM SOLVING

The calculus had its origins in solving real-world problems, particularly those involving motion, but it has become a very powerful tool with a wide range of applications within mathematics and many other fields. I have suggested throughout this book that algebra should be presented in ways which make its meaning and purpose clear and that one way in which this should be done is by using problems of all kinds as starting points. Problem solving, like learning, is often a messy business, which has to be learnt by doing it and by facing the struggle and frequent failures that are involved. It is very easy for students to gain the impression from seeing model solutions to problems presented effortlessly by teachers and textbooks that it is all a straightforward matter if you know enough. Clearly, fluency and understanding with appropriate ideas and skills are necessary, as are qualities like determination and persistence, but they are not sufficient.

Polya (1945), in his book *How to Solve It*, suggested a four-part strategy for solving problems:

- understanding the problem;
- devising a plan;
- carrying out the plan;
- looking back.

This is expressed in a rather terse form, but it offers some very sound advice. However, one must add the proviso that there is likely to be a lot of looping back to earlier stages of the strategy. In practice, plans do not always work out and attempts to solve a problem sometimes reveal aspects that were not fully understood at the start. The element of looking back is important throughout the process and it is also useful to look forward as well. It is useful to review what you have done, where you started from and where you are trying to go. It is very easy for an overall strategy, such as Polya's, to become lost in the technical details of the individual steps. Students should be encouraged to engage in this reviewing process as they proceed and they need to be given ideas about where to search for inspiration when they are stuck.

Although many standard mathematics problems can become routine tasks when the ideas and procedures are familiar, every teacher knows that they can present considerable difficulties before that desirable state is achieved. I discuss here a standard problem which involves calculus to draw attention to some of these difficulties and ways of helping students with them.

Problems like this are often carefully structured for students by telling them what variables to use and what intermediate steps to take, often with statements that say 'show that' so that in effect answers are given at each stage. This removes much of the problem element by making the task one of following instructions. Whilst this may have its place at times, students will not learn how to solve unstructured problems if they are always given detailed instructions on how to solve them.

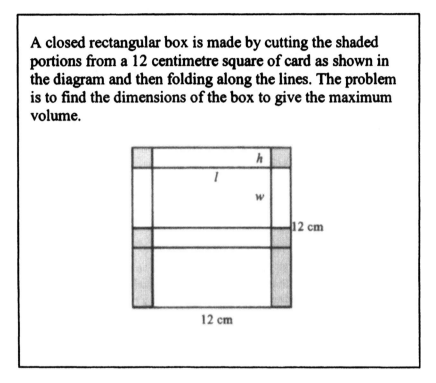

A closed rectangular box is made by cutting the shaded portions from a 12 centimetre square of card as shown in the diagram and then folding along the lines. The problem is to find the dimensions of the box to give the maximum volume.

Figure 12.14 *Maximizing the volume of a box*

Figure 12.14 shows a simple unstructured problem which I will use to focus on how students can be helped to think about solution strategies. I would suggest that the variables l, w and h, for length, width and height, should not appear on the diagram when the problem is first encountered, because an essential part of solving a problem lies in deciding what variables are involved and how to represent them. However, before looking at variables, it is necessary to understand the problem and that involves visualizing what the box will look like. For many students, it is very helpful to make a simple model with a square of card or paper, although others will have no need of such an aid. The discussion can then focus on what we are trying to find, namely the volume and when it is at a maximum value. At this point it is worth discussing the constraints on the size of the parts that are cut out and how the volume varies accordingly. Sketching a graph of the volume against one of the variables is a good way of focusing attention on this.

To make further progress we need to write down an expression for the volume and find where it takes its maximum value, something which should suggest to students that they will need to find a derivative and set it equal to zero. We now have a basic solution strategy:

- find an expression for the volume;
- find a derivative and set it equal to zero;
- solve the equation.

To find an expression for the volume it is necessary to choose what variables to use. Students will recognize how to calculate the volume of a box, so it is natural for them to suggest the variables *l, w* and *h* that have been indicated on the diagram. The next step is more difficult, because they will realize that they cannot find a suitable derivative from the formula $V = lwh$ for the volume. We need to have an expression in terms of a single variable, so can they see any relationships between the variables? This question should lead to two equations $l + 2h = 12$ and $2w + 2h = 12$, or alternative forms of them. A decision is now needed about which variable to work with and, of course, there are three to choose from. The fact that *l* can immediately be written as $12 - 2h$ and *w* as $6 - h$ might suggest that it is best to work in terms of *h*. Let us proceed with that, although we could equally have chosen either of the other variables and it would indeed be instructive to compare more than one way of arriving at a solution.

Our working will now proceed something like this:

$$V = lwh$$
$$= h(12 - 2h)(6 - h)$$
$$= 72h - 24h^2 + 2h^3$$

There will be variations in how the final step is arrived at, but it is a routine application of a standard skill that will not be a major stumbling block. Typically, many students will not know what to do next. This is point where they have to learn to review what they have done, and what they are aiming to do, in order to decide how to proceed. With luck they will then realize that they must find the derivative and produce an equation to solve, as follows:

$$V = 72h - 24h^2 + 2h^3$$
$$\frac{dV}{dh} = 72 - 48h + 6h^2$$
$$\frac{dV}{dh} = 0 \Rightarrow 72 - 48h + 6h^2 = 0$$

We are now at the third stage of our plan: there is an equation to solve which should be recognized as a quadratic equation, although the numbers may make it seem complicated to some students. It is good to encourage the habit of modifying expressions to look as simple and familiar as far as possible, so dividing by 6 and rearranging so that the square term comes first are sensible steps. In this case the equation can easily be solved using factors to give two solutions for *h*:

$$72 - 48h + 6h^2 = 0$$
$$h^2 - 8h + 12 = 0$$
$$(h - 2)(h - 6) = 0$$
$$h = 2 \text{ or } 6$$

The solution $h = 2$ leads to $l = 8$ and $w = 4$, giving $V = 64$. The other solution corresponds to a volume of zero because $h = 6$ would result in the whole of the square being eliminated. Since $V = 0$ when $h = 0$ and $h = 6$, something that should have been established with a sketch graph earlier, the value $V = 64$ when $h = 2$ must be the maximum value. So, we have a volume of 64 cubic centimetres for a box with dimensions of 8, 4 and 2 centimetres, which seems a very plausible solution to the problem.

It is always valuable to look back and see whether there are other aspects of the problem that may be of interest or which offer possible extensions. In this case, we might note, for instance, that $l = 2w$ and, less obviously, that the maximum volume arises when the value of h is one sixth of the length of the edge of the original square. Using a rectangle rather than a square provides an alternative problem of the same kind and a more demanding problem might involve a box with some trapezoidal faces.

We have followed Polya's four-part strategy here, giving particular emphasis to the initial stage of understanding the problem as a prelude to devising a plan. Carrying out the plan may seem a straightforward matter, but there are two major sources of difficulty. The first is one of losing the thread of the argument and failing to see what to do next and the second is when there is a lack of fluency with appropriate skills and an awareness of when they are relevant. The first is helped by encouraging students to step back from the problem and review their original plan and the second, the importance of fluency and understanding, has been constantly emphasized in earlier chapters.

CONCLUSION

Although this chapter has of necessity only been able to touch upon a small sample of topics and ideas from elementary calculus, it has brought together many aspects of teaching and learning algebra that have been constant themes throughout the book. The quotation at the start of the chapter states how important the early stages are in learning calculus, something that is equally true of algebra. The constant danger in learning mathematics is that the perceived pressure to develop fluency takes priority over the need to build relational understanding and the ability to apply ideas in a wide variety of situations. Fluency and understanding are both crucially important and there is a vital balance between them that has to be maintained.

Derivatives and integrals are the two key ideas of the calculus: I have discussed in detail some introductory approaches to both that draw on numerical and graphical ideas to reinforce essential algebraic arguments and results. Students need to investigate the gradient of a curve and the area under a curve numerically in order to acquire a strong feel for the meaning of the key results of the calculus and how they emerge from limiting processes. This intuitive feel for what is going on is an essential precursor to understanding more formal algebraic arguments and to being able to apply the ideas to new situations. Fluency with procedures and skills can never be sufficient on its own.

Appreciating the links and connections between different ideas is an important aspect of understanding and using them. The calculus brings together a very wide range of ideas with some often very surprising connections of which the link between derivatives and integrals is so important that it is referred to as the fundamental theorem. There are, however, many surprising results in the calculus: cosine as the derivative of sine, the derivative of the exponential function and the integral of the reciprocal function have all been discussed in this chapter. Students need to see these as part of a whole interconnected web of ideas and not just as a lot of discrete formulae and procedures used for solving routine problems.

As I argued in Chapter 1, the essence of algebra is that it is a symbolic tool for representing expressions and relationships and using them in constructing arguments to predict, to explain, to prove and to solve problems. Proficiency in using this tool is very dependent both on fluency with rules and procedures and relational understanding, which embraces knowing how to do things and what lies behind the ideas, why they work and how they are interrelated. Algebra is a very economical language: making sense of an expression, a step in an argument or a complete argument is very dependent on a deep understanding of all the component parts as well as the overall logic of the argument. This has been illustrated by my discussion of the volume problem, which is very simple to solve when you are familiar with all the appropriate ideas and strategies, but provides a daunting array of stumbling blocks to the learner who does not have this ready familiarity. In the same way, making sense of new ideas and following algebraic arguments, like many of those presented in this chapter and elsewhere in this book, poses exactly the same difficulty for the learner.

Whilst fluency and understanding are crucial to success with algebra, there is a more fundamental requirement implicit in the question 'Why learn algebra?' posed at the start of Chapter 1. Students need to see meaning and purpose in what they are doing and for most this needs to be immediate, rather than something that is promised for the future. By developing real understanding and fluency, algebraic ideas can become meaningful to students, but alongside this a sense of purpose must be engendered by constantly seeking to catch students' interest and stimulate their curiosity, whether it be through problems and puzzles of all kinds or through the intrinsic fascination of a subject that is so powerful and such a rich source of surprises.

Bibliography

Adey, P. and Shayer, M. (1994) *Really Raising Standards: Cognitive Intervention and Academic Achievement*. London and New York: Routledge.

Andrews, P. and Sinkinson, A. (2000) 'Continuity, coherence and curricular entitlement', *Mathematics Teaching*, **172**, 52–5.

Arcavi, A. (1994) 'Symbol sense: informal sense-making in formal mathematics', *For the Learning of Mathematics*, **14**(3), 24–35.

Askew, M., Rhodes, V., Brown, M., Wiliam, D. and Johnson, D. (1997) *Effective Teachers of Numeracy*. London: King's College, London, for the Teacher Training Agency.

Askew, M. and Wiliam, D. (1995) *Ofsted Reviews of Recent Research: Recent Research in Mathematics Education 5–16*. London: HMSO.

Association of Teachers of Mathematics (1970) *Mathematical Reflections*. Cambridge: Cambridge University Press.

Ausubel, D. (1968) *Educational Psychology: a Cognitive View*. New York: Holt, Rinehart and Winston.

Bednarz, N., Kieran, C. and Lee, L. (1996) *Approaches to Algebra: Perspectives for Research and Teaching*. Dordrecht, Boston and London: Kluwer.

Bell, A., Malone, J. and Taylor, P. (1988) *Algebra: an Exploratory Teaching Experiment*. Nottingham, UK: Shell Centre for Mathematical Education; Perth, Australia: Science and Mathematics Education Centre, Curtin University.

Bell, A. (1996) 'Problem-Solving Approaches to Algebra', in Bednarz, N., Kieran, C. and Lee, L. (eds) *Approaches to Algebra: Perspectives for Research and Teaching*. Dordrecht, Boston and London: Kluwer.

Berry, J. and Monaghan, J. (eds) (1997) *The State of Computer Algebra in Mathematics Education*. Bromley: Chartwell Bratt.

Billington, J. and Evans, P. (1987) 'Levels of knowing 2: the handshake', *Mathematics Teaching*, **120**, 12–19.

Booth, L.R. (1984) *Algebra: Children's Strategies and Errors*. Windsor: NFER-Nelson.

Boyer, C.B. and Merzbach, U.C. (1991) *A History of Mathematics* (2nd edition). New York: John Wiley.

Clement, J. (1982) 'Algebra word problem solutions: thought processes underlying a common misconception', *Journal for Research in Mathematics Education*, **14**, 16–30.

Cockcroft, W. (1982) *Mathematics Counts: Report of the Committee of Enquiry into the Teaching of Mathematics*. London: HMSO.

Davis, P.J. and Hersh, R. (1983). *The Mathematical Experience*. Harmondsworth, UK: Penguin.

Davis, R.B. (1984) *Learning Mathematics*. Beckenham, UK: Croom Helm.

DfEE (2001) *Key Stage 3 National Strategy Framework for Teaching Mathematics: Years 7, 8 and 9.* London: Department for Education and Employment.

DfEE/QCA (1999) *Mathematics: the National Curriculum for England.* London: Department for Education and Employment/Qualifications and Curriculum Authority.

Dickson, L., Brown, M. and Gibson, O. (1984) *Children Learning Mathematics: a Teacher's Guide to Recent Research.* Eastbourne, UK: Holt, Rinehart and Winston.

Driscoll, M. (1999) *Fostering Algebraic Thinking: A Guide for Teachers, Grades 6–10.* Portsmouth, NH: Heinemann.

Euclid (translated by Heath, T.L.) (1967) *The Thirteen Books of Euclid's Elements.* New York: Dover Publications.

Fauvel, J. and Gray, J. (1987) *The History of Mathematics: a Reader.* London: Macmillan.

French, D. (1990) 'Sums of squares and cubes', *Mathematics in School*, **19**(3), 34–7.

French, D. (1992) 'A number and its cube', *Mathematics in School*, **21**(2), 38–41.

French, D. (1995) 'Two and a bit', *Mathematics in School*, **24**(2), 5–7.

French, D. (1997) 'The difference of two squares', *Mathematics in School*, **26**(1), 30–4.

French, D. (1999) 'Factorizing with a TI92', *Mathematics in School*, **28**(1), 30–4.

French, D. and Stripp, C. (eds) (1997) *Are You Sure? Learning about Proof.* Leicester: The Mathematical Association.

Frobisher, L. (1999) 'Primary school children's knowledge of odd and even numbers', in Orton, A. (ed.) *Pattern in the Teaching and learning of Mathematics.* London: Cassell.

Gray, E. and Tall, D. (1991) 'Duality, ambiguity and flexibility in successful mathematics teaching', *Proceedings of PME 15, Assisi, Italy*, **Vol II**, 72–9.

Gray, E. and Tall, D. (1993) 'Success and failure in mathematics: the flexible meaning of symbols as process and concept', *Mathematics Teaching*, **142**, 6–10

Hardy, G.H. (1967) *A Mathematician's Apology.* Cambridge: Cambridge University Press.

Hart, K.M. (ed.) (1981) *Children's Understanding of Mathematics: 11–16.* London: John Murray.

Hart, K.M. (1984) *Ratio: Children's Strategies and Errors.* Windsor: NFER-Nelson.

Hergel, W., Heugl, H., Kutzler, B. and Lehmann, H. (2001) 'Indispensable written skills in a CAS environment', *Mathematics in School*, **30**(2), 2–6.

Herscovics, N. and Kieran, C. (1999) 'Constructing meaning for the concept of equation', in Moses, B. (ed.) *Algebraic Thinking: Readings from NCTM's School-based Journal and Other Publications.* Reston, VA: National Council of Teachers of Mathematics.

Hewitt, D. (1992) 'Train spotter's paradise', *Mathematics Teaching*, **140**, 6–8.

Hewitt, D. (1996) 'Mathematical fluency: the nature of practice and the role of subordination', *For the Learning of Mathematics*, **16**(2), 28–35.

Holt, J. (1958) *How Children Fail.* Harmondsworth, UK: Penguin.

Howson, G. (1991) *National Curricula in Mathematics.* Leicester, UK: The Mathematical Association.

Johnson, D.C. (ed.) (1989) *Children's Mathematical Frameworks 8–13: a Study of Classroom Teaching.* Windsor, UK: NFER-Nelson.

Kaiser, G., Lunn, E. and Huntley, I. (1999) *International Comparisons in Mathematics Education.* London: Falmer Press.

Kaner, P.A. (1964) 'The addition and subtraction of negative numbers', *The Mathematical Gazette*, **47**(364), 183–5.

Kaplan, R. (1999) *The Nothing that is: a Natural History of Zero.* Harmondsworth: Penguin Books.

Kent, D. (1978) 'The dynamics of put', *Mathematics Teaching*, **82**, 32–6.

Kerslake, D. (1981) 'Graphs', in Hart, K.M. (ed.) (1981) *Children's Understanding of Mathematics: 11–16.* London: John Murray.

Kieran, C. (1999) 'The learning and teaching of school algebra', in Moses, B.(ed.) *Algebraic Thinking: Readings from NCTM's School-Based Journal and Other Publications.* Reston, VA: National Council of Teachers of Mathematics.

Küchemann, D.E. (1981a) 'Algebra', in Hart, K.M. (ed.) *Children's Understanding of Mathematics: 11–16.* London: John Murray.

Küchemann, D.E. (1981b) 'Positive and Negative Numbers', in Hart, K.M. (ed.) *Children's Understanding of Mathematics: 11–16*. London: John Murray.

Kutzler, B. (1996) *Improving Mathematics Teaching with DERIVE*. Bromley, UK: Chartwell-Bratt.

LMS/IMA/RSS (1995) *Tackling the Mathematics Problem*. London: London Mathematical Society/Institute for Mathematics and its Applications/Royal Statistical Society.

Ma, Liping (1999) *Knowing and Teaching Elementary Mathematics*. Mahwah, New Jersey: Lawrence Erlbaum.

Maor, E. (1998) *Trigonometric Delights*. New Jersey: Princeton University Press.

Mason, J. (1988) *Learning and Doing Mathematics*. London: Macmillan.

Mason, J. (1996) 'Expressing generality and roots of algebra', in Bednarz, N., Kieran, C. and Lee, L. (eds) *Approaches to Algebra: Perspectives for Research and Teaching*. Dordrecht, Boston and London: Kluwer.

Mathematical Association (1934) *The Teaching of Algebra in Schools*. London: G. Bell and Sons.

Mathematical Association (1950) *The Teaching of Trigonometry in Schools*. London: G. Bell and Sons.

Mathematical Association (1951) *The Teaching of Calculus in Schools*. London: G. Bell and Sons.

Mathematical Association (1995) *Why What How: Some Basic Questions for Mathematics Teaching*. Leicester: The Mathematical Association.

Ministry of Education (1958) *Teaching Mathematics in Secondary Schools*. London: HMSO.

Moses, B. (ed.) (1999) *Algebraic Thinking: Readings from NCTM's School-Based Journal and Other Publications*. Reston, VA: National Council of Teachers of Mathematics.

NCET (National Council for Educational Technology) (1995) *Algebra at A Level: How the Curriculum Might Change with Computer Algebra Systems*. Derby: Association of Teachers of Mathematics.

NCTM (1988) *The Ideas of Algebra, K–12: 1988 Yearbook*. Reston, VA: National Council of Teachers of Mathematics.

NCTM (1989) *Curriculum and Evaluation Standards for School Mathematics*. Reston, VA: National Council of Teachers of Mathematics.

NCTM (1991) *Professional Standards for Teaching Mathematics*. Reston, VA: National Council of Teachers of Mathematics.

NCTM (1992) *Calculators in Mathematics Education: 1992 Yearbook*. Reston, VA: National Council of Teachers of Mathematics.

NCTM (1999) *Developing Mathematical Reasoning in Grades K–12: 1999 Yearbook*. Reston, VA: National Council of Teachers of Mathematics.

NCTM (2000a) *Principles and Standards for School Mathematics*. Reston, VA: National Council of Teachers of Mathematics.

NCTM (2000b) *Learning Mathematics for a New Century: 2000 Yearbook*. Reston, VA: National Council of Teachers of Mathematics.

Nelsen, R.B. (1993) *Proofs without Words: Exercises in Visual Thinking*. Washington, DC: The Mathematical Association of America.

Nemirovsky, R. (1996) 'A functional approach to algebra: two issues that emerge', in Bednarz, N., Kieran, C. and Lee, L. (eds) *Approaches to Algebra: Perspectives for Research and Teaching*. Dordrecht, Boston and London: Kluwer.

Nickson, M. (2000) *Teaching and Learning Mathematics: a Teacher's Guide to Recent Research and its Application*. London: Cassell.

Nunn, T.P. (1919) *The Teaching of Algebra*. London: Longmans, Green and Co.

Orton, A. (1999) *Pattern in the Teaching and Learning of Mathematics*. London: Cassell.

Pimm, D. (1995) *Symbols and Meanings in School Mathematics*. London and New York: Routledge.

Polya, G. (1945) *How to Solve It*. Princeton, NJ: Princeton University Press.

RS/JMC (1997) *Teaching and Learning Algebra pre-19*. London: Royal Society/Joint Mathematical Council.

Sawyer, W.W. (1964) *Vision in Elementary Mathematics*. Harmondsworth, UK: Penguin.

Shuard, H. and Neill, H. (1977) *The Mathematics Curriculum: From Graphs to Calculus*. Glasgow and London: Blackie.

Shuard, H. and Neill, H. (1982) *Teaching Calculus*. Glasgow and London: Blackie.

Sillitto, A.G. (1970) 'An introduction to trigonometry', in Association of Teachers of Mathematics (eds) *Mathematical Reflections*. Cambridge: Cambridge University Press.

Skemp, R. (1976) 'Relational and instrumental understanding', *Mathematics Teaching*, 77, 20–6.

SMP (1966) *The School Mathematics Project, Book 2*. Cambridge: Cambridge University Press.

SMP (2000) *SMP Interact, Book 1*. Cambridge: Cambridge University Press.

Stewart, I. (1987) *The Problems of Mathematics*. Oxford: Oxford University Press.

Swan, M. (2000) 'Making sense of algebra', *Mathematics Teaching*, 171, 16–19.

Tall, D. (1986) *Graphic Calculus I, Graphic Calculus II, Graphic Calculus III*. Barnet, UK: Glentop.

Tall, D. (1991) *Advanced Mathematical Thinking*. Dordrecht, Boston and London: Kluwer.

Tall, D. (1995) 'Cognitive growth in elementary and advanced mathematical thinking', *Proceedings of PME 19, Recife, Brazil*, Vol I, 61–75.

Tall, D. and Thomas, M. (1991) 'Encouraging versatile thinking in algebra using the computer', *Educational Studies in Mathematics*, 22(2), 125–47.

Thompson, S.P. and Gardner, M. (1999) *Calculus Made Easy* Basingstoke, UK: Palgrave/Macmillan.

Usiskin, Z. (1999) 'Why is algebra important to learn', in Moses, B. (ed.) *Algebraic Thinking: Readings from NCTM's School-Based Journal and Other Publications*. Reston, VA: National Council of Teachers of Mathematics.

Wagner, S. (1981) 'Conservation of equations and functions under transformations of variable', *Journal of Research in Mathematics Education*, 12, 107–18.

Wells, H.G. (1910) *The History of Mr Polly*. London: Thomas Nelson.

Wheeler D. (1996) 'Rough or smooth? The transition from arithmetic to algebra in problem solving', in Bednarz, N., Kieran, C. and Lee, L. (eds) *Approaches to Algebra: Perspectives for Research and Teaching*. Dordrecht, Boston and London: Kluwer.

Index

acceleration 86, 129
Adey, P. 12
algebraic fractions 61–3, 95–8
Andrews, P. 132
applications 3, 18, 98, 121–4, 175
Arcavi, A 8, 12
area 111, 135–40, 174–5, 178–82
area functions, *see* functions
arithmetic sequences 161–3, 167, 173
arithmetic series 34, 37, 161–3, 168, 173
Askew, M. 14, 19
assessment 6, 24
asymptote 96–7
Ausubel, D. 10

Babylonians 138
Berry, J. 22
Billington, J. 37
binomial theorem 76–80, 184
Booth, L.R. 11, 26
Boyer, C.B. 2, 114
brackets 29, 50, 54–6, 67

calculators 6, 21–4, 30, 48–50, 65–6, 81–2, 97, 102–3, 107, 111–12, 127, 146, 150, 175, 180
calculator based ranger 85
calculus 4, 84, 86, 94, 157, 174–90
Calculus Made Easy 175
CBR, *see* calculator based ranger
China 9, 138
circular functions, *see* functions
Clements, J. 12
closure 15–16

Cockcroft, W. 3, 17
coefficients 76, 78, 109
cognitive conflict 12, 24, 48, 50, 66
complex numbers 151
complication 101, 108–9, 127, 163, 173
computers 3, 24, 26, 30, 81, 82, 146, 175–6, 179
Concepts in Secondary Mathematics and Science 11, 14
conceptual difficulties 7, 50
conceptual understanding 9
conjectures 74
connectionist 19
connections 8, 19–21, 24, 77, 179, 189
consecutive numbers 2, 33–5, 69, 71, 74–5, 167–8
context 8, 17–21, 24, 38, 44–5, 56, 63, 98, 143, 168
convergence 112–13, 181
co-ordinates 31, 37, 154, 176
cosecant, *see* functions
cosine formula 153
cosine function, *see* functions
cotangent, *see* functions
CSMS, *see* Concepts in Secondary Mathematics and Science
cubes 49, 75–6, 80, 168–73
cube roots 112
cubic functions, *see* functions
curriculum 2–7

data logging devices 85
decay functions, *see* functions
derivative 157, 175, 178, 180, 182, 187–9

Derive (computer algebra software) 22
Descartes, R. 2
Department for Education and
    Employment 4, 146
DfEE, *see* Department for Education and
    Employment
diagonals of polygons 18–19, 37, 133, 136–8
difference of two cubes 70, 138
difference of two squares 21, 65, 67–72, 128,
    141, 143
differential equations 174, 185
differentiation 174–90
direct proportion 4, 120–1, 151
discriminant 108
discussion 7, 18, 38–9, 43, 47–8, 61, 67, 73, 82,
    84, 98, 101, 162
distance-time graphs 85–7, 175
distributive law 47, 168
divisibility 33
Driscoll, M. 31
dynamic geometry software 130, 132, 140

Egyptians 114
ellipse 92
enlargement 53, 117, 119, 145, 148, 151, 159
equations 4, 15, 26–30, 37–8, 81–2, 86–94, 98–
    115
    approximate solutions 87, 111–114, 150
    exact solutions 113–14
    graphical methods 107
    linear equations 99–104, 114
    literal equations 103
    quadratic equations 4, 19, 106–14
    simultaneous equations 4, 19, 50, 104–6, 114
    trigonometrical equations 114, 155
errors 10, 12, 14, 24, 33, 47, 61, 63, 66–7, 108,
    116–17, 120, 152, 154, 161
Evans, P. 37
even numbers 32–3, 37, 40, 44, 59, 69, 75
expanding expressions 28, 47, 58–60, 63, 70–4,
    114, 165
expected answer obstacle 15–16
explanation 2–3, 7, 38–40, 44–5, 54, 59, 63–80,
    98, 155–6, 190
exponential functions, *see* functions

factorial 78
factors 19, 21, 23, 28, 46, 58–61, 73
factorizing expressions 22, 58, 63, 69–75, 87,
    94, 107–8, 114, 188
Fauvel, J. 2, 145

feedback 47, 84, 152, 160
Fibonacci sequence 113–14
flow diagram 60, 100–4
fluency 7, 16–17, 46–7, 54–6, 63, 73–4, 97, 99–
    101, 114–15, 186, 189–90
formulae 18, 29–31, 45, 108, 145, 149, 161–4,
    167
fractions 10, 19, 23–4, 50, 61–3, 70, 78, 95–8
French, D. 63, 69, 73, 75, 169
Frobisher, L. 32, 33
functions 2–4, 15, 27, 31, 32, 60–1, 81–98, 114,
    128, 175
    area functions 179–80
    circular functions 3–4, 93, 145–60, 182–3
    cosecant 157
    cosine 3, 90–93, 145–160, 189
    cotangent 157
    cubic functions 4, 93–5, 114
    decay functions 124–5
    exponential functions 3–4, 124, 127
    gradient functions 175–8, 182–4
    growth functions 124–5
    linear functions 3–4
    logarithmic functions 3–4, 183–6
    polynomial functions 3–4, 76, 180
    quadratic functions 3–4, 21, 72–4, 79, 87–
        90, 106–10
    rational functions 3–4, 95–8
    reciprocal function 4, 62, 98, 185, 198
    secant 156–7
    sine 3, 90–3, 145–60, 182–3, 189
    tangent 144, 150, 151
fundamental theorem of the calculus 174, 189

Gardner, M. 175
generalization 1, 8, 15, 19, 20, 23–4, 27, 31, 37,
    43, 62–3, 65, 77, 131, 153, 164, 169
geometric sequences and series 163–6, 173
geometry 1, 18, 24, 119, 128–44, 145, 160, 173
golden ratio 113, 137
gradient 82, 84–6, 121, 150–1, 159, 174–7
gradient functions, *see* functions
graph plotters 6, 50, 59, 81–4, 88–9, 96, 98,
    134, 176, 182
graphical calculators, *see* calculators *and* graph
    plotters
graphs 4, 21, 24, 37–8, 45, 53, 59–60, 81–98,
    107, 112–4, 120–8, 133–4, 145–7, 154–6,
    175–6, 179–84
graph sketching 82, 86, 89, 93–4, 98, 109, 155,
    176, 187–8

Gray, E. 10, 16, 44, 96
Gray, J. 2, 145
growth functions, *see* functions

handshake problem 37
Hart, K.M. 11, 14, 117
Hergel, W. 22
Heron's method 111–13
Hewitt, D. 17, 31, 46
Holt, J. 10
Howson, G. 4
How to Solve It 190
Humber Bridge 90

identities 3, 20–1, 59, 62, 65–8, 74, 79, 155–8, 160
IMA, *see* Institute of Mathematics and its Applications
Institute of Mathematics and its Applications 15
indices 4, 123–4, 127, 185
inductive definition 31, 161–2
infinity 98, 165, 172
insight 3, 98, 128, 136, 139, 166, 169, 173
instrumental understanding 9, 24
integration 174–90
inverse 51, 52, 73, 98, 99, 116, 121, 122, 150
inverse proportion 4, 98, 121
isosceles triangles 130–3, 136, 138, 143
iterative processes 111–15

Johnson, D.C. 13
Joint Mathematical Council 4
JMC, *see* Joint Mathematical Council
juxtaposition 11, 24

Kaiser, G. 9
Kaner, P. 51
Kent, D. 11
Kerslake, D. 85
Key Stage 3 National Strategy 146
Kieran, C. 13
Küchemann, D. 14–15, 51
Kutzler, B. 22

lack of closure obstacle 15–16
letters as objects 11, 15, 24, 26–7, 54
limits 95, 166, 172, 175–7, 180, 182, 184, 189
linear functions, *see* functions
linear equations, *see* equations
links 19–21, 24, 77, 80–2, 97–8, 128–44, 189

LMS, *see* London Mathematical Society
loci 4
logarithmic functions, *see* functions
London Mathematical Society 16
Lucas sequence 113

magic numbers 38–9, 45, 56
Ma, Liping 8–9
manipulation 8, 16, 22, 24–5, 30, 32, 38, 62–3, 97–8, 111, 152–3, 168
Maor, E. 145, 160
Mason, J. 20, 31
Mathematical Association 27, 29–30, 174
maximum value 187–9
mean 111, 113, 136, 162, 168, 172, 178–9
meaningful learning 10, 24
mental algebra 47, 63, 68, 74, 75, 77, 86, 98, 152
mental calculation 22, 24, 46–7, 63, 66, 68, 79, 161
Merzbach, U.C. 2, 114
mid-ordinate rule 179–80
Ministry of Education 1
misconceptions 5, 10, 12, 13, 24, 31, 48, 54, 67, 117, 122, 151–2, 157, 159–60, 173
mismatches 9
modelling 4, 127, 160
Monaghan, J. 22
motion 84–6, 175, 186
motivation 8, 18, 19, 28, 38, 43, 46, 49, 54, 44, 64, 80, 97, 100, 114, 163, 177
Multilink cubes 66, 69
multiples 1, 2, 33–4, 40, 54, 68–70, 75, 161
multiplication table square 169–70
multiplicative relationships 116–20, 125

National Council for Educational Technology 22
National Council of Teachers of Mathematics 4, 8–9, 22
National Curriculum (England) 4, 9
natural numbers 36–7, 167, 169
NCET, *see* National Council for Educational Technology
NCTM, *see* National Council of Teachers of Mathematics
negative numbers 10, 24, 40, 43, 50–4, 63, 71, 75, 78–9, 86, 100, 110, 123
Neill, H. 175
Nelsen, R.B. 166, 169
Nemirovsky, R. 17

Newton-Raphson formula   113
Newton, Sir Isaac   78
Nickson, M.   13
notation   4, 37, 123, 130, 158–9, 167–73, 180
number line   51
Nunn, T.P.   30, 145

odd numbers   32–38, 40, 44, 47–8, 54, 59, 68–9, 75, 161–2, 167–8
Orton, A.   31, 40, 42

parsing obstacle   15
parabola   86, 89
parameters   82, 92, 93, 98
Pascal's triangle   40, 76–80
patterns   1, 4, 6, 8, 20, 22–3, 27, 31–2, 35, 51, 54, 62–6, 71, 74–5, 78, 80–1, 173
percentages   116, 121–3, 127
perimeter   27, 30, 31, 56–8, 135–6, 143
period   91, 154–5
Pimm, D.   5
pocket money problem   163–5, 167
Polya, G.   186, 189
polygons   18–19, 37, 133–5, 143
polynomial functions, *see* functions
powers   40, 43, 77–8, 80, 122–4, 127
pre-calculus   4
prediction   2–4, 31, 38–9, 56, 190
Principles and Standards for School Mathematics (USA)   4, 8
problem solving   2–7, 17, 20, 22, 24, 27, 29, 40, 44, 47, 61, 63–4, 74, 79, 80, 87, 89, 98, 99–115, 122, 127–33, 136, 141–5, 148, 152–4, 159–60, 163–5, 173–4, 186–90
procept   16, 44
process   16, 22, 24, 73, 96
process-product obstacle   15, 16
proof   2–4, 6, 7, 65–80, 98, 128, 132–3, 136, 139, 141, 143–4, 153, 165, 169, 172–3
proportionality   41, 116–27, 143
purpose   6, 8, 22, 24–27, 30–1, 37–8, 43–6, 54–6, 62–3, 80, 106, 115, 127, 143, 159–60, 173–4, 186, 190
puzzles   24, 28, 43, 56–7, 99–115, 190
Pythagoras' theorem   110–11, 138–44, 153–5, 160

QCA, *see* Qualifications and Curriculum Authority
quadratic equations, *see* equations
quadratic functions, *see* functions

Qualifications and Curriculum Authority   4, 9

radians   182–3
rate of change   84, 175
ratio   116, 118–21, 125, 136, 141, 143, 145, 149, 154, 159
rational functions, *see* functions
real world   3, 17, 18, 24, 26, 125, 186
reasoning   1, 4, 74, 75, 88, 98, 128
reciprocal function, *see* functions
reflection   124
Regiomontanus   145
relational understanding   9, 24, 46, 189–90
relationships   1–4, 44, 48, 54, 63, 73, 120, 135, 190
representation   2, 31, 39, 40, 43, 50, 65, 81, 92, 156, 160, 189
research   4, 6, 7, 13, 14, 19
rote learning   10, 24
Royal Society   4
Royal Statistical Society   15
RS, *see* Royal Society
RSS, *see* Royal Statistical Society
rules to remember   6, 9, 77, 150, 190

Sawyer, W.W.   104, 105
Schools Inquiry Commission   1
scale factor   53, 116–21, 125–7, 136, 143, 145, 148, 151
School Mathematics Project   42
science   3, 85, 121
secant, *see* functions
sequences   1, 4, 27, 31, 33, 38, 40–2, 44–5, 54, 56, 62, 73, 81, 111, 113, 122–3, 131–2, 163–73, 177
series   163–73
Shayer, M.   12
Shuard, H.   175
sigma notation   37, 167–73, 180
similarity   116, 119, 136–8, 143, 144
simplicity   80, 100, 127, 153, 163, 188
simplification   11, 19, 28, 32, 34, 38–9, 46, 54–8, 61–63, 70, 75, 114, 136, 168, 178
simultaneous equations, *see* equations
sine formula   154
sine function, *see* functions
Sinkinson, A.   132
Skemp, R.   9, 10
sketching graphs, *see* graph sketching
SMP, *see* School Mathematics Project
software   50, 82, 130, 146

specialization 20, 24
speed 86, 110, 110, 116, 117, 121
spreadsheet 30, 59, 106, 111–12, 134, 177–8, 184
Stewart, I. 17
square roots 43, 87, 104, 106, 111–12, 150
squares 34, 65, 66, 68, 70, 79, 87, 104, 108, 138–40, 143, 168–73
staircase diagram 112
standard deviation 168
statistical formulae 167–8
strategies
  learning and teaching 7, 20, 28, 153, 169
  problem solving 186–90
stretch 87–93, 96, 124
structures 8, 162–3, 167, 173
substitution 19, 30, 32–3, 46–8, 54, 61, 63, 67, 114, 130, 163
Swan, M. 6–7
symbols 1–4, 20, 27, 31–2, 41, 44–5, 48, 50, 56, 63, 81, 98–9, 129, 139, 155, 172, 180, 189
symmetry 135, 147, 155

table of values 81–2, 112, 146, 164, 169
Tackling the Mathematics Problem 16
Tall, D. 2, 10, 15, 16, 25, 44, 175
tangent, *see* functions
technology 21–4, 81, 86, 146, 175
text books 5–6, 8, 24, 28, 30, 37, 46–7, 51–2, 54, 67–8, 70, 81, 100, 118, 145, 149, 160, 162, 168, 175, 186
Thomas, M. 2, 15, 25, 58
Thompson, S.P. 175
TI-89/TI-92 calculators 22–3, 60–1, 85, 96, 102–3, 107, 155, 178–80

transformation
  expressions 2, 62
  formulae 104
  functions 4
  graphs 87–93, 124, 127, 154
translation 87–93, 96, 124, 179
trapezium 136, 137, 178, 179
trapezium rule 178–9
trial and improvement 106–7, 114–15
triangle numbers 35–37, 45, 68, 167, 169–72
trigonometry 116, 144–160
Trigonometric Delights 160

understanding 7–10, 16, 21, 22, 24, 29, 31, 41–2, 46–8, 50, 53–6, 62–3, 74, 79, 82–3, 86, 98, 100–1, 114, 127, 135, 143, 145, 153, 156, 160, 165, 173–5, 183, 186–7, 190
undoing 100, 101, 116, 122
unitary method 118
United States 4, 8, 9
unknowns 14, 15, 24, 29, 101, 114, 118
Usiskin, Z. 3

variable 1, 2, 15, 24–5, 27, 29, 30, 37, 44, 58, 84, 103, 114, 120–1, 128–9, 143, 154, 161, 178, 186–7
vectors 151
velocity 86, 124, 149, 175
velocity-time graphs 86
Venn diagram 4–5
volume 94, 138, 143, 187–90

Wagner, S. 15
Wells, H.G. 12
Wheeler, D. 7
Wiliam, D. 14
word problems 99

Lightning Source UK Ltd.
Milton Keynes UK
UKOW021416150513

210718UK00002B/4/P

9 780826 477491